This book is about political culture. It examines developments in the social sciences and integrates them into a theoretical explanation of historical changes in political values. The starting point is the premise that political culture is rooted in the interaction between individual thinking and social norms. Individual reasoning develops according to Piagetian principles. Conceptions of social life reflect the way thought is organized; they are expressed, however, through symbolic forms constructed from prevailing cultural orientations. Social norms reflect the reasoning capability of society's members but are not organized conceptually in the same manner. They also serve institutional purposes by providing moral justifications, comprehensible to all of society's members, for inequality and solidarity. Institutional efficiency is enhanced when status arrangements are considered legitimate. Moral criteria that justify compliance thus serve to reduce friction in, and hence the costs of, organized activity. Moral justifications, however, as an aspect of cultural orientations in general, may be challenged following technological innovation that alters institutional arrangements. In the turmoil that accompanies change new moral guideposts are debated. Through discourse, individual conceptions of social life are transformed and, interactively, social norms and cultural orientations as well.

The first two parts of the book explore these issues theoretically. The second two examine them empirically by showing the ways that political cultures have changed over time. In the modern period the differences in the political cultures of capitalist and communist systems are contrasted; although both conceptualize social life in terms of property accumulation, they utilize different cultural orientations to reduce institutional transaction costs. The way the tensions between these two systems can be resolved is also explored.

T0370789

Compliance ideologies

Compliance ideologies
Rethinking political culture

RICHARD W. WILSON
Rutgers University

CAMBRIDGE
UNIVERSITY PRESS

CAMBRIDGE UNIVERSITY PRESS
Cambridge, New York, Melbourne, Madrid, Cape Town, Singapore,
São Paulo, Delhi, Dubai, Tokyo, Mexico City

Cambridge University Press
The Edinburgh Building, Cambridge CB2 8RU, UK

Published in the United States of America by Cambridge University Press, New York

www.cambridge.org
Information on this title: www.cambridge.org/9780521144841

First published 1992
First paperback printing 2010

A catalogue record for this publication is available from the British Library

Library of Congress Cataloguing in Publication data
Wilson, Richard W., 1933–
Compliance ideologies : rethinking political culture / Richard W.
Wilson.
p.   cm.
ISBN 0-521-41581-0
1. Political culture.   2. Political development.   I. Title.
JA75.7.W553   1992
306.2 – dc20   91-27178

ISBN 978-0-521-41581-1 Hardback
ISBN 978-0-521-14484-1 Paperback

To the memory of my parents,
Richard Henry Wilson and Susan Agnes Pasley Wilson

Contents

Preface

Differences among societies have fascinated observers since ancient times. Customs vary, words convey subtle, not quite familiar meanings, and responses are often unpredictable. Even our own close ancestors can seem remote. Photographs from a century ago reveal people who are near in time yet, somehow, far in spirit. Their letters and poetry, speeches and novels, speak to concerns that we understand, but to us they are strangers whose lives have a fabric and rhythm different from our own.

In politics knowledge of how others interpret events is vital. All too often great plans for peace and war have gone awry because intentions were misjudged; knowing the mind of an opponent is truly the first key to victory. Yet this means understanding the perceptions of others; it means putting aside our convictions about what is desirable and, instead, seeing the world through a different set of lenses. Broadly speaking, this is what is meant by cultural analysis, determining how others think and feel and what it is that societies consider significant.

Those who study political life are aware that culture is important. Few concepts, however, have so bedeviled research. Problems have been both theoretical and methodological. For instance, how do cultural norms come to exist and how do they affect the ways that people think? Indeed, what is thinking itself? What kinds of propositions can make sense of the diversity of human experience? These are only a few of the questions that must be asked. So thorny have these problems been that many have simply stepped around them, preferring to believe that all people think in roughly the same way and are motivated to obtain similar goals. Then unforeseen events occur, such as the recent turning away from communism in Eastern Europe or the confrontation in the Persian Gulf. The importance of understanding political cultures then becomes clear and immediate.

This book is about political culture. It takes a fresh look at theoretical developments in the social sciences and seeks to integrate them into a new frame of reference. The starting point is the premise that political culture is rooted in the interaction between individual thinking and social norms in contexts that are deeply affected by considerations of economic efficiency. How choices are constrained by the norms that govern organized activity, how organized activity influences the shape of norms, and, finally, how norms are transformed by the choices that are made in response to social changes are crucial matters for inquiry.

The focus of the book is on historical changes in cultural norms and in the related patterns of right and obligation in social and political life. Following a theoretical discussion in the first half of the book, the second half discusses historical transformations in political cultures and lays out the probable trajectories of future change. Although political cultures are shown to be exceptionally diverse, they nevertheless all change in ways that are theoretically commensurable.

In writing this book I have incurred a debt of gratitude to many. I would especially like to thank Stephen Chilton, Thomas A. Metzger, and Andrew J. Nathan, who criticized my ideas as I was developing them in various papers. At a later period James C. Davies made detailed comments on the manuscript from beginning to end. His contribution to my understanding has been matched only by his unstinting support. I am indeed profoundly in his debt. My gratitude goes also to Lucian W. Pye and Shawn W. Rosenberg, whose thinking has deeply influenced my own. Thanks are also due to Emily Loose of Cambridge University Press for valuable suggestions and for patience in steering the manuscript toward publication. My appreciation goes to the Faculty Academic Study Program of Rutgers University for providing me with the time for research and writing. I wish also to express gratitude to Phyllis Moditz of the Rutgers Political Science Department for her extraordinary care in typing numerous drafts. And my deepest thanks go to my wife, Myoung Chung Wilson, who throughout has been a constant and unfailing source of encouragement.

Introduction

Across time far greater than humankind's recorded history huge mountains reared their noble spires. Slow and stately in their growth, their rise was accompanied by rivers of fire, sudden cleavages, and shocks that left those who lived on the slopes in ruin and desolation. So also has it been with new forms of social, political, and economic life. There is, indeed, a specter that haunts contemporary man – it is nothing less than the creation of a new world.

The great tide that raises some and destroys others has no boundary. Change in the modern world is uneven, to be sure, but it is also inexorable and universal. Dikes can be built, levees to protect the privileges of the favored, but they have nowhere held. New institutional forms, novel ideas, and an explosion of aspirations all ceaselessly overwhelm those who cling to the past.

Explanations of change

There is no easy way to summarize the great variety of studies about change, for different thinkers have addressed a multiplicity of problems. For Machiavelli and Hobbes the question was how to maintain order and extend power. Locke and Marx, poles apart otherwise, both focused on ownership or control of property. For Locke the free use of property was the key to political participation, whereas for Marx class struggle, between groups whose identities were determined by their relationship to the control of the means of production, set the stage for political change. Max Weber studied the development of new institutional forms and the formal rationality that characterizes modern bureaucratic operations. Sigmund Freud revealed how the unconscious affects decision making and how great myths become the totems and taboos of civilized life.

In answering questions about change there has been a persistent effort, dating from the classical Greeks, to type societies. Among the better-known modern designations are Ferdinand Tönnies's *Gemeinschaft* and *Gesellschaft;*

1

Sir Henry Maine's status and contract; Herbert Spencer's militant and industrial; Charles H. Cooley's primary and (implicitly) secondary; Emile Durkheim's mechanical and organic; Robert Redfield's folk and urban; and Howard Becker's sacred and secular.[1] The echo of these typologies in contemporary times is found in Mao Zedong's comments about first-, second-, and third-world countries. In constructing typologies thinkers have focused on the individual, the family, the workplace, the market, government, and society. How these various levels are linked and the styles of authority exercised within and among them (e.g., persuasion, fiat, and exchange) are often the basis for the typological distinctions.

Recognizing that individual motivation is often crucial for understanding change, different theories have employed various models. Harry Eckstein has suggested that these fall into two broad categories, the culturist and the rationalist.[2] Culturists focus on collective constructions of meaning. Individual dispositions are aggregated into social level norms and these delimit the possibilities of, and the constraints on, both individual and social action. For rationalists uniformity is in terms of individual motivation. Assuming individual rational calculation of means and ends, rationalists have developed models that purport to explain choices in situations as diverse as policymaking and voting. In dealing with motivation, therefore, the culturist and rationalist positions impose uniformity at two different levels of analysis. In both cases the rich possibilities that exist when a range of psychological inputs are considered are eschewed in the interest of parsimony. Eckstein feels that a resolution of this difficulty is foremost on the agenda of political science.

In the post–World War II era one of the most promising approaches in comparative politics came to be called "political culture." Culturist in orientation, political culture was a union of anthropology, political science and psychology. From anthropology it borrowed the idea that values, cognitions, and feelings, aggregated as generalized dispositions, are crucial variables for understanding behavior. From political science came the idea that the relationship of values to authority is a significant one for understanding political action. From psychology a social learning model was borrowed that helped explain, through socialization studies, how values, cognitions, and feelings are acquired and with what strength and consistency.

Although few doubt that understanding values is important for political analysis, political culture has declined as a dominant paradigm, replaced by

---

[1] Ferdinand Tönnies, *Community and Society*, trans. and ed. Charles P. Loomis (New York: Harper & Row, 1963). From the Introduction by John C. McKinney and Charles P. Loomis, p. 12.

[2] Harry Eckstein, "A Culturist Theory of Political Change," *American Political Science Review* 82, no. 3 (September 1988):789.

rationalist models that provide greater empirical rigor in areas such as policy analysis. A lack of stability over time in value orientations, difficulties in linking complex behavior patterns in diverse areas (e.g., the family and society), and an inability to pinpoint the most crucial socialization influences have all been cited, among others, as reasons for the failure of political culture to achieve its early promise. As a consequence, political culture has become a residual category, something that everyone knows is important but is referred to only to fill in the gaps that remain after harder analysis.

Requirements for a theory

Long ago Sir Francis Bacon pointed out that our knowledge is shaped more by the questions we ask than the theories we propose.[3] In beginning an inquiry into political culture it is appropriate first to frame general questions and the ways to answer these before proposing any specific theory. Mustering empirical data to support the theoretical argument is the last step. The paramount and overriding requirement is how to organize knowledge in such a way that it commands the hidden potential in the issue at question.

Is there an underlying dimension to political culture? Should we focus on a concept such as power, which Bertrand Russell suggested is fundamental to political analysis?[4] Or should we search for a dimension that is less tied to political science, one that applies more generally to all the social science disciplines? Power, for example, may help us to understand the exercise of authority, but except in its most naked aspects it is less useful for understanding obedience. Still less does it tell us about reciprocal exchange, an issue of importance in politics but even more so in economics.

This book focuses on ethical concerns as central to political culture. This is hardly a novel proposition, however, being as it is a point of view developed by Aristotle many centuries ago. How, then, can we hope to say anything new? A reasonable question, therefore, is whether there have been advances in areas of knowledge, or changes in the nature of societies, that justify a continuing search along these lines.

Two developments of the past hundred years are significant. At the individual level psychology as a discipline has become increasingly sophisticated in its explanations of cognition and motivation. We now have a body of theoretical and empirical data that provides greater understanding regarding the wellsprings of human behavior. At the same time, separate analytically from the individual level of analysis is the emergence in social life of giant, complex organizations. As sociologists have long pointed out, such institutions

---

[3] William J. Chambliss, "Toward A Radical Criminology," in *The Politics of Law: A Progressive Critique,* ed. David Kairys (New York: Pantheon, 1982), p. 230.

[4] Bertrand Russell, *Power, A New Social Analysis* (New York: Norton, 1962), p. 9.

have radically altered the ways people relate to each other. Their existence has required novel justifications for elite legitimacy and fresh explanations for group solidarity.

Is political culture, however, equivalent to psychological or social factors, a reflection either of inner psychological processes or of sociological influences? Reductionism is not necessarily the evil that some portray, but it is an important issue to consider in the development of theory. In this book I eschew a reductionist approach. It is more reasonable and fruitful, I believe, to analyze both the motives of individuals and the nature of social institutions and to derive a concept of political culture from the interaction between them.

Causal thinking, especially about human beings, is extremely difficult. The data needed for testing theory are often incomplete. Historical material, whose use in examining virtually any subject has been in vogue since the days of Hegel, is often subject to alternate interpretations. Survey data appear hard in comparison and can be subjected to statistical manipulation. Yet they, too, are rarely complete. Even when they are sufficient from a mathematical standpoint, aggregated data give no clue about specific individuals and are often unhelpful as indicators of future variation.[5]

Some of these difficulties are partially overcome by the use of ideal types. This approach mirrors that of scientific endeavor generally in its attempt to construct simple models that, although they do not replicate the real world, are nonetheless complex enough to serve as explanatory models for the phenomena under consideration. Ideal types abstract the essential features of a situation considered as a whole and organize them into a coherent explanation. Although deficient as a tool for understanding particular preferences or specific relationships, they provide general schemes that are assumed to be probabilistically relevant. These assumptions are then matched against historical or other data for confirmation or disconfirmation.

Constructing ideal types is thus a perfectly valid scientific method for pursuing knowledge. They, too, however, are burdened with qualifications. If intruded upon by pretheoretical assumptions (e.g., racial or gender superiority), the usefulness of ideal types is severely degraded, if not completely obviated. Some absolute prior conditions may be assumed in the construction of an ideal type, but the condition must be bedrock and not spurious. Positing a capacity for moral development, for example, is not the same as a statement that all men and women seek to do good. The former is the basis for constructing a general theoretical model of ethical judgments. The latter assumes a particular type of motivation; it thus restricts theoretical development to a model of causality formulated on the basis of an unexamined assumption.

[5] Shawn W. Rosenberg, *Ideology, Reason and Politics* (Princeton, N.J.: Princeton University Press, 1988), pp. 40–41.

Ideal typification must also avoid the danger of overinclusiveness, of assumptions, implicit or explicit, that there is any complete theory of human behavior. This problem is most severe when a complex reality is dealt with in terms of only two or three categories. The solution, however, is not to leap in despair into the thicket of configurative analysis. Complete description with the aim of avoiding oversimplification runs as much risk of creating confusion as does the model that describes complex variations in dichotomous or trichotomous terms. The balance lies somewhere in between, in the development of ideal categories that direct attention away from inessentials yet are themselves sufficiently textured that they can deal with multiple levels of causation.

Ultimately, and finally, every theory must have at its core a set of assumptions about the roots, ingredients, or elements of behavior. Failure in this area is not trivial. Many theories in the social sciences have lots of sail but no mast. At the heart of the human condition is a human being, and whether that person is said to be motivated by a priori knowledge, by libidinal drives, or by a withering alienation from the products of his or her own labor, that human must be explained. The goal is nothing less than to replace a sense of bewildering diversity with one of far-reaching uniformity, of the particularity of experience with what is truly universal.

Plan of the book

This volume is divided into four parts; the first two deal with theoretical issues while the last two examine and interpret these issues in terms of historical and contemporary data. The goal is to return political culture to a position of central consideration. There is no assumption here that this book completes the task or that its propositions are beyond disconfirmation. The object, rather, is to show how a redirection of attention can enrich our understanding of social life.

Part I contains just one chapter, in which I briefly develop a set of ideas showing how political cultures stabilize the institutional processes of societies. Stabilization is related to elite legitimacy, which, in turn, is a function of institutional form and of property relations. Political culture, I suggest, is synonymous with a concept I label "compliance ideology." Such ideologies reduce institutional transaction costs and thus stabilize institutional arrangements. They are a critical link between the individual and the social environment.

Part II is composed of three chapters that expand the understanding of compliance ideology by examining its psychological and sociological parameters. Neither, I suggest, is reducible to the other; rather, they interact. Chapters 2 and 3, therefore, explore psychological growth and the development of social values. These two developmental patterns are not mirror images, nor do they follow the same dynamic. Disjunctions between the two processes are fostered by changes in institutional forms and technological capabilities and by a continuous process of social discourse. When disjunction occurs it is the source of an interactive effect that influences both individual development and social values. Chapter 4 is directly concerned with this interaction. Although compliance ideologies follow no uniform pattern of development, the diversity we recognize is not unstructured. Rather, compliance ideologies develop, and can only develop, in ways that are appropriate for group interaction in given historical conditions and that do not violate the psychological limits of the human personality. They can thus be categorized in terms of these two limitations.

Part III shifts attention to the historical record of various societies and to the different ways in which compliance ideologies have changed with the development of large, complex organizations. Chapter 5 studies the traditional pattern and the early phase of transition to the modern period. It points out how traditional agricultural techniques and rural family organization corresponded to a generally lower level of ethical development in both the psychological and social areas. As Chapter 6 points out, however, development away from this pattern was highly disjunctive. Compliance ideologies diverged, leading to social tension, revolution, and war.

Part IV is a conclusion, but not in the sense of a summary; rather, it is a discussion of future possibilities. Chapter 7 presents material showing why changes in compliance ideologies have been difficult but also why such ideologies are continuing to change in the contemporary world. Chapter 8 continues this argument, showing the limits of future change and the possibilities for eventual convergence.

Throughout this work a particular definition of political culture will apply, and it is appropriate at this point to state it. Political culture is a set of values that stabilize institutional forms and hierarchical social relationships in terms of ethical constructs; over time these values reflect developmental changes in individual psychology and in social norms of legitimation; they evolve as a consequence of the interaction between them. The definition offered is not a simple one, but by tracing its various components it can serve as the starting point for the development of comprehensive theory.

Concluding comments

It is fashionable to speak of the end of ideology. Such talk supposes that ideological considerations are no longer the engine of world politics. I disagree. As in times of great religious differences, the world today is riven by ideological confrontation. Conflict in many parts of the globe testifies eloquently to a clash of ideas and values.

A desperate scramble has begun for an understanding that will combine our knowledge of the human condition with our hope for a progressive politics. The history of genocide, of bureaucratic encroachment on freedom of dissent, of affluence next to starvation – to name but of few of the ills of our time – deprives us of any easy belief that mankind is rational and free and able to construct nonrepressive cultures. Indeed, men and women are both irrational and unfree and have nowhere ever created a culture free of repression. But if this is so, they nevertheless have one gift that holds out hope, not for a perfect world but for a better one. It is knowledge, not of ultimate ends but of the processes that govern our lives.

Should the societies of today pass successfully through this age of potential Armageddon, there is the possibility of a vastly different world. It will not be one where all people are uniformly alike for each part of the world will bear the stamp of its own unique heritage. It will, however, be a world where major categories of consideration are shared to a degree that renders meaningless the present sources of conflict. Part of the reason for this will surely be a greater shared prosperity. As important, however, will be transformations in the values that define compliance. Such shifts will reflect changes in technology, in work environments and work patterns, and in understandings of social relations. From these, in a continuous process of interaction, flows the possibility for the transformation of societies to higher and better forms.

I

Compliance ideologies

1

Political culture as ideology

Social life is given meaning from individual interpretations of it that are made in terms of a collective standard. Culture is the beliefs, values, and definitions that make up that standard. Although individuals are different, their particular beliefs and values are said to have relative interpersonal consistency and mutual intelligibility through reference to common cultural definitions.[1]

A focus on shared values and beliefs is as old as social analysis itself. Although the manner of this sharing is now being subjected to reevaluation,[2] some set of commonly recognized objective standards seems clearly requisite for the stable functioning of societies. In the broadest sense this collective standard has been called a civil religion; more analytically, it has been referred to as publicly common ways of relating.[3] When narrowed to the domain of politics, this standard has been defined as "the system of empirical beliefs, expressive symbols, and values which defines the situation in which political action takes place."[4] Political culture, as it was traditionally formulated, had at its core the assumption that every collectivity has a set of orientations that are used by its members in authority contexts to make choices, resolve dilemmas, and accept particular resolutions as valid.

Investigating the beliefs, symbols, and values that are relevant in authority contexts has proven not to be easy. Because power and responsibility are features of almost all human interaction, the research task is overwhelming

---

[1] Shawn W. Rosenberg, *Reason, Ideology and Politics* (Princeton, N.J.: Princeton University Press, 1988), pp. 3, 5.

[2] Ibid.

[3] W. Lance Bennett, "Invitation, Ambiguity, and Drama in Political Life: Civil Religion and the Dilemmas of Public Morality," *Journal of Politics* 41, no. 1 (February 1979):111. Stephen Chilton, *Defining Political Development* (Boulder, Colo.: Lynne Reinner, 1988), p. 14.

[4] Sidney Verba, "Comparative Political Culture," in *Political Culture and Political Development,* ed. Lucian W. Pye and Sidney Verba (Princeton, N.J.: Princeton University Press, 1965), p. 513.

without further specification. Political socialization developed as a major area of research in order to deal with this problem. Those cognitions, feelings, and schemes of evaluation that are important for cultural continuity generally and political behavior specifically are said to be formed in a learning process where already socialized carriers of culture impart their knowledge to younger generations.[5] Socialization studies, however, were only partially successful in fulfilling the task allotted them. Questions arose over which cognitions, feelings, and schemes of evaluation are important for explaining specific adult political behaviors and, indeed, whether orientations acquired early in life persist to later periods.

A major failure of the political culture approach, in my view, has been an overconcentration on values and behavior per se at the expense of other variables. We may, for example, agree that the stability of authority systems requires a belief in the legitimacy of leaders along with supportive values of loyalty, trust, and the like. But this does not tell us very much. Social systems have particular forms of organization and it is within these groupings that significant political behavior occurs. We must ask, therefore, what these forms are and what maintains them. Political culture, I suggest, is part of the answer.

If political culture is concerned with subgroups, how shall these be defined? Are they, as Marxists would insist, social classes, historically shaped, that contend in a context where the ideas of the ruling class are the major ideas in society? Or are they, as I argue, more concrete entities, the productive organizations of society? Although broad classifications of have and have-not may surely be discerned in any society, it is actual institutional contexts that tell us about the nature of hierarchy, the needs of elites and subordinates, and the nature of social contention. In these contexts, especially, political culture is vital and immediate. It stipulates the meaning of relationships and defines the purposes of individual and institutional existence.

The meaning of institution

Subgroups can be classified by a number of terms including "family," "class," "association," "organization," "subsystem," and "institution." Some, such as organization, are thought of as relatively fixed and formal, whereas others, such as kinship, are more elastic. Although the bureaucratic organization is an exceptionally important subgroup in modern times, its current centrality as a social institution has no analogue in traditional experience, even bearing in mind the great historical bureaucracies of the Chinese and the Byzantines. As a consequence, I primarily, and in a general sense,

[5] Harry Eckstein, "A Culturist Theory of Political Change," *American Political Science Review* 82, no. 3 (September 1988):791, 792, 802.

use the term "institution" when speaking of subgroups, reserving the right to use more specific titles as appropriate. An institution, as I define the term, is a set of roles whose interaction is specifically designed to achieve particular goals.

The functional role of institutions is to take advantage of the superior productivity that occurs as a consequence of joint effort. Work design and overall institutional structure are related to the goals of the institution, whereas its efficiency is related to its internal organization, the technical capability that is available, and the general amount of knowledge that exists. Institutions all have informal attributes (internally and in terms of their external relations), but it is the formal goal (e.g., procreation, molding of beliefs, production of goods, military superiority, etc.) that establishes what general subgroup category the institution belongs to.

In achieving their stated ends institutions set constraints on behavior. On the one hand, such restrictions are general and apply to the membership as a whole; on the other hand, they are specific in terms of a person's role in the institution's division of labor. It is the incumbents of leadership positions who are responsible for enforcing constraints, specifying incentives and disincentives, and devising rules that will promote institutional efficiency. By surrounding power with a halo of legitimacy, leaders are able to uphold moral and ethical guidelines for cooperative endeavor that reduce the costs of enforcing compliance.

Institutions, then, even diffuse ones, have structures of power and responsibility that are clearly "political" from the standpoint of the institution's members. In complex societies, however, a person is a member of multiple institutions, some of which may be political in the formal sense. Although not all institutions are legitimate within a polity (e.g., the Mafia), those that are acquire their legitimacy in terms of the polity's moral and ethical norms in the same manner that roles are legitimated within an institution (i.e., by reference to a collective standard). Indeed, for social stability, the moral criteria in both areas must be broadly congruent, given the multiple institutional memberships of individuals and the fact that institutions are nested hierarchically within the polity.

The moral and ethical norms of institutions are thus behavioral rules that govern internal relational patterns. Put in other words, institutions are the relational patterns and can be described in terms of the behavioral rules that govern these patterns. Although astonishing diversity may exist in the forms of institutions, their rules provide standardized information. At the most general level, rules define the division of labor; they also set forth how members are mobilized to achieve stated goals, how rewards and punishments are established, how competing behavioral rules are preempted, and how legitimacy to ongoing arrangements is provided.

Institutional costs and the origin of rules

If rules describe institutions, how do they come into being and under what constraints do they function? Clearly, because institutions are embedded in societies, factors exogenous to the institution itself may be of importance. In this section, however, attention is directed primarily at the relational patterns within institutions. External influences are discussed with the purpose of illuminating the nature of internal interactions.

Control, as an aspect of relationships, is ubiquitous; it is always exercised relative to the particular conditions that inhere in exchanges among individuals. Because all decisions are constrained by scarcity, in goods, prestige, or whatever, all relationships are bounded by costs that must be apportioned among those who are parties to exchange. Within institutions apportionment is by rules enforced by those in authority.

Economic matters account for a large proportion of the concerns that people have. How scarce and indivisible resources are allocated and whose demands have highest priority are issues of great importance, both for individuals and for societies. Fundamentally, such questions regard property rights and are central to any economy.[6] But property rights are themselves nothing but a set of rules, which is to say they are regulations that specify and enforce a particular pattern of distribution.[7] They are, therefore, political. Regulation (politics) and allocation (economics) are thus reciprocally joined. This is clear even when the matter at hand does not involve tangible resources. Participation in governance, for example, requires a particular type of property right, one related to the privilege of exercising authority. When allocation with regard to this right is relatively unrestricted, participation (if exercised) will be widespread.[8]

The role of authority is to coordinate the activities of the members of an institution by upholding rules that structure "publicly relevant behavior."[9] Organizations are hierarchical because social action depends on the differential distribution of power; authority is centralized because this economizes on the costs associated with issuing directives. Those who govern, by control over the special kind of property called authority, have, as it were, a power cachement they can drawn on to fulfill their leadership role.

If power is a cachement whose use depends on role occupancy, then those who function at the state level have rights to it superior to those of all others

[6] Lester C. Thurow, *The Zero-Sum Society: Distribution and the Possibilities for Economic Change* (New York: Basic Books, 1980), p. 130.

[7] Douglass C. North, *Structure and Change in Economic History* (New York: Norton, 1981), p. 17.

[8] David Lyons, *Ethics and the Rule of Law* (Cambridge: Cambridge University Press, 1984), p. 208.

[9] John Gerard Ruggie, "Complexity, Planning, and Public Order," in *Organized Social Complexity: Challenge to Politics and Policy,* ed. Todd R. La Porte (Princeton, N.J.: Princeton University Press, 1975), p. 147.

(when not unchecked by specific rules). State power appears as a natural monopoly because its holders are responsible for protecting the property rights of subordinate individuals along the multiple dimensions by which property can be defined. The state has a monopoly on the use of coercive force, and control over institutions such as the police, because of the great economy of scale that results from the use of coercion in protecting rights. In exchange for tax revenues the state assumes responsibility for the enforcement of general institutional arrangements (preventing cheating, free riding, etc.); for monitoring exchanges among subordinate political, economic, and social institutions (maintaining courts for contract disputes, etc.); and for supplying services to reduce the costs of exchanges (maintaining a military establishment, customs offices, a treasury, etc.).

Prestige, income, and power do not vary at random. In some combination they are found in all societies, representing structured inequalities that can be used to define social groups. Disproportionate shares of wealth and income and control over major political, economic, and social institutions correlate with beliefs that support such arrangements; these beliefs bolster the institutional processes that shield the privileged from the preferences and pressures of the less advantaged.[10] Although rules, as Isaiah Berlin has pointed out, enjoin uniform behavior in identical cases and thus entail a measure of equality,[11] they do so within the framework of an underlying specification of property rights. This specification sets forth the modes and limits of distribution and delineates the system of protection governing distribution. Societies, says the economist James M. Buchanan, exist when property rights are defined and boundaries are drawn.[12] Rules, then, establish the modalities of behavior within that definition.

Rules also criminalize – with the intent to repress – activities that violate the prevailing specification of property rights. Criminologists tend to agree that, by and large, it is the affluent and the influential who define what behavior is to be officially regarded as criminally deviant.[13] Monitoring agencies that deal with deviance are an important part of the institutional matrix that develops and within which elites exercise, and often work to increase, control. Of course, not the least of the reasons why elites criminalize certain kinds of behavior is that they themselves, as individuals, have personally ascribed to the legitimacy of prevailing property rights in order to reach the top. If institutional stability is to be maintained and their own

[10] Joan Huber and William H. Form, *Income and Ideology: An Analysis of the American Political Formula* (New York: Free Press), 1973, p. 61.

[11] Cited in Douglas Rae et al., *Equalities* (Cambridge, Mass.: Harvard University Press, 1981), p. 21.

[12] Gareth Locksley, "Individuals, Contracts and Constitutions: The Political Economy of James M. Buchanan," in *Twelve Contemporary Economists*, ed. J. R. Shackleton and Gareth Locksley (New York: Wiley, 1981), p. 39.

[13] Ronald Chester, *Inheritance, Wealth, and Society* (Bloomington: Indiana University Press, 1982), p. 149.

positions legitimized, an equal willingness by others to adhere to the rules is essential.

The elite, which may, of course, dominate a number of different types of institutions, is often socially homogeneous. There is a tendency for elites to recruit new members in their own image, according to criteria that validate elite status and that justify, in the elites' view, the unequal rewards they enjoy. Indeed, they also often establish the extent of these rewards. In the United States, for example, top executives set their own very high incomes, in accordance with standards these same executives consider right and proper.[14] Such desires to utilize control in order to augment prestige and distinction have long been noted. Unger, for one, states that the basic impulse of institutional leaders is "everywhere and always the same: to ensure maximum leeway for their own instrumental rationality and to limit the discretion of other groups."[15] The urges for influence and affluence are said to go hand in hand, with wealth the key to influence and influence the lever that pries loose the lid to wealth.[16] Even the heroes of bygone ages were not exempt from these tendencies. Adam Smith, in *Wealth of Nations*, put forth that legal, economic, and constitutional arguments often mask deeper motives for position and power. Said he of America's founders, "The leading men of America, like those of all other countries, desire to preserve their own importance."[17]

Transaction costs are related to how property rights are structured and managed. As Douglass North puts it, "The state will specify rules to maximize the income of the ruler and his group and then, subject to that constraint, will devise rules that would lower transaction costs."[18] The form that property rights take is the result of the tension between these two conditions.[19] Elite rewards, therefore, are justified in the context of the costs (i.e., transaction costs) of organizing, maintaining, and enforcing the rules of a particular institutional arrangement. These costs exist in areas of enforcing compliance to rules and adherence to agreements, restraining opportunism and shirking, detecting violations, acquiring information (partly to minimize uncertainty), and organizing institutional activity.

Institutions coordinate the activities of many individuals. Coordination has costs that are related to the general level of technology (e.g., feudal ag-

[14] Sidney Verba and Gary R. Orren, *Equality in America: The View from the Top* (Cambridge, Mass.: Harvard University Press, 1985), p. 150.
[15] Roberto Mangabeira Unger, *Law in Modern Society: Toward a Criticism of Social Theory* (New York: Free Press, 1976), p. 190.
[16] Verba and Orren, *Equality in America*, p. 218.
[17] Cited in J. Bronowski and Bruce Mazlish, *The Western Intellectual Tradition: From Leonardo to Hegel* (New York: Harper, 1960), p. 376.
[18] North, *Structure and Change*, p. 24.
[19] Ibid., p. 18.

ricultural techniques versus those of bureaucratic industrialism), the size of enterprise, the amount of available capital, educational levels, and the degree to which the state can provide a system of uniform weights and measures, judicial services, and so on. Coordination also depends on the degree to which agency problems (to use the economist's term) exist. This is perhaps the most crucial area. Maximizing institutional efficiency depends greatly on the perceived legitimacy of institutional arrangements. The rules facilitating exchanges among superiors and inferiors, defining role requirements, and curtailing the damage that deviance may entail, must be nested within a framework of shared ideas regarding goals, status, and appropriate rewards. Should this overall framework be lacking, the transaction costs involved in enforcing compliance will rise markedly.

Interestingly, those who are subordinate generally accept prevailing institutional arrangements as fair, especially if they believe those in authority are guided by rational standards that serve common ends. In such cases, profound resentment about inequality does not arise. Workers in the United States, for example, rarely question the premises of ownership claims, not least because they feel that doing so might jeopardize the claims they make in other areas of life, such as asking an undesirable visitor to leave one's private home.[20] In fact, in the very sense that Antonio Gramsci meant it, hegemony is most effective when both the privileged and the underprivileged alike believe that the way things are is the way they ought to be. For the powerful to be beyond reproach and their challengers evil, the interests of those who exercise control in institutions must appear as general interests, while other interests are merely particular and (potentially) unworthy.

Every society, in its socialization mechanisms, inculcates support for the beliefs that bolster the interests of those who exercise control in institutions. These beliefs may be phrased in kinship terms, as religious tenets, as codes for a warrior society, or as a comprehensive ideology for a multifaceted secular state. Shared cognitive orientations are part of the psychological basis for feelings of belongingness; they are also guideposts that describe an individual's place in society, justify allegiance, and spell out the goals and means of group activity. Additionally, they are part of specific rules that compel particular forms of loyalty and participation. Acquiring these beliefs is an aspect of the learning experience of those who will later be selected for leadership and who, in their turn, will uphold these beliefs and their associated institutional forms. In fact, of course, the dominant group in society no more specifies property rights solely according to its interests than does any other group. It seeks its interests, rather, within an ongoing form of economic organization in which the need to minimize transaction costs requires shared

---

[20] Robert W. Gordon, "New Developments in Legal Theory," in *The Politics of Law: A Progressive Critique*, ed. David Kairys (New York: Pantheon, 1982), p. 287.

standards that both limit the degree of elite aggrandizement and bolster the loyalty of subordinates. There are, of course, many possible variations, and rulers have often ignored the needs of subordinates in seeking to maintain or secure specific advantages. The history of rebellion and revolution, however, is a cautionary tale for those who perpetually ignore the needs of followers.

The beliefs and values that uphold a particular institutional arrangement in a manner that reduces transaction costs are a significant component of what I define as political culture. They are not, of course, all of the cognitions and evaluative patterns to be found in a society, although there are links between them and the core ones of the culture as a whole. They are, nevertheless, those that concern the stable and efficient operation of social institutions. I label these particular beliefs and values a "compliance ideology."

Political culture as ideology

Ideology as a term came into being around 1800 to describe the work of a group of French philosophers who were interested in the science of ideas.[21] For Americans, however, ideology has generally been used in a pejorative sense, to describe closed and inflexible ideas. This has had the unfortunate consequence of limiting the use of this term solely because it smacks of the passions of doctrinaire debate rather than scholarly discourse.

An additional difficulty with the term "ideology," however, is the multitude of meanings given it. Shils, for example, says that ideology is different from the term "creed," which affirms the existing order of society.[22] An ideology is more extensive, carrying images of a reconstituted society, a set of ideas that can be used by reformists or revolutionaries to describe the ills of current society, the virtues of the society to be, and the ways that the transformation between the two can be achieved.[23] Ideology, in fact, has often been used to describe those ideas which make explicit the nature of a good society in opposition to the one that actually exists.

Other definitions of ideology are more specific. Ideology has been said, for example, to be a structure of signification that defines roles and the purpose of individual activity. In this sense ideology functions as a system of communication using a common language and providing common categories of thought.[24] Somewhat more broadly, ideology is said to be a systematized, integrated, relatively inflexible, and authoritative set of opinions, attitudes,

[21] George C. Lodge, *The New American Ideology* (New York: Knopf, 1975), p. 22.

[22] Edward Shils, "Ideology," in *The Intellectuals and the Powers and Other Essays*, ed. Edward Shils (Chicago: University of Chicago Press, 1972), p. 24.

[23] John Bryan Starr, *Ideology and Culture: An Introduction to the Dialectic of Contemporary Chinese Politics* (New York: Harper & Row, 1973), pp. 10–11.

[24] Franz Schurmann, *Ideology and Organization in Communist China* (Berkeley and Los Angeles: University of California Press, 1966), pp. 18, 58.

and values that touch a number of different areas of social life, including politics, economics, religion, and so on.[25]

By combining these various definitional strands ideology can be termed an economizing device that incorporates a world view that legitimizes the existing order and provides a framework for a consensus on the general purposes of community life. An ideology is a set of ideas with affective overtones that describe both the world that is and the world that ought to be. The feature of ideology that permits this is the moral and ethical judgments about fairness that are interwoven into it. Such judgments give ideology its distinctive characteristic as an explanation for the ways in which people relate and as a measuring rod that clarifies inconsistencies between experience and what could and ought to be.

Ideologies are "the framework by which a community defines and applies values."[26] Karl Mannheim, in *Ideology and Utopia,* describes them as myths that justify existing governments and that are, in some sense, false.[27] Although most authors today reject the idea of false consciousness or delusionary belief, ideologies do serve the function of defending social institutions and rationalizing group interests, often in the face of inconsistencies. They tell who should rule and why and explain stratification in ways that are meaningful for individuals. Because they justify the generational persistence of inequality, they legitimize, in Clifford Geertz's sense, both the search for power (interest theory) and the ways to reduce anxiety (strain theory).[28] They thus function, as Mannheim early suggested, in both a particular and a total sense, as an explanation of social arrangements and as a rationale for the rights and duties of individuals in society. Ideology, in this sense, is that aspect of the collective standard which serves to elicit predictable patterns of behavior in terms of an ongoing definition of status arrangements.

One behavior that ideology is expected to justify is compliance. A compliance ideology, therefore, as part of ideology in general, bolsters stable institutional arrangements by explaining, justifying, and prompting support for a particular stratification system whose failure or demise will lead to the disintegration of a particular pattern of control. The idea that a compliance ideology serves social maintenance purposes, however, should not be confused with the concept of a dominant ideology that primarily reflects the ideas and interests of a ruling class. To be sure, a compliance ideology does bind elites together; more important by far, however, it justifies institutional arrangements, including stratification, in a way that reduces transaction costs, thus

[25] T. W. Adorno, Else Frenkel-Brunswick, Daniel J. Levinson, and R. Nevitt Sanford, *The Authoritarian Personality,* pt. 1 (New York: Wiley, 1964), p. 2.

[26] Lodge, *New American Ideology,* p. 7.

[27] Karl Mannheim, *Ideology and Utopia* (London: Routledge & Kegan Paul, 1936).

[28] Clifford Geertz, *The Interpretation of Culture* (New York: Basic Books, 1973).

serving the interests, in different ways, of various groups. Although elites may (and do) use a compliance ideology to legitimize their status, the ideology itself serves the more neutral purposes of institutional stability more than it does the conspiratorial (or even unconscious) drive for power on the part of a particular group. Sanctions alone are not normally the most effective way to enforce authority. Control, after all, is costly in the absence of trust and cooperation. Efficiency and economic value do not reside in situations where there is a continuous need for coercion.[29] A compliance ideology, in short, serves the interests of the less privileged as well as the more favored.

Compliance ideologies are important because they function to meet ends deemed desirable by a large cross section of a society. They infuse relationships within institutions with an aura of justice, thereby engendering a sense of fairness that is as important for the disadvantaged as it is for elites. By connecting values with the context of an institutional setting, a compliance ideology gives values meaning. "Ought" is combined with "is"; a particular kind of fair arrangement that should be honored is, in fact, shown to be actually in practice. Compliance ideologies thus help mobilize people to participate in institutional activities; they tap energies, check free riders, and channel behavior in the direction of fulfilling institutional goals. In addition, they connect institutional activities. Internally, as an aspect of institutional operating rules, they make meaningful the necessary coordination among various activities (e.g., budget allocation, personnel assignment, and selection of an appropriate communication channel and format). Externally, the general features of compliance ideologies permit the members of different institutions to communicate effectively with each other. They are the basis for interinstitutional coordination, dispute settlement, and the ranking of interinstitutional priorities. Without an effective overarching compliance ideology, societies would fragment, a consequence that is noted in revolutionary situations where agreement about an appropriate compliance ideology has ceased to exist.

Law as a compliance ideology

A compliance ideology is broader than the law per se although ideas, attitudes, and beliefs about law (i.e., a legal culture) are an important part of the ideology. A compliance ideology is infused with conceptions of justice that involve broad definitions of the appropriate interests of individuals and of the community. In this sense, a compliance ideology is an ethos that always subordinates some interests that might otherwise be acted upon. Law, specifically, through its structure of courts and rules, mediates conflicts of in-

---

[29] Kenneth J. Arrow, *The Limits of Organization* (New York: Norton, 1974), p. 72.

terest and adjudicates among diverse claims. As an aspect of compliance, law is never neutral; it is never totally blind and impartial for it always reflects the overarching ethos of compliance. It does, however, strive for predictability within the framework of that ethos and, when codified, for impersonality as well. Norms are encoded as rules, which then function as a logic for an authoritative definition of appropriate and inappropriate behavior.

Law is not all norms but only those that are authoritative.[30] As such, laws may be highly formal (e.g., the Napoleonic Code) and apply to activities within large, diverse societies; or they may be less structured and inclusive, as with the regulations of a social club or a corporation, or even the customs embodied in the oral tradition of a tribal group. Law embodies "is" and "ought" in that it is a reciprocal expectation regarding conduct arising from a recurring mode of interaction among individuals and groups.[31] It is thus a factor in the power, or lack of it, of all members of a society. In the establishment of reciprocal expectations, certain outcomes become established as primary (substance); these are linked to acceptable and established modes for their attainment (procedure). For much of recorded history reciprocal expectations often varied very little over time. In these circumstances law served primarily to establish and defend social hierarchies and class divisions. When expectations change, however, law may become the defense of the rights of emerging groups. When these rights have been codified in constitutions and in laws governing private interactions (e.g., contract law), they may again become the vehicle for the protection of privilege.

In reducing the transaction costs of institutions, law operates through constitutions as regulations that govern the range and mode of acceptable behavior. A constitution establishes the nature of property rights, the rights of government vis-à-vis those of individual citizens, and what goods fall within the public domain and how they will be provided and financed. There are, in addition, bodies of regulatory law that apply to specific institutional arrangements and that affect the operations of particular organizations. These organizations, in turn, have further regulations, distillations of requirements established at higher levels that aim to maintain a specified pattern of property rights and of individual and community rights within an institution.

Along with the development of specialized legal norms and legal institutions, there also develops a legal profession. Although this profession is most clearly observed in modern, bureaucratic states, all societies, even quite primitive ones, usually have someone or some group responsible for interpreting the rules of society. Historically, such people have been called wise men, shamans, advisers to the king, and, of course, lawyers.

[30] Lawrence M. Friedman, *Law and Society: An Introduction* (Englewood Cliffs, N.J.: Prentice-Hall, 1977), p. 4.
[31] Unger, *Law in Modern Society*, p. 49.

In understanding compliance we cannot downplay the role of those who advise about the law. In times of rapid change knowing who such people are (e.g., jurists, revolutionary ideologues, etc.) is critical. Forty-five percent of the signers of the American Declaration of Independence and 56 percent of the members of the Constitutional Convention in Philadelphia, for instance, were lawyers.[32] The members of prestige law firms in the United States, those whose legal work is in the service of corporations, have annual incomes far larger than the senior executives of the same institutions.[33] As protectors of the institutions of society, lawyers sit at the very heart of compliance. Those who frame rules, and who are authorized disputants in conflicts over rules, are the true guardians of whatever theory of property rights prevails.

Law is founded on a conception of fairness and in turn affects that conception. Dedicated primarily to social control, to effective government, law is nevertheless not an autonomous entity, any more than it is a mere reflection of the interests of a particular group. It evolves in societies as a mechanism for regulating behavior by restricting choices, and it does this in a manner that reflects, ultimately, the ideas, attitudes, beliefs, and expectations that people in general have about their social relationships. Law is thus rooted in particular forms of social life. As a major component of any compliance ideology, it teaches us, as few other bodies of empirical data can, what a society does and does not value.

Compliance ideology and social change

Compliance ideologies are not static. They change historically, usually gradually but at other times in sharp jumps that involve violent, dramatic changes in stratification patterns, and the destruction of a society's physical assets. Yet understanding change is a vexatious problem.

A compliance ideology is a set of rules regarding institutional arrangements. The beliefs embedded in the ideology are acquired during socialization, including formal education, and are relevant to aspirations about work and reward, the form of the division of labor, and so on. In seeking reasons for changes in compliance ideologies, therefore, we must look both at the human factor – the changes that occur in the way people evaluate their social world – and at underlying changes in institutional arrangements that lead to incongruities with people's expectations. The link between these two interrelated sources of change is a complicated and nonintuitive one.

[32] Seymour M. Lipset, *The First New Nation: The United States in Historical and Comparative Perspective* (New York: Norton, 1979), p. 70.
[33] John A. Byrne, "Executive Pay: Who Got What In '86," *International Business Week*, no. 2995–325 (May 4, 1987):56.

People's views about institutional arrangements change when they are able to conceptualize those arrangements in a new way. The nature of arrangements is largely determined by the general technological level of society and its institutional complexity. Agricultural societies and information-age societies have institutional arrangements with different relationship patterns. These differences correlate with concepts of social life that differ in their degrees of abstractness, consistency, and coherence. Although any given individual's capacity to reevaluate social life is idiosyncratic, for reasons that are partly innate and also partly due to education and the nature of personal experiences, the ways in which people overall view social arrangements do alter as institutional patterns change.

Shifts in the way that people evaluate social life can also arise as a consequence of the behavior of particular individuals or groups. An obvious example is when leaders deprive subordinates of what the latter feel is their fair share. Leadership, of course, need not be self-consciously opportunistic for subordinates to develop such feelings. Power may flow increasingly into the hands of some because they have a relative abundance of time, money, and interest to devote to institutional arrangements. In such cases an increasing inequality may be less the result of deliberate policy than of a subtle shift of responsibility. Michel's "iron law of oligarchy" speaks eloquently to this issue.[34]

In compliance ideologies moral and efficiency criteria are joined in a way that provides rationalizations for success and failure. The seeming inevitability and neutrality of these rationalizations is broken when procedural or substantive rules become divorced from the vocabulary of morality. When law protects the interests of some at the expense of others in a way that has become repugnant, then the compliance ideology is compromised as a mechanism for reducing institutional transaction costs. Although this type of situation can exist for a long time, there develops, nevertheless, a strain whose resolution may ultimately involve a reform of compliance criteria.

Compliance ideologies thus change as a consequence of the influence of various and often interrelated factors. The basic cause, however, is continuous social discourse about the rules that govern institutional arrangements. In times of stability this discourse has the appearance of affirmation and approval of received wisdom. At other times institutional arrangements may change owing to technological innovation or human agency. These changes alter relationship patterns and call into question the validity of institutional rules. In the dialogue that ensues a discontinuity is revealed between the way individuals think about rules and the rules themselves. This disjunction can

---

[34] Robert Michels, *Political Parties* (New York: Free Press, 1962).

ultimately lead to changes in the way people think as well as in the ways the rules themselves are formulated.

Summary

A compliance ideology is a special category of ideology as a whole. It embodies the beliefs and evaluations that people have about authority within the context of the institutions that structure their lives. It is not all beliefs and evaluations, nor is it the specific knowledge that people acquire about particular institutions (e.g., the presidency, political parties, etc.), important though that knowledge is for understanding the framework of compliance. Nor is a compliance ideology all publicly common ways of relating, to use Chilton's term.[35] Rather, a compliance ideology rests both on generalized notions of what is morally acceptable and on regulations (customary or codified) that translate what is acceptable into specific guides for action. The study of political culture, as I use the term, is the study of compliance ideologies and the way they legitimize systems of institutional control.

In seeking to understand how compliance ideologies justify particular patterns of authority, several levels of analysis are involved. A compliance ideology is rooted in individuals, yet it is not simply a summation of individual values; it can be articulated independently of individuals as a body of regulative principles. There is, in fact, a complex pattern of interaction between individual evaluative capabilities and social frameworks of knowledge, the boundaries of which must be explored. No simple mechanism, such as class interest, will suffice as an explanation. Rather, we must analyze the psychological variables that underlie individual cognitive and evaluative frameworks, the way in which social factors affect these frameworks (and vice versa), how institutional arrangements are influenced by general technological and productive capabilities, how ideas that minimize transaction costs are developed and maintained by institutions, and how these ideas become articulated and challenged as legitimations for control in institutional life.[36] These various strands are the subject of discussion in Part II.

[35] Chilton, *Defining Political Development*, p. 14.
[36] Based in part on ideas set forth by J. Hartley, "Ideology and Organizational Behavior," *International Studies of Management and Organization* 13, no. 3 (Fall 1983):26–7.

II

Theoretical issues

2

Psychological limits

Just as the earth once stood in the center of the universe, surpassed only by the heavenly kingdom, so also did man once stand as the finest work of creation. This conceit has long since passed. Man has been revealed as a creature among creatures, occupying but a peripheral speck in a vast universe. Qualities once thought to be unique are now known to be possessed by others. Man the upright animal, the thinker, communicator and toolmaker – these are no longer the special possessions of humans.

Yet for all the traits that are lowly and shared, mankind is more than *primus inter pares*. Characteristics must be judged by their quality as well as their uniqueness. There are degrees of logical thought and of toolmaking that set mankind apart. Men and women may share their basic drives with other creatures, but the capacity to think about these drives, define, order, and discuss them in terms of their causal significance, this indeed may be unique in time and place. In fact, as a species, humans are insatiable in their pursuit of knowledge, accumulating wisdom just as so many other objects are acquired. Collecting is itself, in fact, another noteworthy drive. Objects and honors are sought after as distinctions, the lack of which in whatever degree leads to anxiety, the motivation that Freud described as "always present somewhere or other behind every symptom."[1]

How one behaves, thinks, and feels defines the individual personality, an ancient word first used by the early Christian church to designate the three masks or modes of being of the Trinity.[2] The capacity to act in a uniquely self-determined way and to rationalize one's actions and deliberate on the anxieties that may be aroused are part of the special ego identity of every person, constructed and reconstructed throughout life. These evolving reconstructions come from solutions to the problems each person faces. They come also from the developing capabilities of the mind to construct general

---

[1] Sigmund Freud, *Civilization and Its Discontents*, trans. and ed. James Strachey (New York: Norton, 1961), p. 82.

[2] George C. Lodge, *The New American Ideology* (New York: Knopf, 1975), p. 55.

guiding principles and its corollary capability to direct behavior autonomously toward fulfillment of feelings of affiliation, achievement, privacy, creativity, and so on.

According to Gordon Allport, anxiety flows from the dependency into which all people are born.[3] There is, at the beginning of every human life, an inclusive, all-embracing, and intimate bond between the ego and the world that surrounds it. The separation of ego and world, however, is intrinsic to normal growth. Leaving a state of complete and unconceptualized dependency is the source of the search for meaning, for understanding regarding the anxiety that accompanies the inevitable process of individuation. It is the source as well for all of the dualities that define existence – indeed, for the conceptions of duality and dialectic (or growth from duality) themselves. As the ancient *Dao De Jing* says:

> Being and non-being produce each other;
> Difficult and easy complete each other;
> Long and short contrast each other;
> High and low distinguish each other;
> Sound and voice harmonize with each other;
> Front and back follow each other.[4]

Such mundane opposite forces can be elevated into loftier dualities that touch the very definition of life: masculinity–femininity; order–disorder; affiliative–agonistic; activity–passivity; and, of course, the greatest of all, eros–thanatos, the life-giving and life-taking urges that Freud in his later years spoke of as the polar meanings of existence. It is the separate quality of these dualities that causes anxiety; it is the contemplation of their relationship that begins the process of understanding of the world one has been separated from and of one's own place in it as a developing, acting, and feeling person.

Of all the dualities that have meaning for social life perhaps none is as important as individuality–sociability. As Charles H. Cooley said years ago, "self and society are twin born."[5] If every person is born into dependency, as Allport stated, they are also, as autonomous beings, born into opposition to it. For as Nobel laureate Gerald M. Edelman put it, "Individuality is not an epiphenomenon, it's at the very center of our humanness."[6] This individuality, however, as Freud noted in *Civilization and Its Discontents*, is in inescapable

---

[3] Gordon Allport, *Pattern and Growth in Personality* (New York: Holt, Rinehart & Winston, 1963), pp. 556–7.

[4] Cited in John Bryan Starr, *Continuing the Revolution: The Political Thought of Mao* (Princeton, N.J.: Princeton University Press, 1979), p. 8.

[5] Ferdinand Tönnies, *Community and Society*, trans. and ed. Charles P. Loomis (New York: Harper & Row, 1963). From the Introduction by John C. McKinney and Charles P. Loomis, p. 15.

[6] Cited in David Hellerstein, "Plotting a Theory of the Brain," *New York Times Magazine*, May 22, 1988, sec. 6, p. 64.

permanent tension with society. More accurately, perhaps, we can say that this tension is not with society per se but with demands to conform to expectations that concern the needs of the group.[7]

A person is thus torn between individuality and sociability. On the one hand there are, clearly, deeply felt needs for others. This is not merely a genetic sociability such as is found among the social insects for whom dependence is all-embracing from the beginning of life to its end. Rather, because of the balance that must be maintained with individuality, sociability is an articulated, self-determined quality that derives from early, complete dependence, is shaped by socialization influences, and is progressively modified and redefined as the personality matures and develops. In tension with sociability is a need for self-identification, an equally deeply felt need for personal expression, self-assertion and self-satisfaction. However, because all normal human beings are socially oriented, the need for individuality is rarely carried to the extreme of isolated existence, to a life apart from others except for purposes of procreation. Independence, therefore, is always independence within a group and is thus in tension with dependence on the group.

Some authors, in their attempts to explain social life, have emphasized either individuality or sociability. They have, for example, discussed a need for privacy as a component of an "individualistic complex."[8] Or, like Schopenhauer, they have interpreted men's actions as springing from some boundless and unqualified egoism.[9] In the contemporary world of social science rational choice theory (based on self-interested value maximization) is much in vogue. In an older tradition, David McClelland has discussed the need for power, how it serves egoistic cravings but also how it can take prosocial forms.[10]

Others have stressed sociability. In the late nineteenth century P. Kropotkin, who debated Darwin's ideas with the British biologist T. H. Huxley, said that species survival depended more on cooperation than on competition.[11] In the interaction between the urge for union and the urge for autonomy there develops the capability for altruistic thinking and for reciprocity, for an understanding of how the self is related to others, and of the kinds of

---

[7] Cited in Karl Dietrich Bracher, *The Age of Ideologies: A History of Political Thought in the Twentieth Century* (New York: St. Martin's, 1982), p. 140.

[8] Anita L. Allen, *Uneasy Access: Privacy for Women in a Free Society* (Totowa, N.J.: Rowman & Littlefield, 1988), p. 50, citing J. Ronald Pennock.

[9] Arthur Schopenhauer, *On the Basis of Morality*, trans. E. F. J. Payne (Indianapolis: Bobbs-Merrill, 1965), p. 131.

[10] David C. McClelland, *Power: The Inner Experience* (New York: Irvington Publishers, 1975), pp. 15, 67.

[11] James Youniss, "Piaget and the Self Constituted Through Relations," in *The Relationship Between Social and Cognitive Development*, ed. Willis F. Overton (Hillsdale, N.J.: Erlbaum, 1983), pp. 201–2.

behavior that foster cooperative relationships. Jerome Kagan claims that underlying the capability to relate with others is a capacity for empathy that is universally inherent in the possibilities for development.[12]

An overemphasis on individualism can arouse anxiety that becomes, as an aspect of conscience, a force for social cohesion. On the other hand, too much emphasis on sociability can arouse impulses for autonomy that are a source of the redefinition of relationships. Every child in every culture experiences the stress associated with the sociability–individuation dichotomy and must, with the aid of cultural markers, find an appropriate balance. In this regard, as Robert Hogan has pointed out, obedience to parental commands facilitates interactions with others and improves the child's chances for survival.[13] As these commands are internalized, they become the basis for developmental shifts in the salience of needs from early requirements for love and belonging in a world where self and society are imperfectly coordinated to later demands for self-esteem and self-actualization in a known and secure social environment.[14]

In a search for a resolution of the tension between individuality and sociabilty we find the source of growth in personalities, and, in the interaction among individuals, the source of change in societies. Small wonder that Jürgen Habermas noted in his inaugural lecture at Frankfurt University in June 1965 that "autonomy and responsibility together [*Mundigkeit*] comprise the only idea we possess a priori in the sense of the philosophical tradition,"[15] or that Barrington Moore, Jr., should write that "the conflict between the desire for independent and even 'selfish' behavior and the objective need to depend on others remains a central aspect . . . in any human society with *any* painful obligations."[16]

The paradox of human growth is the development of a capability for independent action out of (indeed, based on) an original dependency. The identity that develops, however, is always in tension. As individuals change over their life-spans, their needs shift and require redefinition. Both within the personality and within societies, therefore, we find no state of Pareto optimality. Instead, people constantly strive for equilibrium in order to give stability to their lives. In social life they balance their alternate needs by de-

---

[12] Jerome Kagan, "Presuppositions in Developmental Inquiry," in *Value Presuppositions in Theories of Human Development*, ed. Leonard Cirillo and Seymour Wapner (Hillsdale, N.J.: Erlbaum, 1986), p. 87 (from his comments during a discussion of his paper).

[13] Robert Hogan, "Dialectical Aspects of Moral Development," in *Dialectic: Humanistic Rationale for Behavior and Development*, ed. J. F. Rychlak (Basel: S. Karger, 1976), p. 58.

[14] Joel Aronoff, *Psychological Needs and Cultural Systems: A Case Study* (New York: Van Nostrand Reinhold, 1967), p. 6.

[15] Jürgen Habermas, *Communication and the Evolution of Society*, trans. Thomas McCarthy (Boston: Beacon Press, 1979), p. xvii (from the Introduction by Thomas McCarthy).

[16] Barrington Moore, Jr., *Privacy: Studies in Social and Cultural History* (Armonk, N.Y.: M. E. Sharpe, 1984), p. 5 (italics in original).

veloping codes of permissible and impermissible behavior, by ranking these behaviors in order of priority, and by elaborate designations of those to whom they apply. What begins as a set of contradictory tendencies ends in ideas like justice and freedom, in conceptions of rights, and in the careful articulation of moral principles that define the limits of individuality and community expectations.

What makes humans unique, therefore, is their ability to set forth abstractly fundamental and limiting ideas about life and to imbue these notions with an ethical dimension. Ethics, the right and wrong of behavior, is in fact central to all issues of social existence because it deals with the basic question of how to take the claims of others into account in relation to one's own. How to determine the appropriate balance between being free to pursue individual claims and restricting one's own goals in favor of criteria of fairness regarding all claims is the root of moral reasoning and the law. It is the basis of theories of entitlements and rights and the source of endless arguments about what people fondly call "the truth."

As far as we know, people differ from all other creatures in their capacity to develop, and live by, normative laws. They are, preeminently, lawmaking creatures. Born into an existing world of laws, they nevertheless have the capability, through their understanding, of devising new laws for different modes of behavior. Although slow and uneven, this process of normative development holds out the possibility of change from patterns of blind conformity, group hatred, and individual greed toward those that embody respect, trust, cooperation, and mercy. How people normatively evaluate competing claims, then, is of critical importance. In the tension between individuality and sociability that underlies all human existence, the way people think normatively about this duality ultimately structures the different compliance ideologies that guide social life.

Reasoning about the world

What is knowledge and how do we apprehend it? In what way do we understand our world and in what way is that understanding shared? Because such questions are fundamental to our comprehension of behavior, they have bedeviled serious thinkers over the centuries. Theories regarding understanding reflect knowledge of human psychology, of the ways people can think about why they think.

From Locke and the English empiricists came the idea that the only kind of valid knowledge is that which comes from the senses. Dialectical reasoning, which had no hard grounding in the physical world, fell from favor. Instead, the concept of mind was mathematized. People, it was said, reason in a similar fashion; understanding is a subjective process of awareness of phenomena that are external to the self.[17] This model still functions today as the basic paradigm of academic psychology.[18] Postulates regarding dialectical reasoning continued, of course, but only as an aspect of developmental theories.[19]

In the prevailing Lockean view people absorb representations of reality in a passive sense, by observing and listening; the tendency, therefore, has been to look at what happens to people rather than at how they think. People, it is said, are exposed to different experiences and thus develop different attitudes and beliefs about reality. However, because the members of specific cultures share the same sorts of experiences, their attitudes and beliefs will be roughly similar and this similarity will characterize them as a group. Moreover, because humans behave in terms of their attitudes and beliefs, the behaviors of the members of particular groups will also be similar. Although studies have shown that beliefs are sometimes inconsistent, and that attitudes are unreliable as predictors of behavior, the proponents of "social learning" see the problem in methodological rather than theoretical terms. As James Kluegel and Eliot Smith state, "When attitudes and behaviors are properly and reliably measured . . . when the attitudes are based on direct experience with the attitude object . . . and when the individual has a vested interest in the attitude object . . . attitudes do reliably and strongly predict the relevant behaviors."[20]

In the social learning approach the members of different groups differ in the ways in which they relate to experience, but they do not differ in the way they think. The cognitive processes of people, historically and among different cultures, are thought to be basically the same. From these ideas there has developed a rich literature about the values of different peoples and a vast industry that surveys attitudes in the conviction that doing so reveals people's feelings about events and the behavior they will subsequently exhibit.

The conceptions about human thinking that underlie belief and attitude studies have never been universally accepted. Experience, some have argued, is never impersonal and the knowledge that derives from experience is therefore not the direct reflection of it. For Kant this meant affirming the significance, important since Aristotle, of nonsensory or a priori knowledge. For Hegel knowledge was the continuous revelation of potentialities that develop as a consequence of the resolution of tension between historically situated dualities. William James was of the opinion that "the intellectual life of man

[17] Shawn W. Rosenberg, *Reason, Ideology and Politics* (Princeton, N.J.: Princeton University Press, 1988), pp. 44–5.
[18] Joseph F. Rychlak, "The Multiple Meanings of 'Dialectic,' " in *Dialectic: Humanistic Rationale for Behavior and Development*, ed. J. F. Rychlak (Basel: S. Karger, 1976), p. 9.
[19] Hogan, "Dialectical Aspects of Moral Development," pp. 53–4.
[20] James R. Kluegel and Eliot R. Smith, *Beliefs About Inequality: Americans' Views of What Is and What Ought to Be* (New York: Aldine De Gruyter, 1986), p. 246.

consists almost wholly in his substitution of a conceptual order for the perceptual order in which his experience originally comes."[21] The conceptual order to which James referred is a set of consistent terms that group the diverse attributes of properties in a higher order of abstraction; the terms then permit the attributes of properties to be related to or distinguished from other aspects of experience.[22]

The most influential contemporary critic of the Lockean model of knowledge has been Jean Piaget, the Swiss scholar who devoted much of his life to reformulating conceptions of cognitive processes. For Piaget, knowledge is not simply a reflection of objective reality. Between the act of experiencing and the process of understanding is a mental activity, a process of subjective definition, whose purpose is to maintain an adaptive, survival-enhancing relationship between the individual and his environment.[23] Knowledge is not passive, therefore, but is sustained by an active intelligence; that intelligence operates on experience, continuously.

According to the Piagetian conception of knowledge, attitudes are epiphenomenal. They are the direct consequence not of experience but rather of the subjective definitions a person makes of experience. Attitudes can thus lack consistency precisely because they are derivative. They are an aspect of the content of thought whose importance is grasped by reference not to experience alone but, more importantly, to the underlying structure of reasoning that a person employs. This structure is the *way* a person thinks. It is different from content, which constitutes the myriad forms, appropriate for different circumstances, a person utilizes when giving expression to a structure of reasoning. Behavior and attitudes, therefore, can only truly be understood by reference to the reasoning that produces them.

The content of thinking is made up of ideas, beliefs, and social orientations acquired during learning. These must be differentiated from the mind considered as a system of cognitive processes that actively works to interpret and give meaning to reality. Ideas, beliefs, and social orientations are an organization of elements and relations that are defined and made meaningful by reference to a more basic structure of reasoning. How a person articulates ideas about political processes or the relationships among physical objects, for example, is related to a mode of reasoning, a generative structure, that establishes the way derivative systems of thought are organized and expressed.[24] As the mind is increasingly able to integrate the properties of events and things in terms of higher orders of abstraction, there is a propogation, or horizontal *décalage*, among cognitive areas. Although this process

[21] Cited in Daniel Bell, *The Coming of Post-Industrial Society: A Venture in Social Forecasting* (New York: Basic Books, 1973), p. 301.
[22] Ibid., p. 301.   [23] Rosenberg, *Reason, Ideology and Politics*, p. 72.
[24] Ibid., pp. 6, 21.

is not synchronous (i.e., it may be difficult to apply a mode of reasoning to a specific area of reality), the tendency is for a particular structure of reasoning increasingly to apply in different concrete domains. The correlative of this conception is that reasoning develops in a sequence of stages. Piaget called these the sensorimotor, the preoperational, the concrete-operational, and the formal-operational.[25]

In the process of development the mind is increasingly able to evaluate reality abstractly using categories that organize and give meaning to it. For example, at the preoperational level a person is a conceptual realist; there is no mastery of the logic of class inclusion, transitivity, or reversible and compensatory relations. Reasoning is transducive (i.e., from particular to particular) rather than inductive or deductive. There is an inability to think of parts individually and simultaneously in a way that can relate them in terms of a larger whole. Causation, therefore, is not a property of the relations among objects but inheres in each object separately. Groups of items may have functional complimentarity (e.g., swords and guns) but they are united by their use function and not by a concept that rises above the separate elements. Reasoning, therefore, may employ associative complexes but these are not stable systems of relations.[26]

As development proceeds to the concrete-operational state the individual becomes able to conceive of absolute versus relative properties, and to see the contradictions that may inhere in symbolic and metaphoric representations. Although reasoning is still in terms of physical objects and events (e.g., a building, a person), it is no longer one-dimensional but takes into account absent objects and future states by the use of concepts with no immediate relationship to physical reality. Constancy of size and shape conceptualized as weight, volume, and the like, become part of the reasoning repertoire. Spatiotemporal constraints are reduced as one develops the ability to conserve the permanency of objects by reference to abstract concepts. Ultimately, although earlier levels of reasoning may persist and be evident in unfamiliar or less demanding situations, there is a further development of cognitive structure that involves the progressive liberation from the concrete and phenomenal toward the ability to reason and make judgments in a completely conceptual manner.[27]

Individuals make their social and physical environments meaningful by constructing representations of reality. Meaning is thus linked to reality; understanding and knowledge are of the environment and cognitive growth

---

[25] Ibid., pp. 11–12. Also Stephen Chilton, *Defining Political Development* (Boulder, Colo.: Lynne Rienner, 1988), pp. 61–2.

[26] C. R. Hallpike, *The Foundations of Primitive Thought* (Oxford: Clarendon Press, 1979), pp. 15–16, 179.

[27] Ibid., pp. 13, 20, 33, 171–2.

proceeds as the consequence of the way preferences are fulfilled and sustained in interactions with reality. As Piaget put it, "logic is not isolated from life."[28] Developmental stages occur in a sequential pattern common to all people, although not all will attain the highest stages. Because each new stage is a response to inadequacies of reasoning at preceding stages, the order of development does not vary but is always toward greater conceptual abstraction and more appropriate adaptation (i.e., understanding) to the environment. However, because environments vary, individual structures of reasoning change at different rates and individuals thus may attain different levels of development.[29]

The dialectical, Hegelian quality of Piaget's ideas is implicit in his view of development. For Piaget, growth is the consequence of an interactive process, in language and role learning as Habermas notes,[30] but also in relation to social life in general. Rather than their being merely acted on, individuals employ abstract conceptions of reality that allow them to act on the environment. Their reasoning mirrors the possibilities presented by that environment but at higher levels is able to recombine parts according to a conceptual vision of a future state. This is destabilizing, both for individuals and, in some historical circumstances, for societies.

Thought is self-regulating. It strives for equilibrium through the construction of stable representations that transcend situational variability. But thought is also assimilative and active and seeks to make sense of environmental contradictions through the development and reorganization of conceptual schema. Knowledge reflects how physical objects act on one another as well as the attempts made to understand and make sense of these acts. Disorder, when perceived, is anxiety provoking; it is threatening unless absorbed into a framework of understanding that permits adjustment and adaptation. "Equilibration" is the term Piaget uses to describe the process whereby one initially suppresses comprehension of disorder, then compromises with it in a manner that affects existing structures of reasoning, and finally creates new conceptual categories that lead to acceptance and reequilibration of a new structure. Development occurs in the attempt to end the contradiction between subjective meaning and objective reality. The goal of equilibrium is approached, therefore, through states of disequilibration.[31]

The process of reequilibration involves reflexive abstraction. This has been described by Rosenberg as "a process of reflecting on how one thinks rather than simply focusing on the objects of one's thought."[32] Through this

---

[28] B. Inhelder and J. Piaget, *The Growth of Logical Thinking: From Childhood to Adolescence* (New York: Basic Books, 1958). Cited in Rosenberg, *Reason, Ideology and Politics*, p. 69.
[29] Rosenberg, ibid., p. 19.
[30] Habermas, *Communication and the Evolution of Society*, pp. 53, 109.
[31] Rosenberg, *Reason*, pp. 69, 71, 129.   [32] Ibid., p. 12.

process "the structure of the individual's thought is transformed."[33] Transformation involves a progressive decentering of the initial egocentric view of the world by the development of perspectives that are informed by ever greater abstraction. In so doing, a person enters upon, in Piaget's words, "an uninterrupted process of coordinating and setting reciprocal relations. It is that latter process which is the true generator of structures."[34]

In conceptualizing motivation, psychologists have often employed developmental models. Freud was no exception to this when he spoke of the development of the superego in individual personalities. David McClelland posited four stages in the development of power orientations. One of the best-known developmental models is that of need hierarchies put forth by Abraham Maslow. Piaget, therefore, is hardly alone in his characterization of development as following, in general, a Darwinian path: Complex categories arise by selection out of variation, from the bottom up. In that sense a cognitive structure, serving an adaptive purpose, is a mechanism, a schema, for reasoning about a variety of objects in different situations. It becomes more generalized as it is capable of assimilating new and different objects and relating them in higher orders of abstraction. But in what sense can we say that structures are socially meaningful beyond the psychological definitions as set forth by Piaget?

The most interesting work on this problem, in my view, has been done by Shawn W. Rosenberg in his book *Reason, Ideology and Politics*. Rosenberg, in a political analysis that is informed by philosophical and psychological insights, suggests three categories of political reasoners linked hierarchically in a developmental order. They are the sequential, the linear, and the systematic. These three types of reasoners represent an amalgam and redefinition of the structural categories set forth by Piaget.

Sequential reasoners are at the base of the developmental pyramid. They are individuals who do not engage in causal analysis and for whom the structure of groups is simple and fluid. The actions of others are not linked in any ordered fashion but are, rather, viewed in terms of their particularity. Individuals themselves are defined "with reference to their place in a hierarchical order or their membership in a categorical group."[35]

Linear reasoners are more analytical and synthetic than the sequential type, although these two aspects are not integrated in reasoning but, rather, follow each other. Groups are defined relative to what they are and do, but these definitions are concrete abstractions. Individuals are seen not in particular terms but as members of a group or as occupants of particular roles. As such these individuals are conceived abstractly, but reasoning itself is

---

[33] Ibid.
[34] J. Piaget, *Structuralism* (London: Harper & Row, 1970). Cited in Rosenberg, *Reason*, p. 76.
[35] Rosenberg, ibid., pp. 111–13 (quote from p. 113).

from personal experience and from the information others provide. The relations among objects are not defined by abstract, principled concepts and, therefore, although the individual can build on experience, he cannot redefine it. Understanding, as a consequence, is the product of the environment to which one is exposed. Reasoning retains its concreteness because no ideal is conceptualized beyond what is personally experienced or culturally defined. A person is a part in a drama. Life in general and politics specifically are "something of a play, one already written by gods or nature herself."[36]

Systematic reasoners define relationships not in terms of the other person but in terms of an overarching conception of the relationship. These thinkers conceive of themselves both as autonomous individuals, free to act and think on their own, and as members of a larger community in which they participate and to which they owe a contribution. Communities are an empirical base from which conceptual relationships are abstracted. Reasoning is reversible in the sense that the extent to which a hypothetical proposition meets a standard of observed reality can be considered from either direction. In politics the rules that govern interpersonal exchange are accorded primary significance as organizing forces. These rules are conceived of in general terms as laws and principles.[37]

In empirical studies of how people reason about international relations and American politics Rosenberg's data show that individuals do think in different ways and that their thinking is coherent and structured in terms of the types he sets forth. Of 126 cases, evidence of structure was found in 107 of them, 20 at the sequential level, 56 at the linear level, and 31 at the systematic level.[38] Interestingly, these data indicate that even in a modern cosmopolitan and industrial society only 25 percent of those sampled reasoned at the highest level.

The thrust of the Piagetian argument is that people are not nonrational creatures governed by enculturated norms and values in the Parsonian sense, nor are they uniform rational maximizers in the mode of *homo economicus*.[39] People are not at some dim and similar level of consciousness whose level is impossible to raise;[40] at the same time they are not all-enlightened or even consistent. Societies and generations possess a mixture of people with structures of reasoning whose diversity speaks against either psychological or sociological reductionism. This diversity, however, clarifies anomalies in data

---

[36] Ibid., pp. 120, 122, 124, 127–8, 137 (quote from p. 137).
[37] Ibid., pp. 138, 140–1, 150, 153–4.   [38] Ibid., pp. 180, 189–90, 193–5.
[39] Ronald Rogowski, "Rationalist Theories of Politics: A Midterm Report," *World Politics* 30 (January 1978): 297. Rogowski reports that political science has come to favor rational actor theory. For another point of view on this, see Amartya Sen, *On Ethics and Economics* (Oxford: Basil Blackwell, 1987), pp. 14, 19.
[40] Peter L. Berger, *Pyramids of Sacrifice: Political Ethics and Social Change* (New York: Basic Books, 1974), p. xii (no. 13 of 25 theses).

and thus simplifies analysis at the same time that it imposes rigorous requirements on the construction of theories that explain the meaning of behavior.

Meaning must be evaluated at two levels of analysis: as the subjective reasoning processes of individuals, and as the symbolic attributes of an environment revealed through language and ritual. Rituals are sets of multivocal symbolic actions that express the shared values that bind a community together[41] but that, when enacted, also embody the contradictions that disequilibrate individual structures of meaning. There is thus a dynamic interaction between individual reasoning processes and the environment, in which each is both determined and determining. Individuals reflect on their environment and can change it; the environment provides the language, symbols, and context that affect the generative capabilities of individual structures of reasoning.

Although affect is at the root of cognitive activity, in the sense that this activity is driven by anxiety that arises from a perception of disorder in the nature of the relationship among objects, Piaget believed that cognitive processes could be studied without explicit reference to affect. When examining individuals in social environments, however, this is not possible, for understanding affect is a crucial source of information.[42] Social reasoning is reasoning about how to relate to others. But why this reasoning should change from conformism and unilateral respect into cooperation and mutual respect cannot be understood as a cognitive process alone.

Moral development

How do people come to feel that the rules that govern social life are just? What, in fact, is justice? In what way do humans use this term and what do they mean by it when using it? Is justice a logical concept, something learned from one's culture, or an artifact of psychological development? These questions, which are not mutually exclusive, have been the source of endless and searching debate. Of particular interest is the way that justice is linked to morality, to issues of right and wrong in human thought and behavior. If a just society is a moral society, what attributes of morality are part of the concept of justice?

Ancient philosophers like Confucius and Aristotle argued for virtue on the basis of the ideal qualities that were said to define a virtuous person. The argument was from the concept of virtue to humans rather than the reverse.

---

[41] Richard Madsen, *Morality and Power in a Chinese Village* (Berkeley and Los Angeles: University of California Press, 1984), p. 9.

[42] Martin L. Hoffman, "Empathy, Its Limitations, and Its Role in a Comprehensive Moral Theory," in *Morality, Moral Behavior and Moral Development*, ed. William M. Kurtines and Jacob L. Gewirtz, (New York: Wiley 1984), p. 48.

For Confucius the virtuous person was one who, in a rigid hierarchy of roles, fulfilled his own role requirements without reflection. Such people were said to be ordered in their persons and thus were the building blocks for an ordered and moral society. For Aristotle the keystone of the virtuous person was *phronesis*. This quality is one of prudent understanding that guides the individual to behave in different situations in an appropriate, socially beneficial way. Both Confucius and Aristotle believed that moral speech alone is not enough to define a moral individual because speech by itself says nothing about the inner quality that is the true guiding light of the moral person.

Subsequent thinkers have elaborated the qualities that constitute a moral identity. They have made efforts to link these qualities with consequent social conditions and to describe the motivations that impel individuals, consciously or unconsciously, toward creating a more perfect world. Utilitarianism, for example, stresses rational choice in the sum-ranking of all possible utilities and consequentialism in the sense that choices are ultimately determined by the goodness of an imagined future state of affairs. When all people make choices rationally in this way, then, at the social level, a condition of Pareto optimality will be achieved. Consequentialism, however, although it may be deemed a necessary condition for moral decisons, is not a sufficient one. For in addition, beyond utilitarian considerations, are factors relating to respect for others that affect, a priori, the nature of the choices that are made. Kantian deontologists, for example, place emphasis on the principle of respect for persons as the fundamental duty underlying moral decisions. People are to be treated not as means for some consequent social purpose but rather as ends who are due respect in terms of their personhood. That respect calls for rationality, free will, and autonomy, as rights for others and as obligations for the self. Other scholars have elaborated additional conditions in a wide variety of formulations – entitlement theories, agent-relative moralities, need based equity principles, and so on.[43]

The leading contemporary moral philosopher is unquestionably John Rawls, whose theories, although criticized, have focused debate on moral issues. Using an analytic device called the veil of ignorance (i.e., not knowing the consequence for oneself of decisions taken with others regarding the equitable distribution of goods), Rawls has elaborated principles that guide decisions toward optimal individual advantage within the context of maximizing intergroup equity. The difference principle, which regulates equitable distribution, corresponds, in his words, "to a natural meaning of fraternity: namely, to the idea of not wanting to have greater advantages unless this is for the benefit of others who are less well off."[44] The ultimate goal is a just

---

[43] For an interesting discussion of this matter, see Amartya Sen, *Resources, Values and Development* (Cambridge, Mass.: Harvard University Press, 1984), p. 302.

[44] John Rawls, "Distributive Justice: Some Addenda," *Natural Law Forum* 13 (1968): 63.

society governed by principles of justice. In Rawls's words again, these can be viewed "as an understanding between moral persons not to exploit for one's own advantage the contingencies of their world, but to regulate the accidental distributions of nature and social chance in ways that are mutually beneficial for all."[45]

In the Rawlsian world rational choice and moral sensibility as motivations are not clearly differentiated. As the quotations from his work indicate, people have mutual understandings not to exploit others and they do not want to have greater advantages for themselves unless this also benefits the less well off. Why people should have such feelings and why many do not is not proven psychologically. Moral sensibility, as with earlier philosophers, is tinged with ideal-type qualities. If people had such sensibilities combined with a clear understanding of how to calculate their own and others' advantages, then the consequent conditions would be just.

The question of how a person might obtain such sensibilities has been addressed by psychologists whose inquiries take them from the world of logic and ideal relationships into the realm of human development. It would be unfair, of course, to state that psychologists eschew ideal typification and logical inference. Their efforts to unravel the mystery of moral sensibility begin, however, with concepts regarding growth rather than with abstract principles governing moral exchange.

Like many philosophers, psychologists start with the idea that fairness and justice are essentially concepts that balance individual interests and the benefits of cooperation within a group. Moreover, this balance can be maintained only when people can recognize norms regarding shared expectations (established initially in a dependent relationship to a caretaker) and when they accept those norms, albeit unconsciously, in the interest of adapting to and maintaining the social system that supports them. We can speak of this process of cooperation and collaboration as a natural adaptive tendency; it develops alongside other tendencies flowing from egoistic assertive qualities that are also inherent in humans. The anxiety that attends the contradictions between these two tendencies impels a cognitive search for concepts (e.g., reciprocity and equality) that will reconcile them.

Moral thinking is concerned with the limits of cooperation, how it should take place and with what degree of reciprocity. The function of moral thinking is to provide a blueprint for the distribution of social goods; it utilizes concepts that in ever greater degrees of sophistication and inclusiveness define relationships and patterns of interaction between the self and others. Reciprocity, for example, in the Piagetian sense, changes form from complementary (one person's behavior determines another's), through symmetrical

---

[45] Ibid., p. 71.

(one person's rules are as correct as another's), to cooperative (interactions are in terms of mutually agreed upon principles). Moral judgment is said to develop according to the laws of cognitive development, changing form in response to disequilibration and subsequent reflexive abstraction. New modes of moral reasoning come into being as individuals wrestle with the moral implications involved in situations of conflict or choice. As Chilton points out, extensive longitudinal, cross-cultural, and cross-sectional research indicates that the moral reasoning of individuals follows a Piagetian cognitive pattern that applies uniformly across societies. Moral reasoning is structurally differentiated in hierarchical stages that are acquired in sequential order; the higher stages allow individuals to coordinate and organize relationships in accordance with more abstract and inclusive concepts.[46] Ultimately, principles are evolved that permit individuals to coordinate sociability and individuality with increasing degrees of harmony and effectiveness.

The most widely known theory regarding stages of moral development was set forth initially by Lawrence Kohlberg and subsequently elaborated by himself and others.[47] The patterns of structural change that are enumerated follow a general format. Rules, for example, are initially thought of as sacred, inviolable, and situationally specific. There then develops a regard for rules per se, independent of situations, and finally a respect for rules only as they conform to ideal principles governing autonomy, reciprocity, and cooperation. Justice is initially conceived of in highly particular terms. Right and wrong are judged egocentrically in terms of punishments and rewards. Justice then becomes reciprocity in action, where a person does what is required by one's role in an established division of labor with the expectation that others will do what is similarly required of them. Laws, in this case, establish public expectations that are categorical, impartial, and impersonal. Justice then becomes agreements that hypothetical, rational people would accept; lawmaking is a process that justifies social cooperation by the establishment of hypothetical, rational standards. Minimal safeguards for everyone are provided. Ultimately, justice is the adjustment of claims by appeal to abstract principles. These principles are concepts regarding mutual expectations "founded on a logical analysis of the requirements of an ideal system of cooperation."[48]

The stages of moral reasoning are said to form a hierarchy of moral adequacy. In resolving the tensions involved in issues of sociability versus

---

[46] Chilton, *Defining Political Development*, p. 38.
[47] See, for example, Lawrence Kohlberg, *The Philosophy of Moral Development: Moral States and the Idea of Justice*, Volume 1 of *Essays on Moral Development* (San Francisco: Harper & Row, 1981). Also James R. Rest, *Development in Judging Moral Issues* (Minneapolis: University of Minnesota Press, 1979).
[48] Rest, ibid., p. 19.

individuality, people develop cognitive schema that begin normatively to approximate the logical requirements for a moral world that have been worked out by philosophers. This conclusion was the basis for Kohlberg's famous article "From Is to Ought," where he postulated the convergence of these two intellectual traditions.[49] In arriving at this conclusion, however, affect was ignored, being assumed to be a condition that triggers a need for a cognitive response but that is not involved in the response itself. Yet this conclusion is an uncomfortable one.

Although, as Schopenhauer pointed out in his critique of Kant's practical reason and categorical imperative, principles and abstract knowledge may be indispensable to a moral course of life, they are not its original source or first foundation.[50] Compassion, he suggested, is far more important. Piaget himself, for instance, when speaking of the developoment of autonomy as a concept linked ultimately with mutuality, had this to say: "Autonomy, therefore, appears only with reciprocity, when mutual respect is strong enough to make the individual *feel from within* the desire to treat others as he himself would wish to be treated."[51]

The words "feel from within" suggest that even the father of cognitive psychology was aware (as, indeed, he was) of the pervasive role of emotion in human behavior. In fact, a number of modern theorists in their analysis of moral action have noted the importance of motivating (i.e., affective) factors. James Rest, for example, has set forth four components necessary for the production of moral behavior: interpretation of a social situation, judgment as to the appropriate course of action, a decision to make the moral course of action the goal of behavior, and persistence in executing one's intentions.[52] Of these, the second is moral judgment while the third involves moral motivation. Lawrence J. Walker points out that cognitive development is a necessary but not sufficient condition for moral development. In addition to citing the importance of role playing, he notes that perspective taking, the ability to put oneself in the place of another, is also a necessary but not sufficient condition.[53]

Individuals may be extremely able and yet not make moral responses. In some cases this can be explained in traditional moral (cognitive) develop-

---

[49] Lawrence Kohlberg, "From Is to Ought: How to Commit the Naturalistic Fallacy and Get Away with It in the Study of Moral Development," in *Cognitive Development and Epistemology*, ed. Theodore Mischel (New York: Academic Press, 1971).

[50] Schopenhauer, *On the Basis of Morality*, p. 150.

[51] Jean Piaget, *The Moral Judgment of the Child*, trans. Marjorie Gabain (New York: Collier Books, 1962), p. 196 (italics added).

[52] James R. Rest, "The Major Components of Morality," in Kurtines and Gewirtz, *Morality, Moral Behavior and Moral Development*, pp. 24, 27, 28.

[53] Lawrence J. Walker, "Cognitive and Perspective-Taking Prerequisites for Moral Development," *Child Development* 51, no. 1 (March 1980): 137.

ment terms. A person, for example, may have a low level of development and be incapable of judgments that are not egocentric. Or, at a higher stage of development, people may be sociocentric, incapable of comprehending moral solutions outside the framework of their own group's norms and social requirements. Interpretations such as these, however, seem flat and inadequate in the face of certain kinds of behavior. Some individuals, for example, often highly intelligent ones, revel in sadistic and malicious acts. They seem devoid of feelings of sympathy and empathy that would otherwise direct them to more caring behavior.

According to Martin L. Hoffman, empathy and guilt are the quintessential prosocial motives. Empathy is awareness of another's feelings; it elicits a vicarious response. Guilt, which may initially evolve from a capacity for empathic distress but is later separated from it, involves a critical awareness – of others, of being the agent of harm, of a moral norm against harming others, and of having choices related to that norm. Psychologically, the arousal of prosocial sentiments may be developmentally related to direct or symbolic association, to classical conditioning, to mimicry, or to role taking. In the United States guilt over harming others is a typical middle-class response by about ten years of age. Being aware that others have their own personal identities and life experiences that transcend the immediate situation occurs by late childhood or early adolescence.[54]

Empathy is a critical and necessary ingredient for moral behavior. It exists in individual personalities at least partly as a consequence of learning. We need not take a relativist position with regard to morality to hold that the probability of moral acts occurring is related to cultural patterns and beliefs. Recognizing that there are some individuals in even the most malignant environments who develop the highest degrees of moral capability does not, at the same time, invalidate the likelihood that particular social and intellectual traditions reinforce the development of empathy and guilt. As Hobhouse noted long ago, we have, on the one hand, individuals with their own characters and, on the other, social traditions of ways of looking at things. These conditions, he stated, are "the two poles between which we move."[55]

Unfortunately, there is still much that is not known about moral development. What, for instance, is the relative influence of particular kinds of role taking, of formal moral education programs, or of events like war or civil conflict? Data regarding differences in development patterns strongly suggest the crucial importance of social variables. Rest, for example, found

[54] Martin L. Hoffman, "Empathy, Guilt, and Social Cognition" in Overton, *Relationship Between Social and Cognitive Development*, pp. 1–5, 12, 27, 32–3, 36.
[55] L. T. Hobhouse, *Morals in Evolution: A Study in Comparative Ethics* (London: Chapman & Hall, 1915), p. 14.

lower scores on responses to his Defining Issues Test from subjects from the conservative South (in the United States) and from conservative religious groups. Those with fewer years of education also consistently score at lower levels. Education, in fact, is more predictive of results than is age.[56] Findings such as these, which relate moral development to social background factors, are, however, only a beginning. How a person changes as a consequence of a personal conflict, such as might arise from the infidelity of a spouse, or from a large-scale event such as racial turmoil, is much less known. What we do know is that people develop morally over their life-spans, not uniformly and not in some invariant fashion, and that these changes reflect both internal capabilities and the influence of external variables.

Compliance ideologies and psychological boundaries

Compliance ideologies are regulatory values that knit the members of institutions together to achieve shared goals in a manner that minimizes the transaction costs of institutional operation. These values function to coordinate the activities of the members of institutions and to facilitate interactions among institutions. They are not isomorphic with the thinking of specific individuals, but they are not unrelated to that thinking. In that sense compliance ideologies are both bounded by the cognitive capabilities of individuals and themselves set bounds to that capability.

The institutional imperatives of less complex, traditional societies are not those of highly interdependent, technocratic ones. Rosenberg, for example, cites extensive research indicating that individuals who live in less complex social environments will not achieve formal operational thought; a number of authors have presented evidence of differences across cultures in developmental achievement.[57] Other differences among cultures are related to the way compliance ideologies become embedded in general socialization influences (e.g., distinctive patterns of reward and punishment and general social orientations). For Americans, for example, the significance of the individual ego is highly touted from the beginning of life. By contrast, the world of the Chinese child is group-oriented and group-centered with a marked deemphasis on individuality and the outward expression of assertive behavior.[58] The fact that responses to the proposition that "the law should be observed regardless of whether it is a fair or unfair law" varied from 40 pecent agreeing

[56] Rest, *Development in Judging Moral Issues*, p. 250.

[57] Rosenberg, *Reason*, pp. 194, 233 fn. 4 (citing work by N. Peluffo, J. R. Prince, A. R. Luria, and P. Dasen).

[58] Carolyn Lee Baum and Richard Baum, "Creating the New Communist Child: Continuity and Change in Chinese Styles of Early Childhood Socialization," in *Value Change in Chinese Society*, ed. Richard W. Wilson, Amy Auerbacher Wilson, and Sidney L. Greenblatt (New York: Praeger, 1979), pp. 101, 105, 113.

in Canada to 73.4 percent agreeing in Japan is surely not accidental, keeping in mind that obedience to law per se is one type of moral response.[59]

The course of change reflects a dynamic and continuous interaction between individual dispositions and social processes and events. Neither can be ignored. In analyzing the consequences of the interaction between them, holistic ideal types that abstract essential traits must be constructed for both levels. The purpose of this chapter has been to set forth some of the bedrock problems that humans in their development must deal with (e.g., individuality and sociability) and to establish the cognitive and moral patterns that emerge in the development process. At this point it is appropriate to turn to the social world and its compliance ideologies and construct, in turn, the significant ideal types that exist there.

[59] Lawrence M. Friedman, *Law and Society: An Introduction* (Englewood Cliffs, N.J.: Prentice-Hall, 1977), p. 141.

3

Phases of development

If men were hermits, compliance would not be necessary. Nor would a concept of justice. Compliance ideologies arise from the need for people to work together. In the process, distinctive cultural rules and institutional forms have arisen that regulate and structure acceptable patterns of engagement. The nature of these patterns is often so implicit, however, that it is never fully or systematically articulated. Scholars may describe social arrangements, but ordinary people accept them as givens.

The link between compliance ideologies and individual psychology is not self-evident. Indeed, the connection between broad-scale social phenomena in general and psychology is still little understood. Why people universally form hierarchies, stigmatize out-groups, and behave ritualistically is not yet fully known. Descriptions of these phenomena exist, of course, and theories regarding them have been propounded, but the issues involved are far from settled. Regretfully, my own findings set forth in this chapter are largely speculative. Some excellent analyses of the relationship between psychology and culture have, of course, been made, but they are far from definitive. While my conclusions build on the work of others, they are similarly in the nature of insights rather than conclusions.

In arriving at an understanding of compliance ideologies this chapter explores only the link with cognition. The second and equally crucial aspect, the link to ethical judgment, is the subject of Chapter 4. However, that chapter builds on the material presented here. Without an understanding of the interaction between ideology and cognition, we cannot take the additional steps that will more fully enrich our understanding. This chapter, therefore, explores the homologies between ideology and cognitive processes. It describes as well the ways in which compliance ideologies develop independently of cognitive processes, in a manner that structures the pattern of interaction between them.

The nature of the relationship between cognitive processes and compliance ideologies

The proposition that people transform their consciousness requires a particular model of the mind, one that holds that thinking processes change over time in a way that alters the understanding of reality. In this conception the mind both organizes knowledge and interprets it. It does so in ways that vary in terms of levels of abstractness and conceptual clarity.

If humans are uniquely rule-making (i.e., culture-making) creatures, they differ in their capacity to express this uniqueness. Men are not, as Machiavelli would have it, "animated by the same passions" such that human events "ever resemble those of preceding times."[1] Although all people share the same neural organization of the brain, just as they share a similar skeletal configuration, it does not follow that that neural organization produces an equivalent product for all people. Variation occurs by age and among groups. Whether that variation is mapped as stages or in terms of some alternate metaphor is not unimportant but is clearly less so than the more basic proposition that holds for change and variation. The philosopher Habermas, for example, describes shifts by stages in structures of rationality from the symbiotic, to the egocentric, to the sociocentric, to the objectivist and, finally, to the universalistic.[2] Lenin, the revolutionary, saw knowledge as an endless series of circles forming a spiral. Although these conceptions differ, both see people as different in the way they think and the mind as governed by a logic of cognitive development.

Although human growth in general is related to the genetic endowment of the species, a requirement for cognitive development is membership in a society.[3] At the core of any society are norms that govern the ways people interact. These norms structure majority patterns of response; they regulate conflicts and are the basis for intersubjective understanding among society's members. In doing this, norms bolster the authority of parents, teachers, supervisors, and the like in ways that establish the limits of institutional practices and forms.[4] Because norms function to make social life possible and meaningful, individuals learn the norms of their society and internalize them (i.e., make behavior in terms of them automatic). In this process they develop concepts that are used to orient their own reasoning processes. For this development to take place it is not necessary, of course, that the underlying

---

[1] Cited in "Savonarola's Bonfire of Vanities," *Columbia* 13, no. 4 (February 1988): 37. (Essay adapted from Rachel Erlanger, *Unarmed Prophet: Savonarola in Florence* [New York: McGraw-Hill, 1988].)

[2] Jürgen Habermas, *Communication and the Evolution of Society,* trans. Thomas McCarthy (Boston: Beacon Press, 1979), p. 100.

[3] C. R. Hallpike, *The Foundations of Primitive Thought* (Oxford: Clarendon Press, 1979), p. 41.

[4] Serge Moscovici, *The Age of the Crowd: A Historical Treatise on Mass Psychology* (Cambridge: Cambridge University Press, 1985), pp. 61, 69.

structure and logic of the norms and the structure of the individual's cognitive processes be congruent. An interaction between the logic of social rules and the way an individual reasons is predicated not on the existence of isomorphic conceptual structures but rather on the necessary interdependence between them.

A compliance ideology must prompt behavioral uniformities if disruptive behavior is not to occur within the institutions of society. An individual's conception of social conventions becomes related to the concepts that explain social organization by following these prescribed patterns of behavior.[5] The very act of behaving in a prescribed manner becomes, over time, symbolic of legitimate membership in society. Although the behavior patterns have been prompted by the compliance ideology, acceptance of them permits individuals to assign them cultural significance. In this manner the compliance ideology becomes an important influence on cognitive processes. The type, quality, and intensity of socialization influences, of course, also have an important bearing on the degree and rate of acquiescence to social conventions.[6]

Reasoning, then, as Rosenberg points out, is not merely a product of the individual's cognitive development but is also reflective of and constrained by the social environment.[7] There is a dynamic interaction between social learning and behaving and individual cognitive development. Ego, in Habermas's terms, is formed by its relations with others; individual achievements become achievements by their placement within a social world. In its turn, the historical development of a group identity is in part the consequence of the multiple achievements of the group's members. The patterns of these activities demarcate different social worlds.[8] The boundaries of group identity are noted in the content of the explanations that people offer about social activities. Structures of individual reasoning are thus revealed by content that references group identity.

The social world of specific individuals is never completely identical with that of others. What constitutes a group identity, therefore, is the product of multiple individual experiences. Below the societal level the possible permutations are extensive and have been variously related to factors such as generation, gender, class, and so on. From the literature, however, two social conditions emerge that appear to be of central importance in mediating the relationship between individual cognitive development and the social environment. These are, first, the degree and type of exposure to knowledge that

---

[5] Elliot Turiel, "Domains and Categories in Social-Cognitive Development," in *The Relationship Between Social and Cognitive Development*, ed. Willis F. Overton (Hillsdale, N.J.: Erlbaum, 1983), p. 77.

[6] Stephen Chilton, *Defining Political Development* (Boulder, Colo.: Lynne Rienner, 1988), pp. 31–3.

[7] Shawn W. Rosenberg, *Reason, Ideology and Politics* (Princeton, N.J.: Princeton University Press, 1988), pp. 18, 85, 95.

[8] Habermas, *Communication*, pp. 106, 110–11.

is available. In a formal sense this means education, but the pattern is larger than education per se; it includes, critically, all influences that are related to the values of society and, especially, to the conceptual framework that organizes and relates these values. The ways in which a person is exposed to knowledge may range from simple participation in public affairs to formal training in law.

The second major influence that connects individual thinking with the social environment is occupational experience, specifically, the nature of the work environment. While working a person is directly exposed to justifications for institutional arrangements and to prevailing patterns of authority. Learning and work experience are, of course, related. Of importance are the nature and duration of work experiences and the degree to which aspects of the work environment are uniformly shared. Of special interest is how requirements for compliance are articulated in institutional settings; this is a decisive point of contact between individual and social constructions of meaning.[9]

The development of cognitive structures is affected by the role-taking opportunities that are provided within institutions. Although individuals with every level of reasoning live in all societies, there is a connection between the degree of abstraction that is required in order to learn a role and to solve role problems, and the general level of development of a population to higher stages of reasoning. The potential for development is constrained by the way the social environment is organized. Data from Iran, for example, show that Iranian children schooled in Tehran in the same manner as European and American children are cognitively two to three years more developed than illiterate children in the countryside. Disparities of this nature were even greater for some African tribes.[10] In different but suggestive tests Inkeles showed with data from six developing countries that those least exposed to modern institutions were only 2 percent modern in terms of his modernity measure, whereas those most exposed were as high as 90 percent modern.[11]

An interaction between individual subjective processes and the sociocultural system seems well established. Institutional forms and values do affect the ways individuals behave and think and vice versa. The interactive process, however, is not one that leads to sudden changes either in the modal distribution of cognitive structural capabilities or in compliance values. How people define their world, the rules that govern them, and the obligations

[9] For some interesting arguments about education and occupation, see Alex Inkeles, *Exploring Individual Modernity* (New York: Columbia University Press, 1983), pp. 60–1, 103–5, 244, 254.

[10] Charles M. Radding, *A World Made by Men: Cognition and Society, 400–1200* (Chapel Hill: University of North Carolina Press, 1985), p. 273.

[11] Inkeles, *Exploring*, p. 14. On the reverse side of the interaction equation Aronoff's 1966 study of a cane gang on St. Kitts showed how personality factors largely determined the structure of the gang institution. Joel Aronoff, *Psychological Needs and Cultural Systems: A Case Study* (New York: Van Nostrand Reinhold, 1967), pp. 125, 137.

they owe to others are not infinitely elastic. Much of the reason for this is that social cognition is very widely concrete operational in form, especially when particular institutional contexts dominate and overwhelm the general structural aspects of cognition,[12] offering little opportunity for reflective thinking. One reason why Piaget felt the level of thinking in many primitive societies is restricted to that of concrete operations is that the members of these societies have no opportunity to exercise higher-order thinking processes. Hallpike goes further and says that individuals in these societies are largely at the preoperatory stage. Indeed, he suspects that the industrial working classes of modern societies also have restricted opportunities for higher-order thinking.[13] To the extent that social institutions reinforce a learning environment that is unreflective, we may expect that concrete, particular reasoning processes will be largely characteristic of the thinking of the institution's members. Collective representations based on these modes of reasoning are stabilizing and conservative in the sense that they form what Bell, following Eisenstadt and Jaspers, calls the axial principles and structures of the social environment.[14]

Institutional forms are slow to change because compliance, if it is not to be mere naked force, is through rules and ethical codes that make possible the functioning of a society's institutions. Ingrown patterns of behavior develop, which change only incrementally. The evolution of new patterns requires transformations in the basic arrangements of society in conjunction with changes in conceptions of the self in relation to others. Under normal circumstances, therefore, large inertial forces, related to psychic and institutional costs, constrain rapid change. Social transformation arouses individual anxiety at the same time that it raises the transaction costs of institutions. These increased prices, so to speak, tend to lower the desirability of change. Nevertheless, social transformation does occur and may be actively sought, leading to changes in rules and challenges to hierarchical orders.

Because the capacity for solving complex institutional problems is small compared to the magnitude of the problems to be dealt with, especially in modern industrial societies, compliance regulations may change in some institutional contexts faster than in others (e.g., a large-scale corporation at the secondary level versus the family at the primary level). The relative ranking of loyalties may also shift (e.g., from the local community to the state). None of these changes need be self-conscious. However, if compliance configurations become increasingly unbalanced such that commitments to certain in-

---

[12] Frank B. Murray, "Cognition of Physical and Social Events," in Overton, *Relationship*, p. 95.

[13] Hallpike, *Foundations*, pp. 24 fn. 11, 398.

[14] Daniel Bell, *The Coming of Post-Industrial Society: A Venture in Social Forecasting* (New York: Basic Books, 1973), pp. 10, 115; S. N. Eisenstadt, ed., *The Origins and Diversity of Axial Age Civilizations* (Albany: State University of New York Press, 1986); Karl Jaspers, *Vom Ursprung und Ziel der Geschichte* (Munich: Piper Verlag, 1949).

stitutions are eroded, leading to a rise in transaction costs, a point will be reached beyond which inertial forces favoring stasis or reform no long predominate. Individuals and the leaders of institutions will then act to reorganize and redefine social action; new political authority will promulgate new normative structures.

The emergence of individuals who respond to disequilibration by defining new principles of organization is latent in every social order. Whether the thinking of such individuals will become prominent in a sudden, charismatic burst or emerge only slowly over a long, protracted period is to a great extent a function of the severity of the objective conditions that induce changes in compliance ideologies. That such changes have occurred is not open to question. While by no means invariant and unidirectional, a change has occurred in compliance patterns for large portions of the world from custom to law, from loyalty to persons to loyalty to principles of universal justice, and from myth and superstition as the basis for the structuring of institutions to principles of rational science.

The goal of compliance is the stable functioning of institutions. In an important sense the regulatory features of compliance concern economic matters, the distribution of goods and services within a community through commands that tell people what they can and cannot do and that permit benefits to some and not to others. Compliance ideologies are ethical codes that function in the manner of regulations as set forth by rationing boards. These codes differ from individual constructions of meaning that serve to adapt the individual to the environment through the elaboration of conceptual frameworks designed to make sense of the world. Compliance ideologies, although created by people, are articulated differently to meet institutional, not individual, needs. When economic and technological factors change the working environment of institutions, compliance ideologies will also change, barring leadership decisions to the contrary, in order to reduce transaction costs. The ideology, then, may become incongruent with individual constructions of meaning, thus prompting individual efforts to reequilibrate with the new social environment by developing new ways of reasoning. In like manner individual changes in ways of reasoning, fostered by a general process of social discourse, may prompt efforts to restructure institutional codes. The interaction context, therefore, is highly dynamic. Under most circumstances we expect, and the stable functioning of societies requires, a relative congruence between the conceptual framework that people use to give meaning to social existence and the conceptual framework that underlies the regulatory mechanisms of institutional life. When that congruence does not exist, the stage is set for individual and social transformation.

In short, compliance ideologies and individual reasoning processes are tightly linked. The connection, however, is not analytically coercive and mechanistic in the Parsonian sense.[15] Integration and consensus are probabilistic only; the relationship is one of dynamic interaction in which both sides influence the developmental possibilities of the other.

Institutional efficiency and compliance ideologies

Compliance ideologies are constrained by the subjective reasoning processes of individuals. The underlying logic of these ideologies, however, is not isomorphic with the logic that structures individual judgments. There are, in addition, objective environmental factors that must be considered. Both intersubjectivity and social conditions, independently but together, delimit the conceptual framework of compliance.

Although we cannot say, as Joseph Schumpeter did of capitalism, that "all logic is derived from the pattern of economic decision,"[16] it is clear that understanding compliance requires an examination of the problems that arise in carrying out economic activities. Economies regulate labor and distribution (as an aspect of exchange relationships) in accordance with rules that define the stakes of the various participants; they also coordinate individual activities within the framework of constraints imposed by the wider social and physical environment. Efficiency, although not always consciously and deliberately sought – as it usually is in modern economies – bears on the costs of all institutional operations. Improving efficiency, therefore, will generally lower overall operational costs unless doing so has negative social consequences, thus affecting transaction costs. Leaders of institutions, in seeking ways to enhance institutional viability, are thus usually open to suggestions regarding efficiency.

Some activities are so vital that seeking efficiencies in carrying them out is of extreme importance. A shift in hunting from rock throwing to spear throwing is a pertinent example. The improvement in efficiency in such a case is gained through technological advance. In this simple example regarding the "production" of food, the introduction of a new technique changes all of the basic costs and rates of return regarding that productive activity. The repercussions ramify, ultimately affecting institutional structures and relationship patterns, including authority patterns.

Technological improvement also prompts changes, again in terms of efficiency, in other areas of institutional activity. For example, the type of information required by various members may shift as technological change alters the functions of particular roles. If certain bits of information must be channeled to specific users, then compliance rules regarding information

---

[15] Harlan Wilson, "Complexity as a Theoretical Problem: Wider Perspectives in Political Theory," in *Organized Social Complexity: Challenge to Politics and Policy*, ed. Todd R. La Porte (Princeton, N.J.: Princeton University Press, 1975), p. 318.

[16] Cited in Bell, *Coming of Post-Industrial Society*, p. 65.

transmission and reception may also change. Technological improvement, therefore, whether we speak of spears or machines, introduces disequilibrium in behavioral rules, in demands for particular services, and in allied institutional activities. Over time there is, as a consequence, a profound effect on institutional regulatory forms and rules. Although these shifts are sometimes in response to a number of forces in addition to those associated with technological innovation (e.g., political intervention), changes in work patterns that result from the introduction of new work techniques are among the foremost of the factors that must be considered.

Technology changes the nature of the division of labor in terms of the tasks to be performed and the ways those tasks are coordinated and regulated. Technological innovations may simplify procedures (thus enhancing efficiency), but they also inevitably introduce complexities. Frequently these arise from the increased coordination required for group activities to proceed in a manner that can take advantage of the possibilities for improved efficiency. Complexity is handled institutionally by control, which means, in effect, eliminating independence of action in some spheres at the same time that independence may be encouraged in others. Overall, the pattern is one of increasing interdependence brought about by enhanced efficiencies in decision making regarding allocative choices, the coordination and control of a more specialized labor force, and so forth. As complexity increases with continuous technological innovation, regulation to insure efficient interdependence grows with it. This is a pattern well understood in modern industrial societies.

Efficiencies brought about by technological improvement are balanced against increased costs for control and coordination. There is a tension here that lies at the heart of all compliance ideologies. The tension can be resolved only if institutional performance is enhanced to a level that offsets the expanded costs for coordination and control. In part this can occur only if control eschews coercion (which raises transaction costs) in favor of patterns considered to be acceptable and just and thus do not require continuous policing. Sociologically, therefore, what occurs is a long-term shift in institutional patterns from compulsory conformity to forms of constraint that embody cooperative solidarity.[17]

The development of acceptable and just patterns of rule may require changes in the form and content of general education and increased opportunities for specialized training. These changes, in turn, both influence and are influenced by shifts in general normative structures, and by more specific alterations in legal codes and institutions. Compliance ideologies reflect these changes and also are mechanisms for reducing the tensions brought

[17] Jean Piaget, *The Moral Judgment of the Child*, trans. Marjorie Gabain (New York: Collier Books, 1962), pp. 346–7.

about by change. In situations of uncertainty in which various areas of life are being transformed in a pattern of disjointed incrementalism, compliance ideologies help promote cooperation by regularizing institutional procedures, promoting the reliability of individual actions, and ensuring that the appropriate information flows to and from the points where it is to be utilized. If transaction costs are to be kept continuously at a minimum, however, then the compliance ideology itself must change as other social factors change. In this process the possibility for disjunction between the logical structure of the ideology and the structure of reasoning of institutional members may rise.

Transvaluation of compliance ideologies

The logic of social life is revealed in the playing out of all large-scale and long-lasting institutional changes. While social learning theory can account for the acquisition of new knowledge regarding novel social conditions (i.e., content), underlying individual structures of reasoning are likely to be persistent. The development of a new conceptual framework for synthesizing the abstracted traits of a new social environment will not occur readily simply from exposure to a different compliance ideology. These ideologies, after all, regulate the behavior of individuals with different cognitive structures. Indeed, they must do this if institutions are to function, and because of this conventionalizing characteristic individuals may not easily encounter the elements of the ideology that would transform their own structures of reasoning. For this to happen a person, ideally, must engage in a new line of conduct and face new problems that overload the adaptive capacity of the older reasoning process. Clearly, as already noted, the likelihood of this happening is increased when people receive formal education rather than simply participating passively in social life and when they engage in work that exposes them to different justifications for power and prestige, different patterns of control and coordination, and different ways of allocating reward and punishment. Over time, of course, as such experiences become commonplace, the normative structures that specify them will become shared and orientation to them achieved largely through a standard socialization process. At this point individual structures of reasoning will "strain" naturally toward congruence with the logical structure of the compliance ideology.

Development, says Stephen Chilton, lies in "how people coordinate their relations with one another – how they interact."[18] Shifts in relationship patterns may vary area by area, sector by sector, and issue by issue and only gradually merge into a coherent and uniform pattern. Individual reasoning processes change, and new modal patterns develop, when new relationship

[18] Chilton, *Defining Political Development*, p. 28.

patterns are justified by reasons that are at, or one stage above, the cognitive level of those involved. When social explanations seem persuasive but are not well understood, the individual will begin to think differently with regard to the particular issue at hand and, ultimately, with regard to other issues as well.[19]

The human mind cannot perceive all aspects of the environment at the same time; sources of disequilibrium are therefore not understood to the same degree by all people. Negotiation among individuals is protracted and learning is slow. The process is evolutionary. In like manner, in a push–pull pattern, compliance ideologies also evolve. Responding to environmental factors and to inputs from individuals, the ideological conceptions underlying social organization change slowly but dramatically, becoming more coherent and inclusive over time. At a very broad level of description Turiel has described such change as progressing "from rudimentary notions of groups and social institutions based on perceived uniformities and power relations, to a conception of social systems based on concrete regularities in rules, roles, and institutions, to a conception of groups, communities, and institutions as hierarchically organized systems serving to coordinate social interactions."[20]

We call the process of change in compliance ideologies "transvaluation." This term refers to transformations in the conceptual underpinning of social conventions as well as to changes in social values as such. The two, needless to say, are related, for the conceptual framework that knits together the values of a compliance ideology cannot be divorced from the values themselves.

In contemplating historical change Freud wrote that "the process of civilization is . . . a task . . . of uniting separate individuals into a community."[21] In a comment that at first glance seems quite different in spirit, Piaget noted, "As Durkheim himself has pointed out, one cannot explain the passage from the forced conformity of 'segmented' societies to the organic solidarity of differentiated societies without invoking the diminished supervision of the group over the individual as a fundamental psychological factor."[22] If these two statements are *both* to be correct, then the process of transvaluation must be explained as one in which the development of community, and awareness of community, takes place concomitantly with a reduction in overt patterns of community control. This can happen only if the way people think about group life, and the logic of compliance, both reflect in their underlying structures an internalized commitment based on a new definition of community and individuality.

---

[19] Ibid., p. 83; Rosenberg, *Reason*, p. 90.
[20] Turiel, "Domains and Categories," p. 83.
[21] Sigmund Freud, *Civilization and Its Discontents*, trans. and ed. James Strachey (New York: Norton, 1961), p. 86.
[22] Piaget, *Moral Judgment*, p. 336.

The pattern of emergence of new definitions of community and individuality

As societies become more complex as a consequence of changes in productive capabilities, the regulatory infrastructure tends to thicken and to bring ever larger numbers of people under the purview of a central regulatory mechanism. Consciousness of social complexity also increases and with it questions about the validity of customary, and often implicit, regulations that assigned duties and privileges in villages, kinship groupings, and so on. Whether loyalty to an abstract concept of state can exist at the same time that privilege and social rank are justified by laws setting forth duties and entitlements in accordance with traditional face-to-face criteria is an issue that increasingly becomes one of overriding importance. However, change in the criteria that legitimize social rank and privilege and in the laws that assign duties and entitlements requires as well a change in the underlying logic of social organization.

One way to approach this problem is to map the changes that have occurred in law. Sir Henry Maine, for example, in his book *Ancient Law* published in 1861, saw early law as patriarchal. Duties were established by status and individuals had few rights or inviolable entitlements. Modern law, on the other hand, was said to be the law of autonomous individuals; relations are established by free agreement and there is a concomitant growth of individual obligation. There is, in short, a shift in the criteria by which relationships are regulated from status to contract.[23] Emile Durkheim, in a different type of analysis, felt that social solidarity was a moral phenomenon whose visible system is the law. Law reproduces the principle forms of social solidarity, from that based on custom to the type of law which symbolizes the special solidarity of which the division of labor is the cause.[24] In this conception law is the matrix of logic of social organization. Changes in law are thus indicative of transvaluation.

Others have also described the changes in law that are associated with transformations of social life. Roberto M. Unger, for instance, describes the growth of positive law in the area of intergroup relations that developed to limit the power of all groups. This law, he says, has been less completely implemented inside groups. Among groups, however, it enforces the ranking among them and does so by criteria that "pretend" to impartiality. This strain toward impartiality has also led, in some areas of the law, to a reduction of formal distinctions among categories of persons, resulting in a greater

[23] Lawrence M. Friedman, *Law and Society: An Introduction* (Englewood Cliffs, N.J.: Prentice-Hall, 1977), p. 43.
[24] Emile Durkheim, *The Division of Labor in Society*, trans. George Simpson (Glencoe, Ill.: Free Press, 1933), pp. 64, 65, 68.

legal recognition of equal worth. In the modern West, at least, law now assigns duties and entitlements regardless of social rank.[25]

Peter Gabel and Jay M. Feinman show how the ideological imagery associated with contract law has changed over the last three centuries as socioeconomic conditions have changed. When the social order was divided among traditional statuses the imagery of the law stressed natural class positions and implementation of customary moral principles by the legal system. As capital ownership and free competition became significant, voluntary contracts between free and equal citizens based on equality of opportunity were stressed. As monopoly control, government regulation, and class distinctions based on the ownership of capital became important, the imagery of the law shifted again to stress voluntary cooperation among groups and compensation for inequalities through government regulation.[26]

Analyzing the imagery of law rather than descriptively noting changes in its character (e.g., from status to contract) brings us closer to an understanding of the conceptual structures of compliance ideologies. It is helpful in this regard to keep in mind the correspondence (although not congruence) that exists between individual structures of reasoning and the logic that explains social relationships. Thus, in societies with no or only rudimentary forms of law and with conventional kinship organizations (essentially a primary group orientation) where relationships are ordered by status rather than by contract criteria, and where communication is permeated with concrete symbolism, we would expect individuals to have difficulty generalizing in explicit terms about the purposes of institutions and in detecting and explaining inconsistencies in social life.[27] Dialogue would tend to be repetitious and simple in form with a low order of generality and with much dependence on implicit meanings. Because thought processes are tied to the phenomenal properties of things rather than to the abstract relationships underlying appearances, classification of items in the real world would be highly particularistic.[28]

Classifications associated with a "natural" and primary social environment change into ones that are appropriate for a modern political community by a process in which concepts regarding relationships become increasingly inclusive. They are transformed from a personal status orientation, to one where others are classified legally (e.g., by class), to one where the private nature of others is recognized, to one where others are recognized, ultimately, as equal members of a fictive world community. Chilton has described interpersonal relationships as moving from physical force, to feudal fealty, to

[25] Roberto Mangabeira Unger, *Law in Modern Society: Toward a Criticism of Social Theory* (New York: Free Press, 1976), pp. 62–3, 81, 83.
[26] Peter Gabel and Jay M. Feinman, "Contract Law as Ideology," in *The Politics of Law: A Progressive Critique*, ed. David Kairys (New York: Pantheon, 1982), p. 182.
[27] Hallpike, *Foundations*, p. 125.   [28] Ibid., pp. 66, 169.

friendship, to mutual support, to mutual respect, and, finally, to mutual care.[29] Underlying these shifts in relationship patterns is the development of increasingly elaborate conceptions of human worth and of the interrelated nature of the social order. Mutuality rather than status defines relationships, bolstered by the use of abstract symbolism that depends on universalistic classifications. Increasingly judgment is not in terms of the particular qualities of things but, rather, in terms of general principles. Ultimately, in the Kantian sense, the fundamental test is whether the principle guiding one's actions can be a universal law of human nature (the categorical imperative).[30]

The conceptual axes of compliance

The conceptions that underlie the organization of compliance correspond in their developmental progression to the conceptual changes that occur in individual reasoning. They are not, however, so neatly invariant in their development, nor is there a similarity in the way abstractions are organized. Compliance ideologies require anchoring symbols that can be clearly understood by people with different cognitive abilities. They must be simple to grasp (yet capable of being elaborated by sophisticated thinkers), inclusive for all members of the community, and explanatory in terms of the prevailing conditions of existence (e.g., technological levels, patterns of social life, etc.). The rules that structure institutional life must appear to be legitimate in terms of the underlying premises of compliance, that is, they must appear to the membership at large to be unquestionably correct as justifications for the distribution of rewards and the assignment of duties. This is possible only when explanations for social life carry with them a powerful persuasiveness regarding good and evil, articulating reasons for misfortune, and setting forth justifications for why the rules that structure existence are the ones that are appropriate for a good life.

Compliance ideologies are formed around conceptual axes that have both a cognitive and a moral component. In their development there is a change from concepts that link people and objects in a particular sense with their own particular fates, and for whom intervention to change fate is barely possible, to a perception of matter as linked by laws or principles that define a basic commonality and where intervention is encouraged if doing so enhances properties of being that should be universally shared. Between these two positions are intermediate ones that reflect the developing cognitive capabilities of individuals and their increasing control over the social and physical environment. Although there is, normally, one dominant con-

[29] Chilton, *Defining Political Development*, p. 43.
[30] David Lyons, *Ethics and the Rule of Law* (Cambridge: Cambridge University Press, 1984), p. 10.

ceptual axis, others may coexist with it and be utilized in particular circumstances.

Before discussing these conceptual axes in detail it is appropriate to define them briefly and to assess their validity. Four separate phases of development can be identified, keeping in mind that as transvaluation proceeds there will be an overlap between phases. The core conceptual framework within each phase is used to justify a particular pattern of relationships and serves as the warp into which a woof of compliance rules is woven.

Phase one is dominant in pre-state and archaic societies, although residues of it exist even in the most technologically advanced states. In this world the physical environment is basically uncontrolled and the cause of significant events is not well understood. Disease, famine, or the approach of marauding bands are seen as the consequence of fate. Indeed, the world is peopled by a multitude of spirits who inhabit physical objects (trees, mountains, etc.) and who can take up residence within people. These spirits are not much better than men, just greater in power and more mysterious, but because they are like people they can be cajoled and bartered with. Relations with others are on particular terms; what you are entitled to is what you have and what you have is your status. Status is like property. It can be given, taken from you, or sold to another (i.e., slavery). Because relationships are based on status, autonomy is weakly defined. The salient conceptual idea is the importance and prevalence of the spirit world and its dominating effect on the fate of men.

Phase two is the traditional one of the settled cultivator, the peasant. Knowledge of agricultural cycles is far advanced over the pre-state and archaic world. Crop rotation and animal husbandry are practiced. Cause and effect are better understood and find expression in inventions of the waterwheel, the iron plow, spoke-wheeled vehicles, the loom, and so on. Because of these inventions, some specialization of labor occurs and concepts regarding relationships and hierarchies of social control are more elaborate. Although spirits may still be invoked to explain fate, the transcendent world is now far more controlled. One spirit or one supreme essence of power and goodness ("Heaven" in the Confucian sense) becomes dominant and rules over subordinate ethereal entities (e.g., angels, saints, lesser gods). Evil and misfortune are the consequence not solely of actions by particular, largely unrelated spirits but of satanic powers that war with beneficence within an encompassing, theologically comprehensive hierarchy of spiritual force. The godly essence of the supreme deity is available to all, making all spiritually equal. Although the deity can be appealed to for special favors, general pronouncements by the deity are equally binding and are the supreme principles of existence. There is, however, a hierarchy of authority up to the Supreme Being itself in a great chain of being. The privileges of status, therefore, granted by heavenly decree, entail duties to protect the less fortunate, in return for their obedience, in order to create a perfectly ordered and reverential society. All people are bound in their responsibilities to each other in order to create the harmonious whole as defined by the great spiritual being.

Phase three is the world of the city and the machine. It is one where sources of energy are increasingly understood and where specialization of labor in order to utilize that energy is dramatically increased over the preceding traditional phase. Property, as the output from labor specialization and the increased use of energy, multiplies rapidly; accumulation for either individual or shared use becomes a central value. As a source of principles governing work relationships and status, the deity retreats and in its place is man-made knowledge, science, based on man's own thinking and achievement. The knowledge of nature reveals the essential equivalence of persons. People themselves thus become like property, essences that deal with each other by agreement, exchanging the properties associated with their rights independent of any binding, overarching conception of natural hierarchy. Status, therefore, is determined not by heavenly decree, as a divine right, so to speak, but by one's relationship to the common endeavor of accumulating property; it is defined by control of property and of people as property through an interpretation of rights that permits governance by some of the institutions that manipulate energy and coordinate labor. Control may be by ownership of an institution or by designation to a position of authority within an institution. The central underpinning of compliance in either case is the neutral physical quality of property combined with the need to accumulate.

Phase four currently exists only partially. It is a world where levels and supplies of energy are uniformly high and abundant. Knowledge of cause and effect in all domains is extremely sophisticated. Control of institutions still determines status but accumulation of property as the underpinning of that control is no longer the core conceptual device. This occurs because of a redefinition of rights away from a notion of them as property that can be manipulated for purposes of control and toward one of rights as entitlements that are mutually and equally shared. In this phase deserts with regard to rights cannot be enhanced or hedged by contract, by membership in a particular group, by position in an institution, or by reference to some particular personal attribute. Right and obligation transcend spatiotemporal factors; they are completely reversible and unrestricted by particularistic criteria. Indeed, the core conceptual axis hinges on this very reversibility of rights and obligations.

Normative systems take a very long time to change their conceptual axes. The span is not years or decades but centuries. Prodded by some individuals in response to challenges that arise as societies evolve, there is a slow developmental process in which new ideas compete with older ones and succeed only as they come to satisfy both the cognitive and emotional aspects that inhere in the new situation.[31] Even when ideas appear to spread very rapidly (e.g., Europe after the French Revolution), there remains a residue of older ways of conceptualizing relationships that is extremely resistant to change. Some people, of course, may have evolved new concepts about relationships; others, however, will be far behind. Indeed, while the world has witnessed great changes in structures of social meaning, retrogression is also possible in particular instances. The scale of new problems may overwhelm adaptive capabilities; disharmony among groups in the way they think about compliance need not be resolved, in specific instances, in favor of those whose conceptualizations are more in tune with technological advance and increased social complexity. Indeed, highly conservative ideologies may hold sway for long periods.

Habermas has stated that evolutionary processes are reversible.[32] The empirical evidence, however, suggests not only the validity of the phases I have set forth but also their long-run evolutionary inevitability. Although the evidence for this assertion is largely correlative rather than direct, it is nonetheless persuasive. Hallpike, for example, has pointed out the differences between Zulu and European children in their conceptual understanding of projective and Euclidean space in which Zulu children without schooling and literacy are well behind.[33] Rest has noted how pediatric residents from India and Saudi Arabia scored lower on his Defining Issues Test than did Americans.[34] These findings are subject, of course, to various interpretations. What is less open to question is the multicountry tests done by Alex Inkeles on individual measures of modernity (5,500 men in six countries responding to 159 different interview items). Exposure to a modern environment (e.g., working in a factory versus agricultural labor) was clearly related to changes in views of the world. On the basis of his study Inkeles concludes that modernity, barring a catastrophe, is about "as near to being inexorable as any social process can be."[35]

Elaborating the phases of cognition and compliance

In setting forth the phases of development of the conceptual axes of compliance ideologies a necessary step is taken toward the specification of political cultures, establishing a bedrock from which further definition can evolve.

---

[31] Barrington Moore, Jr., *The Causes of Human Misery* (Boston: Beacon Press, 1970), p. 172.
[32] Habermas, *Communication*, p. 141.
[33] Hallpike, *Foundations*, pp. 334–5.
[34] James R. Rest, *Development in Judging Moral Issues* (Minneapolis: University of Minnesota Press, 1979), p. 115.
[35] Inkeles, *Exploring*, pp. 83, 318.

An elaboration of the phases, articulating more fully their basic features, is thus called for.

Phase one: the pre-state and archaic phase of spirits and imposed fate

When Socrates was asked why he had not entered politics he replied that he had been held back, in this as in many aspects of his life, by a sort of voice, divine and spiritual, that spoke to him at such moments.[36] One is reminded by this statement of what Julian Jaynes has called the bicameral mind, a type of thinking characteristic of earlier people where the gods were not figments of the imagination but internally heard voices that were thought to be part of every person's volition, a divine component that ordered behavior.[37]

In the time spoken of here – a period encapsulating the diverse experiences of hunter-gatherers, primitive horticulturists, preliterate agrarian states, and even literate societies that we term archaic to differentiate the early stage of state development – close personal relationships, defined almost exclusively by kinship terms, served virtually all of an individual's interests. Social position in this network demarcated roles, with special emphasis on the obligations owed by people to each other. Although individuals were responsible for personal failings (cheating, stealing, etc.) and were answerable for them, there was no conception that social roles and duties could be legitimately questioned. Instead, the social system had a mystical quality, authenticated by sacred symbols, whose inviolate nature was sanctified by rituals enacted at important seasonal, social and life events to ensure fertility, prosperity, peace, and so forth. When barrenness, illness, death, and other misfortune occurred, a crisis was precipitated that disrupted personal relationships. In seeking an understanding of these calamities two questions were asked: How did the adverse event occur? and Why did it occur? Answering the "how" query involved description. In responding to the "why" question causation was assigned to the omission of ritual, to breaches of taboo, and to sorcery and witchcraft. These explanations provided reasons for the disruption of proper moral relations among people. They described how vagaries of good and ill fortune are associated with personal ancestral spirits who may act to punish the social transgressions of their descendants and how witchcraft, emanating from others, can determine why seemingly chance events such as illness and injury strike some individuals, even virtuous ones, but not others.[38]

[36] Barrington Moore, Jr., *Privacy: Studies in Social and Cultural History* (Armonk, N.Y.: M. E. Sharpe, 1984), pp. 121–2.

[37] Julian Jaynes, *The Origin of Consciousness in the Breakdown of the Bicameral Mind* (Boston: Houghton Mifflin, 1976), pp. 201–3.

[38] Max Gluckman, *Politics, Law and Ritual in Tribal Society* (Oxford: Basil Blackwell, 1967), pp. 226, 239, 243.

Draped over social relations was a heavy mantle of restraint based on a requirement for community consensus. However, this does not mean that societies, especially in archaic times, were without strata that provided some with privileges unavailable to others. There is some disagreement concerning the nature and extent of social differences, but all tend to agree on the greater religious–political power available to those with higher status.[39] In pre-state societies, extending into archaic times, leaders employed this power in rituals and sacrifices as means for airing and remedying grievances with the aim of renewing social consensus.[40] Compliance was thus deeply enmeshed with the spirit world but in a manner that referenced the particularity of spiritual force while simultaneously acknowledging its role as a pervasive determinant of fate.

What type of conceptual underpinning supported the reasoning of people in these diverse societies? From the standpoint of cognitive psychology the work that best discusses this world is C. R. Hallpike's *Foundations of Primitive Thought*.[41] The discussion that follows is largely based on this excellent analysis, which throws light on the thinking processes of those who lived in pre-state and archaic times.

In this phase of development a person was comprehended not as a mind–body duality but as a fusion of the psychical and the physical. Thinking was largely preoperatory in nature, a mode fully capable of dealing with the problems of daily life. There was no necessity to develop coordinated systems of thought that required the conservation of invariant relationships. The representations of reality that developed through daily interactions were, however, expressed by social and cosmological categories whose symbolism had a range and significance far beyond that of the modern world; in later periods such symbols became isolated from each other because distinct legal, constitutional, political, and economic categories, and the like developed that structured interaction in their place.

In the earliest societies, although particular cases were integrated in general classes or propositions, concepts that permitted a reversible nesting of a hierarchy of classes and relations were lacking. Inputs were directly transformed into outputs; symbolic reasoning was thus associated with transductive inference. Argumentation was carried out with little idea of how to derive conclusions from logically constructed premises. Reasoning in terms of assumptions that were outside the realm of individual experience was

---

[39] See, for example, the contrasting arguments of Elman R. Service, "Classical and Modern Theories of the Origins of Government" (pp. 21–34), and Morton H. Fried, "The State, the Chicken, and the Egg: or, What Came First?" (pp. 35–47), in *Origins of the State: An Anthropology of Political Evolution*, ed. Ronald Cohen and Elman R. Service (Philadelphia: Institute for the Study of Human Issues, 1978), pp. 32, 36.

[40] Gluckman, *Politics, Law and Ritual*, pp. 110, 227–8.

[41] Hallpike, *Foundations*.

rejected; generalization was inhibited by the wide use of specific proverbs and allusions that were based on shared experiences and knowledge. Education, largely by participation rather than through formal instruction, tended to promote classificatory thinking of the taxonomic type rather than hypothetical reasoning. Modes of representation did not permit conflict among ideas and there was, in fact, little experience of, and thinking about, alternate belief systems or modes of social organization. A general homogeneity of outlook was accompanied by a repression of questioning and nonconformity.[42]

In the world of spirits and imposed fate technological problems were few in number and complexity and were solved by time-honored means. Questions that arose in daily life chiefly concerned personal interaction. Because technological problems were integrated with social relations generally, they were not often even thought of as problems in and of themselves. Indeed, in a broader framework, natural and human cycles were associated (e.g., life was a passage of seasons) and were resistant to causal analysis. Measurement, explicit planning, and experimentation were little in evidence. People related to each other in terms of status in a social framework that lacked clear specifications of institutional type and function.[43]

When objects were classified the conceptual relationship was functional (e.g., eating utensils, tools, etc.) and was derived from concrete properties and everyday associations. A complex of associated items was thus conceived of in terms of the elements that were associated rather than in terms of a superordinate concept. Qualities of items each had their own independent aspect; hot and cold were not seen as having anything in common, nor were hard and soft or heavy and light. Physical perception governed assessments such that heavy was heavy to lift, hard was hard to cut and hot was hot to the touch. Time was usually in terms of recurring events as reflected in natural processes such as the passage of seasons. Space was noted in terms of proximity, separation, inclusion, and order rather than by Euclidean and projective relations.[44]

The conceptual context of pre-state and archaic societies lent itself to the development of causal ideas that reflected particularity and conceptual realism. Thus, the gods and fates were part of all the circumstances of life because every observable entity had its own particular purpose and inherent vitality. The woods, fields, and streams were peopled with spirits because each and every concrete entity had its own special spiritual force. Small wonder, as even the great thinker Socrates noted, that humans should be thought to have their own independent spirit whose speech, expressed internally,

---

[42] Ibid., pp. 59, 132–4, 140, 144, 408, 489–90.
[43] Ibid., pp. 131–4.
[44] Ibid., pp. 52, 97, 179, 234–5, 343, 356.

guided behavior. People were thus defined in their particularity. Revenge, for example, was a personal affair, at most a family matter, between individuals, and was not tinged with lofty conceptions of crusade, class warfare, or Islamic jihad. If a branch fell on your head, you punished the tree by cutting it or sought to determine who had used witchcraft against you.

Shakespeare, with his timeless understanding, captured the quality of particularity embodied in the art of witchcraft. In *Macbeth* there is a moment when the first witch, speaking to the other two hags, describes her malevolent power. Earlier, the wife of the master of the ship *Tiger*, under way to Aleppo, had refused to give the witch the chestnuts that she, the wife, was eating. In response the witch proclaimed her intent to treat the hapless sailor-husband as follows:

> . . . I'll drain him dry as hay:
> Sleep shall neither night nor day
> Hang upon his pent-house lid;
> He shall live a man forbid.
> Weary se'nnights nine times nine
> Shall he dwindle, peak and pine:
> Though his bark cannot be lost,
> Yet it shall be tempest-tost."[45]

When 167 French children were asked by an associate of Piaget why a child who stole apples fell into the water while running away over a rotten bridge, those under eight years of age answered that it was because the child had stolen the apples (a type of concept formation that Piaget called "immanent justice"). We must suspect that in pre-state and archaic societies the answer would be because the spirit of the bridge was ailing and vindictive, the child's own spirit was bad, or, even more likely, that the accident was caused by witchcraft done by the person from whom the apples had been stolen. The situation could be corrected by making the bridge strong again and by rituals to cleanse the child and the bridge of evil and to ameliorate the wrath of the aggrieved. Rituals had meaning because of the spirit nature of the world. They were an antidote against the vicious feelings of others that set witchcraft to work. Through ritual these feelings were condemned publicly, not merely to reintroduce harmony into relationships so as to alleviate misfortune but also to sustain a code of morality by putting pressure on people generally to control those feelings that, set loose, create disharmony and thus provoke others to witchcraft.[46] Like the cargo cults practiced in certain Melanesian villages as means to obtain Western manufactured goods, it was

[45] W. J. Craig, ed., *Shakespeare: Complete Works* (London: Oxford University Press, 1905), p. 847.
[46] Max Gluckman, *Custom and Conflict in Africa* (Oxford: Basil Blackwell, 1966), pp. 93–4.

the ritual activity (rather than, say, an import-substitution policy) that was used to determine social outcomes.[47]

The particularity that underlay reasoning about cause and effect did not imply any conception of privacy or contract between autonomous persons. Fate for particular persons, in terms of disease, accidents, and the like, was a matter determined by the agents of the largely uncontrollable spirit world. That was what made an individual particular. As a social person, however, an individual was an element of an associational complex in which activities of procreation, role behavior, and social control were defined by kinship. Obligations were highly concrete, beginning with the family and extending to the lineage, the tribe or village, the local community, and so on. Family relationships were paramount, with only the minimal development of religious and political institutions involving members from different communities. How one fulfilled kinship obligations was to a great extent the measure of right and wrong and the touchstone of compliance. In this status-oriented social world the distinction between public and private all but disappeared.[48]

Phase two: the traditional phase of encompassing hierarchy

If we rank the relative importance of compliance ideologies in terms of longevity, then that of the pre-state and archaic phase of spirits and imposed fate would be clearly preeminent. It lasted for thousands of years, in different forms and patterns to be sure, but recognizable in any place where man's antiquity has been explored. The change that ultimately overwhelmed this older way of regulating behavior was not characterized by a sharp cleavage with the past. Phases occur not as discrete bundles but as softly interwoven periods of subtle transformation. A blend of the new and old was thus clearly evident for many centuries (the last vestiges of witchcraft, for example, were not officially banned in Britain until the reign of James II, 1685–8). Certain markers, however, reveal when newer patterns began to emerge. They are preeminently three in number: the development of monotheism, the beginning of law, and the rise of world religions.

As would be expected, the change that took place in the conceptual axes of compliance both reflected and impelled changes in the social and technological environment. The elaboration of writing techniques, for instance, permitted communication over long distances and the keeping of records at home. Advances in methods of warfare (e.g., the invention of the chariot) changed the nature of conflict. Agriculture became a settled occupation subject to control for revenues for military and religious purposes. Towns grew in number and extent. Shipbuilding technology improved, leading to an expansion of trad-

[47] Radding, *A World Made by Men*, pp. 21, 267.
[48] Moore, *Privacy*, pp. 19, 30, 81.

ing. In these and other areas newer patterns of life raised questions about the workableness of the ancient spirits as explanations for the tragedies and triumphs that accompanied events. Fate, once so inexorable, seemed constantly to work against particular groups for reasons that appeared increasingly to be social in origin. How to reinterpret fate and alleviate its harshness in a world where spiritual forces still predominated became, in certain selected places, a major issue.

In the midst of the Exodus, when the children of Israel had gone forth out of the land of Egypt and were gathered at Mount Sinai, God called Moses to the top of the mount and spoke to him saying, "Thou shalt have no other gods before me." Thus did the ancient Hebrews, in a world they still populated with a multitude of spirits, begin the process of denying them legitimacy. This God above all gods was jealous of his power, stern toward those who hid wickedness in their hearts, and demanding in his Commandments that his people take upon themselves the obligation to live righteously, forgoing vengeful murder, honoring their parents, and respecting the wives and property of their neighbors. Obligation did not stop at the front door as it did in most ancient societies. Instead, God's justice demanded compassion for the needy, poor, and unfortunate, whoever they might be.[49]

In this far-reaching moral revolution, undertaken in the context of an increasingly complex social world, the commands that directed behavior no longer came from internal voices, from the particular spirit lying within every person. Instead, Yahweh was separated from men and they, in their turn, separated from the world in which they lived. God was above and he commanded. Individuals below were autonomous in the degree to which they might accept the word of God into their own hearts. Reference to myth and the ritualistic affirmation of the customs of one's own kinship group were thus not enough to ensure God's approval. Instead, a person must live by God's law, made known to all people, through one's own acceptance of it as an ultimate explanation for life. In this way the public and private realms of life were decisively separated; concepts of relationships shifted from concrete particularity to an order regulated by an abstracted reality analytically distinct from, yet conceived of as still concretely part of, individuals as persons. There was, of course, no equality in either God's universe or the world of men. What had come into being was a conception of autonomy within an encompassing hierarchical order. Demands for social consensus, however, were now modified by the possibility of private interpretations of events.

If people have their own personal representations of reality, something that can be thought of only with a conceptual framework that perceives the self as having some degree of autonomy, then conflicts among private

[49] Ibid., pp. 170, 190, 196.

representations are also conceivable. In these circumstances social order requires a tool that is more powerful than traditional social consensus. This was provided by the elaboration of regulatory mechanisms embodied in religious doctrine and public law. The most fully articulated example of the first of these is the Sharia of Islam, the law as it was interpreted from the words of the Prophet Mohammed and the Koran, which binds Islamic societies together as religious–political communities. Of the second, the best example was the development of Roman jurisprudence. In both cases, but more fully independent in the Roman case, law functions to minimize random outcomes in interactions among persons who possess private realms.

In the archaic world law was always intertwined with religious norms and taboos (e.g., Hammurabi's code of 1800 B.C., which actually predated the Old Testament). The Romans were no exception in this regard. Out of their own tradition, which was not monotheistic, they wrestled with the problems of how to control behavior, especially the violence of private vengeance, when interaction in their world increasingly included strangers who lived outside the bounds of informal, face-to-face group pressures. Two lines of development intersected. First, Roman ritual practice became concentrated on intellectual abstraction leading, as Weber has pointed out, to a ceaseless cultivation of a rational, practical casuistry of sacred law, which, in its turn, then sponsored rational juristic thinking.[50] Second, the philosophy of Stoicism outlined a conception of a universal human brotherhood in which all people were equal despite differences of rank, race, and wealth. The polity, according to the Stoics, was an ethical union that united people in bonds of justice.

Roman lawyers, especially those who were Stoics, became increasingly concerned about the issue of slavery. Although slavery was clearly legal in Roman society, these lawyers developed a concept of natural liberty that allowed the development of legal safeguards for slaves and other oppressed people. For Cicero, the best known, if not the greatest, of the Stoic Roman lawyers, natural liberty was a moral requirement, which demanded that some measure of respect and dignity be given to every person, even slaves. These ideas were clearly evident in the movement, which fell short of including slaves, toward worldwide Roman citizenship without class distinctions that was achieved by the edict of the Emperor Caracalla in A.D. 212. Yet a major problem remained, for no one in the ancient world had any sentiment of nationalism as we know it. The law could abolish distinctions and make all free people citizens, but without religious support, the traditional cement of ancient societies, an uncoerced loyalty to a world empire was impossible.

[50] Max Weber, *Economy and Society*, vol. 2, ed. Guenther Roth and Claus Wittich (New York: Bedminster Press, 1968), p. 409.

At their core all major religions are concerned with questions of power. What Christianity did for the declining Roman state was to provide a moral framework for evaluating behavior out of the ancient Jewish religious tradition and to make that framework available to a worldwide community. Of course, another religion might have sufficed, although given the moral power of the Mosaic tradition, Christianity's claim was a strong one. It raised problems, however, that were unknown in the ancient world. Unlike the Roman lawyers who believed that authority came from the people, Christians believed that ultimate authority came from God. For them morality and religion did not meet in the state and its leaders for church and state were separated. Obedience in matters of the flesh was due to an office but not to the person of a ruler. That particular individual, like all individuals, was subject to earthly desire and the requirement for contrition that could not be modified by assumptions of divine status. Law, then, was not just a basis for causal inference; it became moralized, a standard for evaluating the appropriateness of behavior.

What might have happened to the law had the ancient world evolved to our own time in peace will never be known. What did happen, of course, was a violent break between the ancient and medieval periods as successive waves of barbarians overwhelmed the Western Roman world. Cicero's legacy continued, albeit modified. The Stoic doctrine of a universal law of nature was interpreted as arising in equal parts from God's providential government and from the social nature of human beings, binding equally on all people everywhere. The idea of a united Christendom under the parallel powers of *imperium* and *sacerdotum* was never challenged, nor was the idea that natural law is binding on both rulers and subjects, that kings should govern justly in accordance with that law, and that duly constituted authority in both church and state is sanctified. At the same time, however, there was a marked upsurge of phase one reasoning. Faith was entwined with superstition. The law sanctioned ordeals in which winners and losers were determined not objectively but by trials that revealed the inner nature of the litigants. Law in most instances was not universal but personal. Status was integral to all considerations as in the greater *wergild* or man-price that was assigned to higher-ranking persons in the Germanic codes.[51] Once again social life was highly ritualized under the aegis of a hierarchical political order and an all-explaining culture. Not until just before the Renaissance did this pattern begin to change and earlier possibilities, greatly transformed, again begin to evolve.

Compliance in the traditional mode required a concept of an organic community, under God's rule, ordered hierarchically and maintained through a

[51] Radding, *World Made by Men*, p. 91.

system of mutual obligations. It is clearly important whether this pattern was one of feudal authority, as in Western Europe, or a system of bureaucratic imperial dominance under the rule of "Heaven," as in China. In either case, however, rules were associated with the paramount need for a hierarchical order and the requirement to maintain this order as a stable mechanism for the transmission of family status and property. In both locales the generally accepted idea that authority has a religious origin (i.e., a divine right in the European case and a mandate of heaven in the Chinese one) was modified by a residual right to resist the unlawful exercise of power. In Europe this was justified by reference to the ancient tradition of power originating from the people. However, it was only when this tradition became joined to a new idea – that fairness requires like cases to be treated alike – that natural hierarchy was challenged and the stage set for the transvaluation of the traditional concept of compliance.

Phase three: the modern phase of property relations

A Supreme Deity as the linchpin of a compliance ideology meant a view of social life as given and natural. Although every person in this world had an element of individuality, relationships overall (and the rewards available to particular categories of persons) had an immutable aspect based on a cosmological order that was encompassing, hierarchical, and personalized. The idea that relationships might be founded on principles that embody elasticity and reversibility was not part of this vision.

The first break in this pattern came in the eleventh century at the cathedral school at Chartres under Fulbert, and at the law court at Pavia. In these centers, remote from the commercial world, there was a rise in educational standards characterized by an emphasis on creative rather than purely curatorial learning. Law and politics began to be discussed as the affairs of the community, not just of the king. Slowly, monasteries began to encourage the expression of inner feelings in the company of equals, and nature once again became a subject of interest in its own right.[52] The idea of a static, given world began ever so slowly to give way to the notion that ideals have importance and that the social world is subject to discussion and redefinition. These new thoughts connected with the idea handed down from the Middle Ages, that lawful authority is a moral force and as such is legally subject to moral criticism when it has become despotic and tyrannical. The underlying thread of life, therefore, became ever more infused with the idea of questioning, often dangerous to do but increasingly practiced in ever widening spheres.

[52] Ibid., p. 256.

No change, however, was as momentous as the gradual development of the market and of relationships that transcended the boundaries of kinship, village, and locality. The market, of course, was more than just the product of technological advance, although the evolution of local and regional fairs into a general market system depended on technological improvements in such areas as transportation and weaponry.

The market involves groups who are brought together by virtue of material interests satisfied by exchanges that are, ideally, mutually advantageous. The medium of exchange, money, is a commodity with value relative to all of the other commodities that are being exchanged. In the market, relationships are in theory impersonal, governed by a rational pursuit of self-interest that is constrained only by the need to honor the commitments that have been made in good-faith dealings.[53] The honoring of commitments is bolstered by laws, customs, and social arrangements that pertain to asset ownership, specifically to the way property rights can be assigned, enforced, and transferred. Around the idea of property, then, as a definition of and a basis for relationships, there slowly began to develop a system of beliefs that ultimately permeated political, economic, and social life.

No name has been associated with the idea of property as a conceptual device defining relationships more than John Locke's. Locke justified the right to private property as a natural right pertaining to objects with which one's own labor has been mixed. This idea differs from Roman law (property rights begin with the appropriation of things) and from conceptions held in the Middle Ages (common property is more perfect and hence more natural) in the sense that by mixing one's labor with an object, one's personality has been extended, so to speak, into the object that has been produced.[54] Property is, therefore, private, deriving from an individual; it is indivisible from a person's own labor, and thus from the activity of labor. As a consequence, property when abstracted is a bundle of powers over things that have been created, loans, lands and shares, and the like, that depends, crucially, on the right to engage in the activities relating to the creation of property. This right, said Locke, cannot and should not be abridged by civil authority for it is the very basis of community life.

In modern industrial societies of all political persuasions the acquisition of property is a central tenet. Compliance ideologies differ regarding how property should be controlled, but they do not differ in the belief that property and its distribution are central to social life. Nor do they differ in their belief that property is the basis of social differences in terms of the power that its control confers. Although inequality can therefore exist, it is an inequality in

---

[53] Weber, *Economy and Society*, p. 636.
[54] George H. Sabine, *A History of Political Theory*, 3rd ed. (New York: Holt, Rinehart & Winston, 1961), pp. 527–8.

the structure of property relations rather than one foreordained by an encompassing cosmological order. These societies also share values associated with acquisition and exchange, namely the desirability of material benefits, of rationality and achievement, and of the importance of science and technology for social life.

The idea of property as the conceptual axis of a compliance ideology must be sharply differentiated from theories about capital. Capital is property, but it is the basis for a particular theory of rule rather than the underlying logic of an epoch in human history. Capital is a type of property whose relative distribution, enforced by particular laws regarding property rights, defines one type of modern political–economic system. Property, on the other hand, is neutral, conceptually more like the parts of a machine, and people, who cannot be separated concretely from property, are those parts. The functioning of the community is like the functioning of a machine. Both have parts that must work together. In the community, people, as parts, are separate yet rigorously united, different in their functions yet equal abstractly in their relationship to property, which is their activity – in essence, themselves. When property is the logic of compliance, people in groups or as individuals are defined as agents who have an equal right and obligation to engage in the processes of society. Paradoxically, the emphasis on equality may exist alongside a great deal of objective evidence of the lack of it. In different ways both the United States and the Soviet Union are egalitarian in rhetoric but far from it in practice.

The transformations in social patterns that have taken place have involved the breaking down of traditional institutions and structures of meaning and the creation of vast bureaucratic conglomerates welded together by codes infused with secular rationality. Changes in law have been accompanied by hopes for a new type of redemptive community structured around principles of equality.[55] In the moral critique of structures of domination that has accompanied redemptive impulses, both legal institutions and the law itself have developed as means to regularize and rationalize the use of power to protect the dignity of those who are weaker and subordinate. Less than two centuries ago the law was an instrument of coercion. At that time five hundred crimes were punishable by death in England and public executions were commonplace. Unevenly, often in the name of substantive justice working through theories of equal protection that define what differences in treatment are morally justified, the law and legal institutions became instruments both to restrain power and to prompt the betterment of society.[56] Uniformity, predictability, and neutrality, the requirement that like cases be treated alike,

---

[55] Peter L. Berger, *Pyramids of Sacrifice: Political Ethics and Social Change* (New York: Basic Books, 1974), pp. 23–4.
[56] Unger, *Law in Modern Society*, pp. 212–13.

became processual standards. Over time, but increasingly, a dense network of compliance regulations based on these principles spread deeper and deeper into hitherto autonomous realms of social life. Concomitantly, arising from the continuous expansion of the market, new and larger institutional forms grew apace, linked in expanding webs of interaction.

In seeking fulfillment for themselves and others, people in modern times have made acquisition a virtue and participation an obligation. There is an emphasis on timeliness, planning, and technical efficacy. Knowledge is highly honored, especially that which is rational and secular, and is increasingly the criterion that is cited for differences in reward. Above all, there is an emphasis on explicit rules that guarantee rights and enforce obligations.[57] Custom and blind conformity have been put aside; neither blind fate nor an imposed hierarchy of inherited statuses govern the affairs of men. Instead, man as property has emerged, rational and equal, to engage with others in the planning and building of a better world.

Phase four: the emergent phase of ethical worth

In the world of property men "own" equal shares of the rights they enjoy. In their dealings with each other this ownership is the basis for the relationships they form. Workers, for example, sell their labor, which they own, freely, in exchange for employment and remuneration. Citizens participate in politics with a vote equal to everyone else's. At the same time, however, although people enter into relationships with theoretical equality, the context of the exchange relationship may in other respects be unequal. Property, for instance, when it is exercised as control of a single, national political party, may mean that only preselected candidates are placed before the voters for their selection – with their equal votes. Or, ownership of a workplace may mean that those who freely sell their labor in order to work in that place at the same time surrender their claims to the products produced there by them, leading thereby to large disparities in the amounts of physical assets that individuals control. The free-and-equal ownership of rights, therefore, in labor or in political participation, is not a guarantee against effective inequality that derives from the control certain individuals are able to exercise in society. The mere fact of ownership of rights does not protect an individual from abuse by institutional control. Despite theoretical equality, relationships remain hierarchical because of the way that control as a prerogative inheres in concepts of property rights (i.e., control of institutions and their processes). This feature of compliance in the world of property is not amenable to change until the concept of rights as property, as *means* that structure relationships within a context of institutional control, changes into a concept of

[57] Inkeles, *Exploring*, pp. 38–9, 101.

rights as the equivalent of personhood, as the *end* or goal of institutional activity.

As long as rights are a property from which a person can be alienated, the conceptual axis of compliance lacks the reversibility that permits a genuine correspondence between structures of social meaning and the highest forms of individual reasoning. However, when the obligations embodied in the compliance ideology match the full range of rights to which an individual is entitled as a moral being, then social and individual structures of reasoning are congruent at the highest level. The likelihood of this happening is certainly a function of general levels of well-being and of a cultural framework that reinforces developmental changes in individual reasoning processes. Change from conventional patterns of thinking is difficult in worlds where scarcity, hierarchy, and inherited status predominate. And, of course, given the variations that exist in individual patterns of reasoning, there will always be many who will be more comfortable in a world of absolutist orientations. Such people are the constant and ever renewed stumbling blocks to the creation of a compliance ideology based on norms of mutual consent and mutual obligations for reciprocity.

How does the conceptual axis of compliance shift to one of ethical consideration? In the first instance, the change comes about through the actions of individuals like Martin Luther King, Jr., who, in their own search to understand social life, articulate a new vision of it that embodies a change in the normative structure of social meanings. Second, the shift occurs through the structuring of law as enforceable codes to protect equal treatment on the one hand, and, on the other, as a set of standards subject to critique on the basis of moral considerations. Third, the shift may occur because a pattern of institutional processes that protects diversity continuously tests the congruence between obligation and right. This means opening wide the door to pluralism. Here is what Karl Dietrich Bracher said about this matter:

Pluralism means, above all, that the common will is not laid down in an authoritarian or totalitarian manner by the state, but that it is represented and determined by a readiness to set bounds to the plurality of intentions and forces: namely, precisely at the point where the existence or viability of that plurality, its freedom and reciprocal toleration itself are threatened or denied. And conversely, the democratic state can offer full scope for the plurality of aspirations, without being in jeopardy itself, only where that basic agreement is acknowledged.[58]

Moral obligation is more extensive than the law, involving, among other attributes, compassion, mercy, charity, and generosity. As law becomes more fully committed to equity and toleration, however, the differences between morality and law begin to recede. Breaches of legal obligation then become

[58] Karl Dietrich Bracher, *The Age of Ideologies: A History of Political Thought in the Twentieth Century* (New York: St. Martin's, 1982), p. 235.

breaches of moral obligation, acts that are unqualifiedly wrong. The letter of the law and the spirit of the law coincide. Driven by sensitivity to the nature of consequent states of affairs, compliance by and through the law involves judgments made in terms of the needs of people. For the first time, institutions become vehicles for the genuine realization of the full potential of all individuals.

Summary

Compliance ideologies vary historically and from society to society. In the ways they structure interaction they have a profound impact on cognitive development. In turn, the ideology itself is bounded by the structures of reasoning that individuals employ. For although the ideology stimulates the conceptual sophistication of its audience, it cannot explain social problems in ways that surpass the general level of sophistication.

Compliance ideologies, however, are also responses to institutional needs as they evolve with technological change. As institutions change under the impact of environmental influences, they place cognitive demands on their members, who must continue to relate with others in an appropriate way if institutional activities are to be carried out successfully. Requirements are placed on individuals to enlarge their understanding of cooperative endeavor, beyond the concrete requirements of specific relationships.[59] Adaptation involving increasingly sophisticated abstraction, thus proceeds at both the individual and the ideological level, slowly, interactively, incrementally, and disjointedly. In the process of change, inexorable as it may seem in the long view, inconsistencies are rife at any given moment in both individual and social constructions of meaning. Some of this is ephemeral; more fundamentally, it reflects the working out, through continuous social discourse, of appropriate responses across a very wide range of social activities.

Marx was right in his vision of logical processes at work in history but wrong in his belief that cause is ultimately traceable to changes in production relations. That is one part only, albeit an important one, of the solution to the problem of change. The other part is the ceaseless thinking processes of individuals. The agenda of change is set definitively not by either but in the interaction between them. Social life, therefore, does not present itself to us in some monolithic fashion despite the fact that people, faced with similar technological problems, have worked out compliance rules in different societies that are broadly similar in their deep structural attributes.

This chapter has suggested four phases in the development of compliance ideologies labeled, respectively, the pre-state and archaic phase, the traditional phase, the modern phase, and the emergent phase. Concomitant with

[59] Rosenberg, *Reason*, pp. 87–8.

shifts from one phase of social meaning to another have been changes in patterns of compliance, from conformity enforced by social custom, to obedience justified by moralized legal codes based on cosmological imagery, to participation protected by neutral laws of ownership specifying rights in various areas of life, to equal treatment in terms of law as a reflection of moral criteria.

People live in imperfect worlds. How social cooperation is to be effected, and how the burdens and benefits of social life are to be distributed, are the conceptual problems at the heart of compliance ideologies. These problems, however, can never be solved by a structure of meaning alone, by greater abstraction that gives increasing coherence to the elements involved – because issues of cooperation and burden sharing also involve feelings. Fairness in relationships is as much an emotional as it is a cognitive issue. We must now turn, therefore, to a consideration of the moral component that is also part of the conceptual framework of compliance ideologies. For as Albert Einstein once noted, in the last analysis all human values rest on morality.[60]

[60] Moscovici, *Age of the Crowd*, p. 316.

4

Contractual and positional compliance

In the study of cheating made famous by H. Hartshorne and M. A. May, children were left alone, or so they thought, to deal with an ethical problem, the kind that at times faces everyone.[1] The question underlying the experiment was how well people resist temptation when no one is around to see them. As we now know, lots of people, and not just children, will bend "the rules of the game" if they think no one is watching and if doing so will result in reward. In little ways, and sometimes in not so little ways, people cheat; students peek at someone else's exam; drivers go through stop signs; citizens shave their taxes; and, ominously, military leaders conceal atrocities. In short, people really do cheat, sometimes terribly.

When economists look at questions of choice, individual or social, they see a tension – and sometimes an equilibrium – between two forces: values and opportunities.[2] The concepts here are not all that different from the concepts involved in cheating. At issue is whether, in a situation involving choice, the constraints imposed by values will prevail over self-interest.[3] Sometimes, of course, there is no conflict because social values and self-interest coincide. At other times the tension is severe. People understand this and a major goal of childhood socialization is to foster ways of expressing self-interest that will coincide with social values.

Self-interest is a concept not easily specified, for the ways in which it is manifested are multitudinous and vary widely among cultures. The problem is simplified somewhat if it is defined as the rational pursuit of utilities. This definition has the virtue of placing emphasis on a mental state, presumably shared, rather than on an outcome. Yet it fails because rationality is a way of viewing the world, not a disposition with regard to it; the definition tells us

---

[1] H. Hartshorne and M. A. May, *Studies in the Nature of Character. Volume 1: Studies in Deceit* (New York: Macmillan, 1928).

[2] Kenneth J. Arrow, *The Limits of Organization* (New York: Norton, 1974), p. 17.

[3] For the most comprehensive critique of the theory of rational self-interest, see Amitai Etzioni, *The Moral Dimension: Toward a New Economics* (New York: Free Press, 1988).

nothing about the motivation for "pursuit" itself. A more fundamental definition, therefore, involves the needs associated with anxiety and egoism. In Maslow's sense these evolve from primitive physical and emotional demands to types that ultimately involve self-actualization.

Egoism is self-centeredness. When anxiety is attached to it we obtain self-interest. That interest need not, however, consistently take the form of self-preferment or be manifested as "the fatal power of envy" that Thucydides spoke of so eloquently in *The Peloponnesian War*. When directed toward solving general questions of health, security, comfort, and the like, its manifestation may benefit others considerably. These caveats notwithstanding, self-interest by itself is not an effective social organizing concept. It needs supporting social principles, a social morality, if it is not to be ultimately destructive. The dilemmas associated with the distribution of goods cannot be resolved on the basis of self-interest alone. Growth, especially if it rests primarily on an ethos of self-interest, will ultimately result in relative scarcity for some. Given that the self-interest of those who experience scarcity is thereby violated, the foundations of social order will be undermined, barring other factors. Strain on the system of distribution, and on the political mechanism that regulates it, is an inevitable consequence without a compliance ideology to provide a moral justification for the prevailing pattern.[4]

The crux of the issue is the degree of social responsibility that exists and how it is defined. As was pointed out in the preceding chapter, issues regarding social responsibility are conceived of differently by people depending on the way they reason. This reasoning shapes patterns of interaction and by so doing contributes importantly to the nature of social life. Knowing this, however, still tells us little about the "content" of social responsibility for content is the product of conditions that are specific to each culture.[5]

As a social construction of meaning a compliance ideology has a deep structure; it also has content that reflects the particular traditions of a society. What results is an ideology that can be classified according to universally shared development patterns and by specific cultural orientations. These orientations vividly reflect moral stances, especially those that underlie justifications for self-interest and social responsibility.

A compliance ideology, therefore, is not just a bundle of conceptual devices, social constructions of meaning that become increasingly abstract and inclusive over time. At their core these ideologies also contain cultural themes that are specific for each society. In traditional societies, for instance, reciprocity was expressed in terms of an overarching ethos of encompassing

---

[4] Fred Hirsch, *Social Limits to Growth* (Cambridge, Mass.: Harvard University Press, 1976), pp. 12, 134.

[5] C. R. Hallpike, *The Foundations of Primitive Thought* (Oxford: Clarendon Press, 1979), p. 483.

hierarchy. Specifically, within the framework of that ethos, there were then differences among societies in the way reciprocity was expressed, depending upon whether they were feudal, agrarian–bureaucratic, and so on.

In the real world, of course, inconsistencies abound and there is no neat analytical form that encompasses all the dimensions by which a society can be characterized. The tension between self-interest and social responsibility, for example, is never resolved by all people in the same way. Choices are handled differently with consequences that are always variable. Group loyalty may be directed toward the family, clan, religious group, occupational association, and so on. Between society and individual are a number of intermediate groups (i.e., institutions) whose own patterns of compliance may be only partly congruent with other institutions and with society as a whole. For these reasons ideal typification is essential; without it, the complexity associated with diversity is overwhelming.

Fortunately, compliance ideologies are amenable to ideal distinctions. Part of the reason for this is that certain technological conditions, widely experienced, impose similar restrictions on social constructions of meaning. In effect, some types of conceptions regarding compliance are more likely than others under given socioeconomic conditions. In addition, in particular societies a relative emphasis on self-interest or social responsibility as a cultural orientation tends to be persistent over time although the form (content) varies depending on the phase of development. Additionally, at any given phase there is a strain toward congruence in content in that patterns of interaction in the most salient institutional settings subordinate incongruent forms in less salient settings.

To be useful ideal typification needs to be linked to dynamic independent variables that are explanatory of the distinctions that are being made. In a structural sense a beginning in this direction was made in Chapter 3 in the discussion relating to the interaction between individual and social constructions of meaning. These comments, however, did not deal adequately with the content component of compliance. Because that component is bound up with the psychology of individuality versus sociability, discussion at this point will focus on this issue. Questions about choice, involving self-interest and social responsibility, are part of this analysis.

Individuality and sociability

The unfolding of an autonomous self in the growth process is a characteristic of all human development. Individuation is necessary for maturation and in that sense is an experience that is not bounded by time and space. This process, however, is not synonymous with the development of privacy or of individualism as these are known in modern societies. That all cultures have had privacy customs (e.g., with regard to family and sexual matters) does not mean privacy as such has been consciously developed as a major principle governing social life. In like manner, although all humans need some measure of escape from the demands of social interaction, they may nevertheless not see themselves as individuals separate from the groups in which they live or may not raise individualism, as such, to the level of a moral principle. East Asian societies, for example, traditionally and contemporaneously, never developed individualism into an axial principle of social existence.

The concept of moral autonomy, therefore, although it inheres as a potential in the human condition, developed historically in tension with existing moralities of solidarity that were generally stronger and more pervasive. In the status-oriented phases of spirits and imposed fate and encompassing hierarchy, autonomy existed only in certain restricted spheres as a way for individuals to cope with the requirements of living together. The idea of respect for individualism as a concept, however, was barely in evidence.[6] It is only in the modern world, where social relationships have been freed from rigid status conceptions based on a presumed natural order – for instance, women conceived of as natural inferiors – that autonomy as a moral principle has developed into a pillar of social life.

In the English language "individual" originally meant "indivisible." Only slowly, and at first pejoratively, did it come to mean a distinction from, rather than a connection to, others. As a singular noun it first appeared in logic, then in biology as a term for classifying genera into species and species into individuals. In the seventeenth century it was used to classify groups as families or commonwealths. In the nineteenth century the term "individualism" was coined, based on a theory, not of abstract individuals only, but of the primacy of individual interests differentiated from those of the state or society.[7] Individualism as a concept is inseparable, therefore, from conceptions of relationships as they developed in the modern phase of property relations. Although autonomy as a moral principle need not flower in that context, the idea of freedom from the restrictions of a fixed and given order does develop and with it the possibility for the subsequent emergence of the concept of individualism.

Many Western psychologists use "autonomy" as a translation term for individual freedom. So also do a number of Western political philosophers.[8] Americans in general believe that individualism stands for moral freedom,

---

[6] Richard F. Hixson, *Privacy in a Public Society: Human Rights in Conflict* (New York: Oxford University Press, 1987), p. 212; also Anita L. Allen, *Uneasy Access: Privacy for Women in a Free Society* (Totowa, N.J.: Rowman & Littlefield, 1988), pp. 1, 2.

[7] Hixson, *Privacy*, pp. 115–17.

[8] Robert Nozick, *Anarchy, State, and Utopia* (New York: Basic Books, 1974).

the rule of liberty and the dignity of man. But as Jerome Kagan notes, it is not obvious that freedom to act in one's own interest unimpeded by rules of conformity and consensus is better than obligation and participation.[9] Many people, including Western Europeans, see individualism as synonymous with selfishness.[10] For the Chinese and Japanese it is not individualism but love of humanity that is seen as the proper goal of human endeavor.

Individualism, of course, even in societies that most loudly proclaim it as their ideal, never stands unalloyed. The power of the community, as Freud pointed out, is always in opposition to individual claims. Justice, as the first requisite of civilization, "the assurance that a law once made will not be broken in favor of an individual," proclaims the collective strength of the community over the person.[11] Individualism is thus a frame of mind, embodying ideas about existence, but is not in itself a sufficient organizing principle for social life. Even in the mind, however, individuality is never in sole possession but always exists in a dualistic relationship with sociability. It does, however, to the degree that it is a prominent sentiment, affect perceptions of the world. The feeling, for example, that people should have the right to explore possibilities for their lives unimpeded by norms of consensus leads to beliefs about the importance of self-expression. By opposing rote conformity, individualism helps a person to strike a nonconservative stance, one that questions order and stability for their own sake. It disassociates people from the embrace of family, class, religion, or race, loci that have been unchallenged as justifications for privilege and influence for hundreds of years. When linked with the idea of equality, it sponsors the idea of interchangeability: that is, that if people had the requisite training and experience, anyone could take another person's place in work, sport, and so on.[12]

In all societies, however, the individual develops against a backdrop of constraints; there is a balance between individual desires expressed as self-interest and community needs that foster social responsibility. The balance may favor one side or the other, but what exists is neither an individual who is totally dependent on the group, nor one who is totally independent; there is, rather, a condition of interdependence that is woven in complex and varying patterns throughout the groups that make up society. As Freud succinctly put it, "A good part of the struggles of mankind centre round the

[9] Jerome Kagan, "Presuppositions in Developmental Inquiry," in *Value Presuppositions in Theories of Human Development*, ed. Leonard Cirillo and Seymour Wapner (Hillsdale, N.J.: Erlbaum, 1986), p. 75.

[10] Herbert McClosky and John Zaller, *The American Ethos: Public Attitudes Toward Capitalism and Democracy* (Cambridge, Mass.: Harvard University Press, 1984), p. 113.

[11] Sigmund Freud, *Civilization and Its Discontents*, trans. and ed. James Strachey (New York: Norton, 1961), p. 42.

[12] J. R. Pole, *The Pursuit of Equality in American History* (Berkeley and Los Angeles: University of California Press, 1978), p. 293.

single task of finding an expedient accommodation – one, that is, that will bring happiness – between the claims of the individual and the cultural claims of the group."[13]

The compromise that is arrived at between the demands of the group and the needs of individuals is formulated in compliance ideologies as moral guidelines. In terms of conceptual sophistication these guidelines embody the structural characteristics of the ideology, and they evolve historically as an aspect of transformations in compliance norms generally. This link to a structure of reasoning thus constrains the format for moral expression; as a consequence, the manner whereby the needs of individuals as autonomous beings are balanced against the claims of groups for social responsibility varies by phase of development (i.e., pre-state and archaic, traditional, etc.). The development of new forms of moral expression is not, however, simply a passive derivative of institutional changes spurred by technological innovations and the like. At the individual level people with different reasoning capabilities discuss moral guidelines in terms of their adequacy for coordinating institutional arrangements. It is from this process of moral discourse, equally and interactively, that there emerges the possibility for transformations in both the structure and the content of compliance ideologies.

Moral ideas about fairness and the balance between self and society

In the language of game theory, mutual cooperation must be preferred over mutual defection for mutual benefit to exist.[14] In these games the actors are presumed to be rational, able to calculate objectively the consequences of both courses of action. In the real world of the psyche, however, the calculation may be far from objective. Cooperation may be a goal of such overriding importance that it is chosen regardless of benefits or losses. It may also be entered into, of course, out of fear or expediency. Cooperation is most powerfully motivated, however, when it springs from feelings of altruism or benevolent reciprocity, for it is when these motivations are aroused that cooperation as an aspect of social responsibility is especially activated. In what way does this occur?

Morality, as Durkheim pointed out, is never met with except in society; it is, he averred, increasingly the underpinning of social solidarity as institutional complexity increases.[15] Yet morality is more than this. It is related, surely, to Freud's idea about the development of a cultural superego – meaning the development of ethics – which constitutes the attempt to rid society of "the constitutional inclination of human beings to be aggressive towards

---

[13] Freud, *Civilization*, p. 43.
[14] Kenneth A. Oye, "Explaining Cooperation Under Anarchy: Hypotheses and Strategies," *World Politics* 38, no. 1 (October 1985): 6.
[15] Emile Durkheim, *The Division of Labor in Society*, trans. George Simpson (Glencoe, Ill.: Free Press, 1933), pp. 89, 400.

one another."[16] Morality, in other words, becomes more perfect to the degree that relationships are freed from the patterns of compliance that are typical in a traditional society, and as individuals, concomitantly, develop a capacity to subdue propensities toward aggression, cheating, and the like.

Individual moral growth proceeds with the interrelated development of cognitive and affective capabilities in conjunction with an ability to replace naked self-interest with personal responsibility for fulfilling obligations. Increasingly sophisticated conceptions about reciprocity and exchange coordinate the ability to be altruistically aware of the needs of others and to be empathic with regard to those needs.[17] In this developmental process there is a gradual generalization of others, meaning that views about appropriate behavior are less and less informed solely by particularistic criteria. What develops are general obligations, which are acted upon not because of status requirements (obeying a superior), or because of demands arising in a particular social context, or because of particular requirements set forth by law or regulation, but because universal principles deemed to be ethically comprehensive require it. These principles are ultimately internalized and stand conceptually above context; they therefore moralize motives for action.[18]

Many principles, however, apparently universal, can compete in a given situation. By what criteria, for example, should scarce resources be allocated? Is fairness achieved by allocation on the basis of need, or should it be in terms of equity, with distribution according to effort? What constitutes equality? Should it be realized in terms of results or in terms of opportunity? Priority among these principles is difficult, if not impossible, to establish. Moreover, if each can be advocated from a veil-of-ignorance perspective,[19] based on rational calculation, to what degree do moral motives play a part at all?

Difficulties such as these have prompted psychologists to develop theories regarding moral reasoning in which the highest stages of development correspond to a Kantian deontological perspective. That is, the principles that gird true moral reasoning are not, it is said, those that support egocentrism or magnify social criteria (e.g., status, laws) but are those that reference personhood. Reciprocity in action, therefore, is truly moral when others are acknowledged beyond their mere presence in social interaction – when others are treated not as instruments for the fulfillment of another's objectives but rather as moral entities in and of themselves. It is from this standpoint, and

[16] Freud, *Civilization*, p. 89.
[17] Richard W. Wilson, *Labyrinth: An Essay on the Political Psychology of Change* (Armonk, N.Y.: M. E. Sharpe, 1988), chap. 1.
[18] Jürgen Habermas, *Communication and the Evolution of Society*, trans. Thomas McCarthy (Boston: Beacon Press, 1979), p. 136.
[19] Martin L. Hoffman, "Empathy, Its Limitations, and Its Role in a Comprehensive Moral Theory," in *Morality, Moral Behavior and Moral Development*, ed. William M. Kurtines and Jacob L. Gewirtz (New York: Wiley, 1984), p. 298.

only from this standpoint, that a consequentialist argument can be made. For outcomes to be truly and lastingly just, the actions that lead to them must be motivated by the deepest concern for the well-being of others.

In what way can the motivations that foster moral action be conceptualized? One might begin with a list of desirable behaviors and of motivating qualities that are presumably linked with them. This approach, taken from the tradition of personality theory, has proven useful when analyzing individuals. It is far less adequate, however, when an understanding of groups is desired. How to determine a group level of anxiety by aggregating those of individuals has proven to be very difficult. Social learning theories have been more successful in this regard but they have foundered for the opposite reason. By measuring (through surveys, etc.) group responses, they bypass individual motivation that lies at the crux of moral action.

Carol Gilligan's work provides an escape from this dilemma.[20] Faced with the curious and absurd finding from data on moral development that women on average do not progress as far as men, Gilligan proposed that there are two "content" routes to moral maturity. The first involves a social orientation grounded in an ethic of care, which she defined as the "responsibility to discern and alleviate the 'real and recognizable trouble' of this world"; with this path identity "is defined in a context of relationship and judged by a standard of responsibility." The second orientation is termed the ethic of autonomy. This path radiates "the confidence of certain truth" and involves "an injunction to respect the rights of others and thus to protect from interference the rights to life and self-fulfillment."[21] In solving moral dilemmas her two ethics require, variously, a concern for others and autonomous reliance on principle. Gilligan analyzed the incidence of these paths by gender in the United States and determined that content differences in social orientations genuinely reflect differences in motivations for moral behavior. Because American women are oriented toward fulfilling the ethic of care, whereas traditional moral development theory evaluates responses in terms of the ethic of autonomy, the anomalies in the data are made clear.

Gilligan's work, among others, makes clear that different content orientations can characterize groups. Studies of non-American societies suggest strongly that the differences she found by gender in the United States also characterize cultures. In America, for example, as Gilligan notes, the ethic of autonomy is the ideal. In Chinese society the ideal is the ethic of care.[22] In solving moral problems about fairness one cultural approach is by the path of

---

[20] Carol Gilligan, *In a Different Voice: Psychological Theory and Women's Development* (Cambridge, Mass.: Harvard University Press, 1982).

[21] Ibid., pp. 100, 160.

[22] See Richard Madsen, *Morality and Power in a Chinese Village* (Berkeley and Los Angeles: University of California Press, 1984).

sociability, through active and principled concern for others within a matrix of relationships. The other approach is individual, not in the sense of self-interest, but in terms of a person's responsibility to utilize principles autonomously in moral judgments. Each path at its most developed utilizes a humanity principle as a universal minimum moral standard applicable to all human relations. Yet each orientation is insufficient by itself; only when they are joined is moral competence complete for it is in the process of joining that empathy and cognitive maturation play complementary roles. Accepting others into one's moral frame of reference involves concern about the requirements of relationships. Putting that acceptance fully into practice requires conceptualizing requirements in terms of universal principles.

Care – autonomy and rights – obligations

The literature on rights is extensive. What is conceived of as a right by various authors differs, along with considerable variation in terminology. Within this diversity, however, certain themes emerge. A.J.M. Milne, for example, lists six rights that all members of a community are said to possess by virtue of membership: the right to life, to justice in the form of fair treatment, to succor, to honorable treatment, to civility, and to freedom from arbitrary interference. The sources of these rights are said to be seven in number, grouped into two categories: (1) respect for life and respect for justice, and (2) fellowship, social responsibility, freedom from arbitrary interference, honorable treatment, and civility. Despite a troublesome overlap, it seems clear that the *sources* of rights, by and large, are, again, the ethic of autonomy (that is, principled reasoning in terms of the humanity principle) for category one, and the ethic of care or social responsibility (also conceptualized in terms of the humanity principle) for category two.[23] The rights themselves fall into two general categories, the right to action or freedom under the law (e.g., freedom from arbitrary interference), and the right to recipience or equal protection of the law (e.g., the right to life, to justice in the form of fair treatment, to succor, to honorable treatment, and to civility). These two categories are those of negative and positive rights, respectively, made well known by the work of Isaiah Berlin.[24]

Positive rights are associated with the ethic of care and the need for sociability. They speak to fair shares and fair treatment, what Aristotle called proportionate equality, and call for departures from self-interested behavior and for a general strengthening of ethical considerations in dealings with others.

[23] A.J.M. Milne, "Human Rights and the Diversity of Morals: A Philosophical Analysis of Rights and Obligations in the Global System," in *Rights and Obligations in North–South Relations*, ed. Moorhead Wright (New York: St. Martin's, 1986), pp. 9, 20–23, 25.

[24] Isaiah Berlin, *Two Concepts of Liberty* (London: Oxford University Press, 1958).

In compliance ideologies they are mirrored by obligations to work consistently for the benefit of the least advantaged. In social relationships altruistic understanding and empathic concern for others are deemed important. Relationships are thus defined in sociability terms, ultimately toward equals in a community of all persons.

Negative rights are associated with the ethic of autonomy and a need for individual enlargement; they speak to personal responsibility. In order for personal responsibility to flourish, negative rights call for freedom from arbitrary interference, for the right to make choices unimpeded by others. In compliance ideologies these rights are guaranteed by obligations that ensure privacy. In the broadest sense this means that all persons shall have a degree of inaccessibility involving, most crucially, freedom from coercion. In social relationships the governing ideals are equal respect for individuals and equal entitlement to that degree of personal sovereignty that is consistent with others having the same. The moral definition of relationships is thus in terms of individuality.

Just as individual moral maturity requires that the motivations underlying the ethic of care and the ethic of autonomy both be incorporated, so do compliance ideologies become more moral to the degree that positive and negative rights are mutually recognized. In the process, law changes from given and beyond question to negotiable in terms of abstract principles; procedural law with its close relationship to negative rights (i.e., processes to protect persons) and substantive law with its close relationship to positive rights (i.e., ideals regarding distribution) become equally emphasized; entitlements defined arbitrarily by position are altered by an expanded definition of community and by a redefinition of personhood. The rights to aid and to civility, for example, are not "rented" from a feudal lord in return for services, nor granted on suffrance by a social welfare state, but extended as a natural entitlement without regard to the status of the recipient. Freedom from interference cannot be abridged on the basis of some unappealable pretext set forth by a hierarchical superior; it is, again, an entitlement that is attached to personhood. In the reconceptualization of negative and positive rights, therefore, compliance ideologies affirm a commitment to a moral society. Yet the obstacles in the path of this development are severe and the greatest of all comes from compliance itself.

Compliance, obligations, and property rights

Cooperation among the members of institutions is necessary if the technology that is available is to be utilized effectively. Grievances must be adjudicated and anger channeled into nondisruptive forms of behavior. The employment of sanctions, of course, is always part of the means employed to bolster cooperative activity. By themselves, however, sanctions are relatively ineffective. More efficacious by far is when the norms that foster cooperation are linked with those that legitimize constraint, thus reducing the transaction costs associated with enforcing decisions.[25]

Compliance ideologies are relatively stable, therefore, when a pattern of control coincides with beliefs about the legitimacy of that pattern. Inertial factors also foster stability (i.e., carrying out obligations toward others in a time-honored fashion because to do otherwise is confusing and anxiety-provoking). More is at work, however, than mere inertia. Control is most effective when elite status is morally justified by a socially approved emphasis on particular rights and obligations.

In practice, certain rights have always been excluded from the full range that is theoretically possible. The way such exclusion is legitimized is the basis for distinctive patterns of reward. Differentiating leadership positions, necessary for the efficient functioning of institutions, is marked by inequalities in prestige, influence, material possessions, and so on, and is secured by minimizing positive or negative rights respectively (and hence the need to honor the obligations associated with a particular category of right). For example, when positive rights are less honored, the obligation to care for others is reduced and with it the need for concern about fair shares. Unequal status is then made morally legitimate by the emphasis on negative rights (i.e., the ideal of autonomy), which calls for noninterference in the affairs of others, including not interfering with the processes that permit greater distinctions for elites. Conversely, when negative rights are minimized, the obligation to desist from interfering with others is less salient and with it the necessity to refrain from arbitrary dominance. Inequality in degrees of authority (and contingent inequalities of prestige, access to privileges, the use of property, etc.) is justified by emphasizing how community well-being (i.e., positive rights and caring) is assured by the authoritative suppression of self-interest.

Inequality is legitimized, therefore, by stressing either positive or negative rights. Of course, while societies in the contemporary world characteristically favor positive or negative rights, all honor both in some relative degree. The actual admixture determines the ways in which rewards are obtained, whether equalities are narrow or broad, and the relative salience of equality of opportunity versus equality of results.[26] Distinctive patterns of property rights are derived from these particular emphases; they both legitimize elite perquisites and justify subordinate status, thereby providing a rationale for cooperative activity. The ways in which rights over property are secured are

---

[25] Shawn W. Rosenberg, Dana Ward, and Stephen Chilton, *Political Reasoning and Cognition: A Piagetian View* (Durham, N.C.: Duke University Press, 1988), pp. 59–60.
[26] Douglas Rae et al., *Equalities* (Cambridge, Mass.: Harvard University Press, 1981), pp. 48, 134.

thus among the clearest indications of the social orientations that are honored in societies.

Justifications for particular patterns of reward are enshrined in property rights. These are said to be positive in nature when the emphasis is on fulfilling community needs; they are negative in nature when justifications stress the desirability of individual attainment unhampered by social interference. In the first case rewards are obtained from occupying a position of trust within an institution (e.g., being a cadre in the Communist Party or an officer in a ruling military organization); in the second case rewards flow from individual accomplishment. With positive rights access to property derives from status in a social unit, whereas with negative rights status is the consequence of unfettered individual activity.

Differences in property rights correspond to differences in ideals about social orientations. In the case of reward deriving from position in a social unit, ideals stress the unit as a whole and the ties among its members. In the case of reward deriving from personal activity, ideals stress the importance of individual achievement. Some of the flavor of these differences is caught in Ezra Vogel's description of Japanese views of American and Japanese firms – organizations, incidentally, that are usually thought of as functioning within the same type of economic system (i.e., capitalist). Says Vogel,

Japanese firms feel that the American individualistic system of contractual relations between firms has high transaction costs involving lawyers, planning for contingencies if other parties fail to meet their obligations, and inflexibilities. They feel that stronger personal networks, involving broader common communitarian concerns, can link firms and permit greater flexibility, more rapid development of new products, and savings of transactions costs.[27]

Criticisms such as the Japanese one cited by Vogel speak to cultural perceptions as much as to any objective assessment of institutional arrangements. Although particular Japanese techniques of organization might be copied to advantage by Americans (and vice versa), harmony in elite-follower relationships in both America and Japan is derived from a complex web of particular cultural expectations and methods of conflict resolution. American firms' extensive use of lawyers and of contingency planning for cases where others do not meet their obligations reflects a general belief in the desirability of individually based contractual relations. That belief cannot be easily modified simply by stressing a need for stronger personal networks.

In short, although status in societies always involves reliance on a mixture of rights and obligations, the pattern is skewed depending on generalized justifications for inequality. Obligations that stress working together in a

---

[27] Ezra F. Vogel, "Conclusion," in *Ideology and National Competitiveness: An Analysis of Nine Countries*, ed. George C. Lodge and Ezra F. Vogel (Boston: Harvard Business School Press, 1987), pp. 318–19.

group and a strengthening of personal ties, for example, are often paired with less concern for rights that stress noninterference. The reverse is also true. In the admixture distinctive forms of property control – and inequality – are justified.

Positional and contractual modes of compliance

For particular institutional arrangements to be efficient they must be thought of as public goods. Such beliefs need not be universally held, but they must be relatively general and widespread if institutional transaction costs are to be minimal.[28]

Compliance rules vary in accordance with the particular blend of obligations and rights that define social orientations. A relative stress on negative rights and obligations is eminently suited for forms of control that emphasize personal unfettered command over some type of resource. In the formation of relationships an ideal of negotiation between parties is always present. I have therefore labeled this category of obligation and right *contractual*. Positive rights and obligations, on the other hand, refer to a fair distribution of the goods of society. These are suited for forms of control that emanate, as it were, from the community; in the formation of relationships, duties are matched against rights in terms of one's place in society. As a consequence, I have labeled this category of obligation and right *positional*.

In every society there is a mix of contractual and positional obligations, although with tendencies, sometimes marked, to favor one type over the other. Contractual obligations, which stress defined limits to authority, the intrinsic value of the individual, and legal guarantees regarding negotiating processes, are paired, in some ratio, with positional obligations that stress mutuality, community need, and an organic view of society. Contractual obligations carry the flavor of the ethic of autonomy and are based, primarily, on psychological propensities toward individuality. Positional obligations have the tone of the ethic of care and reflect psychological propensities toward sociability.

Positional obligations are not synonomous with communism nor are contractual obligations synonomous with capitalism. Each type of obligation can exist in market or nonmarket economies and can be associated with brutal and authoritarian governments as well as with tolerant and democratic ones. Also, each can exist in a bureaucratic or nonbureaucratic environment. In the broadest sense contractual means simply that there are spheres of life that are to be untrammeled, whereas positional means that there are duties owing to others that cannot be voided by individual volition.

[28] Douglass C. North, *Structure and Change in Economic History* (New York: Norton, 1981), p. 106.

A major reason why positional and contractual obligations can flourish in different environments is that each is subject to redefinition in the way it functions depending on the conceptual phase with which it is associated. For example, in the traditional phase, contractual obligations are defined in hierarchical terms that have the form of clientalism, in which subordinates are unprotected except for negotiated matters. In the modern phase contractual obligations stress rights that are mutually held and the need to develop complex legal procedures to ensure the fulfillment of obligations and to adjudicate conflicts over property. In the emergent phase people are regarded as embodying in themselves the rights that previously were only their property. With ethical consideration contractual obligations begin to stress care and responsibility in relationships; inequalities in the control of resources are reshaped in the direction of equality of consideration and outcome. Contract becomes a mode for universal attainment rather than one for individual fulfillment. As shifts in conceptual development take place the compliance ideology of a previous phase, once seen as absolute, becomes less relevant. The table (p. 91) shows the content of the obligations that are associated with different phases of development.

Change in compliance patterns

To paraphrase Chilton, the development of compliance ideologies is unilinear in structure but multilinear in content.[29] Change does not occur equally and simultaneously in all realms (e.g., economy, polity, culture), nor, when it occurs, is the process sudden and complete. Rather, different types of obligations appropriate for different phases of development can exist side by side for a protracted period. Moreover, although there is a bias toward progress, based in part on a history of continuous technological improvement, regression in one or more areas can take place. What stands especially in the way of change are the patterns of privilege that are tied to particular patterns of right and obligation. The disciplining of subordinates also acts as a potent brake against change when carried out by those at a conventional level of moral reasoning who believe that loyalty to leaders and prevailing norms is the essence of moral virtue.

Deviance from the norms of a compliance ideology defines the ideology's boundaries. What a society considers to be moral is then etched clearly for all to see. In Kai Erikson's words, "morality and immorality meet at the public scaffold, and it is during this meeting that the line between them is drawn."[30]

---

[29] Stephen Chilton, *Defining Political Development* (Boulder, Colo.: Lynne Rienner, 1988), pp. 94, 96.

[30] Cited in Lawrence M. Friedman, *Law and Society: An Introduction* (Englewood Cliffs, N.J.: Prentice-Hall, 1977), p. 152.

Table 1. *Changes in obligation by phase of development*

Phase of development	Positional obligations	Contractual obligations
Pre-state and archaic	Kinship unit paramount Loyalty to particular others Strict status role requirements – punishments for violations	Kinship bonds paramount Bargaining as pleading with overlords and gods Personal oaths sacred – punishments for violations
Traditional	Heavenly harmony obtained by social stability Loyalty to sanctified roles Social gradations define responsibilities Emphasis on obedience by inferiors	Importance of hierarchical ranking Duties associated with class status Religious sanctions enforce agreements Emphasis on deference to superiors
Modern	Rights as property of community Support for rational ends defined by substantive law (ends) Concern for community need Emphasis on solidarity	Rights as property of equal individuals Support for rational ends obtained through procedural law (processes) Concern for privacy Emphasis on autonomy
Emergent	Rights as intrinsic involving recognition of privacy and importance of procedural law Community service through individual attainment Wholistic concerns	Rights as intrinsic involving recognition of community concerns and importance of substantive law Individual fulfillment through community service Wholistic concerns

Although elites may be more vigorous than others in defense of existing norms, challenges to established beliefs are generally resisted by all segments of a society; they are usually deflected or channeled into reforms of current policies and procedures. Only when a comprehensive and desirable counterideology is presented is there a possibility of change and even then only slowly and with difficulty, sometimes involving chaos and violence.

Certain kinds of events, however, do hasten changes in compliance ideologies. A defeat in war, for example, may lead to an open reevaluation of obligations. In the same manner, a sharp rise in scarcity or in criminal activities that cause diseconomies may occasion a similar reexamination. The same may occur when an economy is strained to the full yet is not progressing at the same tempo in all parts. Sectoral imbalances may lead to sharp disagreements that undermine compliance justifications. Increasing social complexity can likewise erode the currency of prevailing criteria; it does so by changing the pattern of payoffs for various activities with implications for the fulfillment of needs in areas including nutrition, health, shelter, sanitation, and education.

Despite all of the conservative factors that support the continuation of a particular compliance ideology, therefore, change does occur. New technology alters work methods and procedures, and along with them, sociodemographic variables. Institutional modifications, in turn, reveal new possibilities for efficient use of technology. Structures of individual and social meaning shift in order to adapt to new conditions. They are reflected in a terminology whose "content" is keyed to new institutional procedures. This content also reflects the new forms that have come into being for the control of property and the obligations important for maintaining such control. Underlying the impulse for change is usually some form of personal moral discontent, provoked because prevailing obligations are being violated or because of an inner sense of the inadequacy of current standards. The process often originates with a single issue whose solution then points the way toward a general reorganization of conceptual categories. In moral discourse those who are truly discontented stand out. In our age of change it has been noted empirically that a central and universally shared characteristic of all reformers and revolutionaries is their keen sense of justice and injustice and their zeal to right wrongs.[31] In the words of R. H. Tawney, "The impetus to reform or revolution springs in every age from the realization of the contrast between the external order of society and the moral standards recognized as valid by the conscience or reason of the individual."[32]

Summary

Over time, as technological capability progresses, institutions become more complex internally and in their interactions with other institutions. Increased demands arise for the coordination of exterior networks and interior relationships. In a push–pull interaction between individual and social constructions of meaning, relationship patterns are reconceptualized through the use of higher-order concepts that are increasingly abstract and inclusive. Concomitantly, rights and obligations, notions about right and wrong, are rephrased in ways that are congruent with new conceptions of social life.

Human beings weave their lives together in rich and complex patterns. There are revealed in the historical record textures of social life that are wonderfully intricate. To know any society in all of its aspects is a process that is

[31] Mostafa Rejai and Kay Phillips, *World Revolutionary Leaders* (New Brunswick, N.J.: Rutgers University Press, 1983), p. 138.
[32] R. H. Tawney, *Religion and the Rise of Capitalism* (New York: Harcourt, Brace; Mentor Books, 1926), p. 109.

both fruitful and endlessly engaging. Within the wide fabric of diversity, complexity increases over time as the institutional focus shifts from family to clan to region, to nation and, ultimately, to the world. Yet while contextual richness thickens as more complex groupings come under survey, other patterns, like the long waves on an oscilloscope, reveal extraordinary continuities. Down through the generations, occurring over and over again like the bold linear strokes of a tartan, designs appear that link the present to the past in a way that is unique for every social order.

III

Compliance in changing societies

5

The end of harmony

Based on the arguments presented in Part II, it is now possible to elaborate the definition of political culture that was given earlier. It is as follows: A political culture is a social construction of meaning termed a compliance ideology, whose structure and content serve to reduce institutional transaction costs by delimiting obligations, expressed in positional and contractual terms, that justify elite status and bolster group solidarity. This definition conforms to Thomas C. Schelling's specification of usefulness as being "simultaneously simple enough to fit a variety of behaviors and complex enough to fit behaviors that need the help of an explanatory model."[1] It is derived from the argument in Part II in which the ideal qualities of compliance ideologies were specified. Before entering the world of concrete phenomena, therefore, we need a form of presentation that can relate any real culture to the ideal-types that have been set forth, that can show the relative salience of contractual versus positional criteria, and that can provide a framework suitable for revealing structural changes in these criteria over time.

I propose at this point to employ a graph format that will highlight my arguments through the rest of this book. The format is a familiar x–y grid with each axis representing, respectively, contractual and positional compliance criteria. Greater values along either axis denote greater structural sophistication (i.e., movement from the pre-state and archaic phase to the traditional phase to the modern phase to the emergent phase). Any point on the graph thus indicates the structure of a compliance ideology and the content of the obligations that inform the prevailing rules of institutional arrangements. The basic form of the graph is as follows:

Figure 1 is not a device that has empirical utility. Given the imprecision in our knowledge about the structural attributes of social constructions of meaning, no units of measurement are noted along either the x or the y axis. What exists, rather, is a device for ordering variables and for showing the

---

[1] Thomas C. Schelling, *Micromotives and Macrobehavior* (New York: Norton, 1978), p. 89.

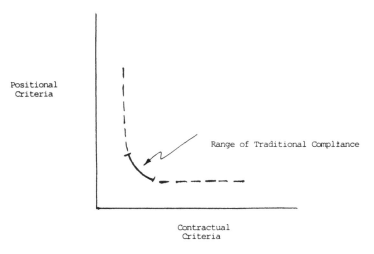

Figure 1. Graphical format for the designation of compliance
ideologies.

comparative relationships among them. I assume that the zero point represents the complete absence of cognitive activity and that there are logical (if
not empirically verifiable) points along both axes that represent the maximum extent of structural development of contractual or positional criteria.
These points, noted as A and B, are the ends of a continuum; they are purely
analytical for neither could exist entirely in isolation. In fact, any actual compliance ideology is always a mixture of both criteria and, if measurable,
would then be located at some point on the grid of the graph. Such a hypothetical point has been indicated at c,d.

It was pointed out earlier that compliance ideologies tend to emphasize
contractual and positional criteria unequally. Theoretically, of course, it is
possible to conceive of contractual and positional criteria keeping pace in
their structural development. In fact, congruence rarely occurs. The logic of
development of social and individual constructions of meaning is different.
At the individual level, through *décalage*, the structure of thinking in different content domains strains toward uniformity. Once movement to a
higher level takes place in any particular domain, that way of thinking will
engulf lower orders of reasoning in other areas. By contrast, the norms of
compliance ideologies conform only partially to this pattern (through the interaction that takes place between individual and social constructions of
meaning). There are, additionally, two related factors that affect social meanings: (1) The social control of institutional activities is based, in part, on normative criteria that must be comprehensible to individuals who reason at
different structural levels; and (2) in times of change norms may be based on

different structures of reasoning depending on whether they emphasize preferences or constraints. Preferences are normative justifications for new patterns of interaction in relationships, whereas constraints are the normative basis of duties within ongoing institutional contexts. The social meanings associated with preferences challenge prevailing compliance criteria; those associated with constraints are articulated at a structural level that is comprehensible to the broadest range of people. In short, when compliance ideologies change developmentally, justifications for preferences (rewards and status) are articulated first at structurally higher levels of meaning (i.e., structurally more comprehensive moral justifications), whereas duties are articulated at a lower or prevailing level (i.e., a level where obedience criteria are widely understood and accepted).

These ideas are explored in these Part III chapters. Because of my concern here and in Part IV with the contemporary period, the present chapter focuses on the transition to the modern phase. Features of the pre-state, archaic, and traditional phases are summarized, but not with an effort to maintain a strict sequence of chronological development. Rather, my comments on these phases serve only as background for understanding today's world.

From archaic to traditional societies

In the archaic period ordinary people survived without wealth, significant freedom of movement, or the hope of change. They toiled in cultivation and in animal husbandry and exchanged with others, as necessary, by means of simple barter. Economies were basically customary in form: that is, there was an emphasis on economic activities carried out without reference to higher-level social bodies or a market system. In the classical world of the West, for example, such things as money using and legal institutions came into being only with the Greek city-state system.[2] The necessities of life (tools, clothing, weapons, utensils) were produced at home with only slight variations in design over very long periods. Even later societies that we think of as relatively advanced and rich in social life, such as the Athenian, were far less differentiated than nineteenth-century England.[3]

For almost all people the activities of life revolved around agriculture. In the interval between sowing and harvesting the risk of adverse weather was often a serious one. There were also risks from disputes with neighbors and from thieves and bandits, all of which put a premium on strong social obligations molded through kinship and neighborhood ties, and on protection by overlords who could enforce decisions in cases of dispute. These overlords often included in their ranks a few who were deemed to be especially wise

[2] John Hicks, *A Theory of Economic History* (Oxford: Clarendon Press, 1969), p. 68.
[3] Barrington Moore, Jr., *Privacy: Studies in Social and Cultural History* (Armonk, N.Y.: M. E. Sharpe, 1984), p. 133.

and knowledgeable (e.g., priests, etc.), but the learning required was often unspecialized in the technical sense. Indeed, there was frequently a hearty skepticism regarding technical experimentation at all levels of society.

In the ancient world kinship systems specified those people with whom one should share goods, dampen hostility, and help in times of need and crisis. The model of relationships was collectivist, marked by a cool and hostile attitude toward individuality and by a requirement to subordinate personal needs to those of the community as a whole. In the words of an old Japanese proverb: "The nail that sticks out is hammered down." People were expected to achieve fulfillment within the hierarchical order of the kinship system. In a very real sense, no person was born equal to others; distinctions of age, sex, and rank prevailed everywhere. This was never more true than for slaves, whose numbers were, at times, extraordinarily large. It has been estimated, for example, that at the time of Julius Caesar, one-third of the population of the Roman state was in bondage.[4]

For most of human history kinship norms were virtually synonymous with ethics; they were always taken for granted and assumed to be primary. People tended to live in close quarters in family units that combined procreational, social, political, and economic functions. Privacy was recognized in areas involving bodily functions (e.g., sex and elimination) but was not tinged with ideas about human dignity or of a right to protection from authority. Vertical relationships entailing unequal obligations and expectations knit the people of this familial world together. Obligations were expected to be honored and violations were often heavily punished. This could lead, as Hobhouse long ago pointed out, to what in modern societies would be considered curious inconsistencies. As he said, "A hospitable savage, who will lend his wife to a guest, would kill her for acting in the same way on her own notion."[5]

The household that one was born into, or became a member of, was a critical determinant of one's chances in life. Within the family, fathers tended to rule, often exercising unlimited authority over wives, children, and servants. Because the family was also the preeminent economic unit of society, nonfamily members attached to the household were also ruled by the master in a familial manner. Children sent to serve others usually assumed a subordinate family role. To be part of a household, however, was also to be part of a wider, albeit often attenuated, network bound by origin, patron–client relations, and friendship ties. For ancient Hebrew males the tribe was the locus of extrafamilial activity. In the Greek polis family origin and property together were the necessary criteria that bound individuals together as citizens.

[4] Stanley H. Cath, "Caesar and His Barren Relationship with Rome," *Psychohistory Review* 16, no. 2 (Winter 1988): 272.
[5] L. T. Hobhouse, *Morals in Evolution: A Study in Comparative Ethics* (London: Chapman & Hall, 1915), p. 11.

Those whose family origin was elsewhere (Metics), or who were themselves property, were ineligible.

In this phase the realm of the mundane was influenced by supernatural force. In *The Iliad*, for example, a work that was listened to and read over many centuries, there is a famous passage describing the fateful day when Achilles met Hector and pursued him beneath the walls of Troy; then "when for the fourth time they had come around to the well springs then the Father balanced his golden scales, and in them he set two fateful portions of death, which lays men prostrate, one for Achilleus, and one for Hektor, breaker of horses, and balanced it by the middle; and Hektor's death-day was heavier and dragged downward toward death, and Phoibos Apollo forsook him."[6] Here is no notion of free will but rather of an imposed fate that comes from the gods.

In the succeeding traditional phase the idea that the supernatural pervades the natural world remained powerful. In Islam, for example, obedience to religious injunctions is coterminous with the whole of life. In both the pagan Roman Empire and in its Christian successor, the Byzantine Empire, the emperor was the object of both a political and a religious cult, standing in a direct relationship to transcendental power. Not all transitions to the traditional phase, however, involved such overt religiosity. As the Chinese state evolved from archaic feudalism toward a proto-empire, compliance was increasingly and explicitly associated with the ideals of social order, harmony, selflessness, cooperation and conformity in which the state itself was unambiguously established over the individual family and clan. For the Chinese it was not the priesthood that attracted those interested in scholarship and in staffing the offices of power, but civil service itself. Heaven existed but it was state officials who had de facto power and who, under the authority of the emperor's heavenly mandate, harmonized social relations.

The transition to the traditional phase

It is in ancient Greece that we most clearly witness, in almost modern guise, how social tension affects prevailing compliance ideologies and prompts transition from a conception of existence governed by particular fate to one of life in an expanded hierarchical order. There, extreme economic polarities had developed by the seventh and sixth centuries B.C., became acute by the fourth century, and resulted in a long series of revolutions that lasted until the Roman Settlement in 146–5 B.C.[7] The common denominator in all of

---

[6] *The Iliad of Homer,* translated with an introduction by Richard Lattimore (Chicago: The University of Chicago Press, 1951), pp. 440–1.

[7] Alexander Fuks, *Social Conflict in Ancient Greece* (Jerusalem: Magnes Press, 1984), pp. 12, 282.

these revolutionary episodes was a striving for equality (political and juridical) and economic liberty, the two being seen as linked. What had occurred was a decline in small and medium land-holdings and a rise of large agricultural properties (usually slave-operated) along with the development of a money-using, price-driven, quasi-capitalist economy in the cities. There was a concomitant rise in the number of landless, a growth of the urban proletariat and of unemployment, and a change in the distribution of wealth, with great possessions being held by only a few, while the number of destitute rose[8] (analogous to what Midlarsky reported on for South China before the modern mass revolution; landlords, who constituted 3 percent of the total number of Chinese families, owned 47 percent of the total acreage, while the poor peasants, who constituted 71 percent of the families, owned but 16 percent).[9] Those who were chattel slaves, rootless, in debt penury, or in that condition of special slavery that Aristotle spoke of – the meaner mechanics or artisans who had no property but their labor and who thus led a servile life – thus became the discontented source of centuries of civil strife.

The consequences flowing from these tensions were a rise of party- or factional-type political activity and the creation of many tyrannies in the fourth and third centuries B.C. These came into being as a result of the strains that developed from the unregulated activities of the customary economy.[10] A number of tyrannies had a social-revolutionary character; they fostered redistribution of land, abolition of debts, the confiscation of property, and the banishment, sometimes killing, of opponents.[11] Tyrannies practiced a type of command economy, which is to say that many decisions crucial to economic arrangements were enacted from above.

These changes in economic relationships underlay some of the most remarkable political thinking the world has known. There was a burst of creative activity that, taken together with the rise in Judea of monotheism and the beginning of an elaboration of law, carried the compliance ideologies of the classical world into the traditional phase. Plato, for example, wrote with the crisis of the first decades of the fourth century B.C. in mind. He condemned both the rich for their avarice and the poor for seeking to possess the property of others, and he saw true reform as lying in the elimination of both riches and poverty. His solution was a new vision of positional authority, a communism of the Guardians.[12] These ideas did not, of course, become reality. Yet one senses their presence in the description George Ostrogorsky

[8] Ibid., pp. 12–14, 51, 60–2.
[9] Manus I. Midlarsky, "Scarcity and Inequality: Prologue to the Onset of Mass Revolution," *Journal of Conflict Resolution* 26, no. 1 (March 1982): 21.
[10] Hicks, *A Theory*, p. 21.
[11] Fuks, *Social Conflict in Ancient Greece*, pp. 30, 26–7, 35.
[12] Ibid., pp. 21, 111.

gives of the encompassing nature of hierarchical control of economic life in the ninth-century Byzantine state:

The principal object of the guild organizations was not, indeed, to serve the interests of the producers and dealers but to facilitate control of economic life by the government in the interests of the State and the consumer. The State appointed the heads of the guilds and employed officials who were especially concerned with their affairs; the government, in fact, in this way controlled the entire economy of the city and the economic processes which took place within it.[13]

Power in traditional societies

In traditional societies the lower classes were often treated with contempt and an utter lack of consideration. In the seventh century in the Byzantine state, villages were regarded as a fiscal unit for tax purposes and the villagers were jointly responsible for a heavy communal tax. The high culture and wealth of the elite were acquired at the expense of a peasantry who lived in misery without freedom and without means of redress.[14] For Tokugawa Iyeyasu, the founder of the last Japanese shogunate, the formula for extraction from the peasantry was "Leave them that they can neither live nor die."[15] In Europe, it has been suggested, force played a central role in feudal societies precisely because the peasants had de facto possession of the means of production and hence the possibility of some real independence from the authority of the landowners.[16] It was necessary, then, to coerce them to their duties.

Power was, indeed, the coinage of relationships. In early medieval Europe, that time of chaotic regression, subordinates had only the barest claim to rights. Codes of law were put together in a completely haphazard fashion. Rights generally had a tribal or kinship basis – they were valid only by virtue of membership in a group that could lay claim to them. Outside of the kinship system of mutual – albeit often skewed – reciprocity there existed few obligations; these essentially ended at one's doorstep. Beyond was the realm Max Weber ascribed to traditional traders, "the will and the wit to employ mercilessly every chance of profit."[17]

[13] George Ostrogorsky, *History of the Byzantine State* (New Brunswick, N.J.: Rutgers University Press, 1957), p. 225.

[14] Ibid., pp. 31, 120–1.

[15] Marion J. Levy, Jr., "Contrasting Factors in the Modernization of China and Japan, Reviewed," paper presented at a conference on "China in a New Era: Continuity and Change," Third International Conference of Professors World Peace Academy, Manila, August 24–9, 1987, p. 12.

[16] Nicholas Abercrombie, Stephen Hill, and Bryan S. Turner, *The Dominant Ideology Thesis* (London: Allen & Unwin, 1980), p. 164.

[17] Max Weber, *Economy and Society*, vol. 2, ed. by Guenther Roth and Claus Wittich (New York: Bedminster Press, 1968), p. 614.

Without a kinship identity a person was truly defenseless. Mohammed's enemies, the Korais, in his early days as a teacher, tried to get his uncle to disown him precisely because he would then be unprotected and could be eliminated without concern. Thus, personal relationships were extremely meaningful, but even so the rule of superiors, including the heads of households generally, was largely unrestrained. God was the great arbiter but was himself awesome and unforgiving, and elites assumed these same attributes for themselves. Pope Gregory I, perhaps the best intellect of his day, could direct that those suspected of adhering to pagan beliefs be jailed and whipped until they were "brought by bodily torments to the desired sanity of mind."[18]

Sagan reports a very high level of cruelty by leaders of early societies, including totally gratuitous and self-indulgent acts that he likens to those of the Red Queen in the story of Alice in Wonderland. Small wonder that subordinates developed servile habits. In archaic-traditional East African kingdoms, for example, wives knelt to greet husbands, and inferiors in general would on occasion grasp the legs of superiors while calling them master or sir.[19] In ancient China, and continuing in modified form down to the early twentieth century, deference in social relations was finely marked. Mikiso Hane reports that premodern Japanese peasants had little idea about rights, freedom, and equality but accepted as absolute truth the idea that they should unquestionably serve a higher entity such as the emperor.[20]

Punishments in traditional societies

In traditional times punishments were severe for infractions of the values cherished by those in authority. The basic integrity of persons was barely considered and, indeed, was hardly an issue; rather, the community and its status structure were of overriding concern. Punishment, therefore, as Durkheim noted, was basically vengeance for acts that outraged community morality. Moral tenets were defined by religious authority and pervaded all judicial proceedings and, indeed, all of social life. Repression in terms of that morality dominated all aspects of the law.[21]

In this environment subordinates quickly learned that their desires should be constrained, whereas elites were generally free, within bounds, to indulge

[18] Charles M. Radding, *A World Made by Men: Cognition and Society: 400–1200* (Chapel Hill: University of North Carolina Press, 1985), pp. 68, 77, 97; Weber, ibid., pp. 645, 880.

[19] Eli Sagan, *At the Dawn of Tyranny: The Origins of Individualism, Political Oppression, and the State* (New York: Knopf, 1985), pp. 163, 280, 292.

[20] Mikiso Hane, *Peasants Rebels and Outcastes: The Underside of Modern Japan* (New York: Pantheon, 1982), p. 62.

[21] Emile Durkheim, *The Division of Labor in Society*, trans. George Simpson (Glencoe, Ill.: Free Press, 1933), pp. 89, 141.

their wishes. Not the least of the reasons for this, of course, were the wide discrepancies that existed in access to coercive force. Machiavelli's ideas about the nature of rulers as being profoundly aggressive, acquisitive, selfish, and egotistical are comprehensible in light of the reality of much of social life in his time.

In this milieu punishments were often hideous and terrifying. Dante's *Inferno* speaks of torments that were a vivid reality. Their like, of course, has been recorded in the unmentionable activities of modern concentration camps, whose social systems are regressive microcosms of earlier patterns. In fact, some contemporary societies still give us a glimpse of traditional punishments. Lionel Tiger reports of a Western man in Saudi Arabia on his way to dinner who stopped to see what he at first thought was a quaint local ceremony. Two large uniformed men in slow and stately fashion were striking a large leather ball hung high above the ground from a stake. Then blood began to flow from the ball. Inside was a woman accused of adultery; had she confessed, she would have been allowed to be killed before being stuffed into the bag.[22]

Law in traditional societies

It was the ancient Greeks and Chinese who began the process of replacing kinship obligations with those based on "higher" laws. Their idea of justice, however, was built around public obligation rather than private right. For the Greeks, only citizenship within the polis guaranteed rights; slaves, for instance, had few or none. The idea of a universal contract binding Greeks of higher status to those of lower status was still nascent.

In the European Middle Ages there were clear obligations binding lords and vassals, although these were largely particular and took the form of specific duties. A lord owed aid and protection; a vassal owed specified payments, service, and attendance as required. These duties were solemnized by personal oaths and were sanctified by the authority of God, from whom rulers received their authority. Outside of specified duties, the ruler's action's were not subject to restraint. Certainly there were no general ideas about welfare or any real concern (beyond charity) for the near complete deprivation that characterized the lives of the rural and urban poor. Subjects, however, were bound to obedience. Even as late as the Reformation, Calvin and Luther could both hold that "resistance to rulers is in all circumstances wicked."[23]

---

[22] Lionel Tiger, *The Manufacture of Evil: Ethics, Evolution, and the Industrial System* (New York: Harper & Row, 1987), p. 247.

[23] George H. Sabine, *A History of Political Theory*, 3rd ed. (New York: Holt, Rinehart & Winston, 1961), p. 358.

Not surprisingly, traditional obligations remained rooted in kinship units. They were then extended to authority in expanded communities (e.g., the city-state), but only after centuries of development did they begin to acquire a nonhierarchical and non-group-related aspect (i.e., a concept of obligation owed among a society of equals). The existence of law alone was no guarantee of this progression. Regulations that lack autonomy (i.e., no sense of law as principles that are transcendent and distinct from policymakers) and that are deficient in generality and uniformity (i.e., they apply with differential rigor to various groups) are mere bureaucratic law as was the *fa* of ancient China. The Chinese concept of *tian*, or heaven, while it ordered the spiritual and secular realms, was too weak to serve as a specific code of transcendent laws.[24] Yet without some unassailable body of rules it is difficult, as Frances Piven and Richard Cloward point out, to wrest from elites the resources that can be used to sustain the articulation of nonelite interests.[25]

In the Roman Republic (c. 200 B.C.) there was still a line between citizens and outsiders (*peregrini*). Over time, however, outsiders (including the conquered) achieved citizenship while mercantile law, applicable to all, slowly penetrated basic Roman law. Parts of this legacy, however battered, were never entirely lost following the collapse of the Western empire. In the Middle Ages a rudimentary sense of mutuality binding the members of society continued. Individuals and collectivities had rights (i.e., liberties) with regard to authority at the same time that there were corresponding obligations to be honored by rulers. Medieval English and continental markets had general mercantile laws against adulteration of goods, speculation, hoarding and monopoly, and secret agreements to control prices and supplies. They also established uniform weights and measures.[26] In time these fragile legacies proved to be the pillars on which modern compliance ideologies were constructed.

Divisions, conflicts, and the possibilities for change in traditional societies

Strict divisions among groups were the general rule for all traditional societies, although they took different forms. Medieval China was controlled by a narrow stratum of families whose position was based on property and the "production" of officials for government service.[27] In later periods scholar

---

[24] Roberto Mangabeira Unger, *Law in Modern Society: Toward a Criticism of Social Theory* (New York: Free Press, 1976), pp. 99–104.

[25] Frances Fox Piven and Richard A. Cloward, *Poor People's Movements: Why They Succeed, How They Fail* (New York: Pantheon, 1977), p. xi.

[26] Dorothy J. Solinger, *Chinese Business Under Socialism: The Politics of Domestic Commerce, 1949–1980* (Berkeley and Los Angeles: University of California Press, 1984), p. 134.

[27] David G. Johnson, *The Medieval Chinese Oligarchy* (Boulder, Colo.: Westview Press, 1977), pp. 2, 31, 112–19.

officials possessed every privilege, including that of reproducing themselves by their monopoly over education. The ruling doctrine, Confucianism, was humane and benevolent in theory but quite authoritarian in practice as regards the common people.[28] In Tokugawa Japan the samurai class, which constituted 6 percent of the population, appropriated for their own use more than 50 percent of the land's bounty.[29] In Europe a person was clearly defined as a member of a specific estate, or *Stände*, which also specified particular rights and obligations.

Conflict over the division of rewards was often severe. In the Byzantine state there were repeated clashes between the Blues, whose leaders came both from the ranks of the great landowners and from the old Graeco-Roman senatorial aristocracy, and the Greens, whose leaders were frequently representatives of trade and industry or from the financial administration.[30] In Japan, between 1590 and 1867, there were more than 2,800 peasant disturbances.[31] The Great Peasants' War, or *Bauernkrieg*, in Germany in the sixteenth century is symbolic in form with other such risings (the English Peasants' Revolt, for example, although the specific causes differed). The European nobility savagely repressed challenges to its rule and never championed the underlings of another class even when they detested that group's leaders (e.g., they rarely took the side of journeymen against their masters even though they expressed harsh opinions about the profits taken by merchants).[32]

Clearly there were great variations in the forms of traditional societies. The *communitas* of Europe differed greatly from the communities of traditional China and elsewhere. What is clear, however, is that these systems were all, to a greater or lesser degree, non-capital creating. They were also ones in which hierarchical relations were characterized by the relative impotence of the less favored. In fact, traditional compliance, although not uniform, was largely informed everywhere by an emphasis on submission, dependence, low empathy, and insecurity. The group orientation was familial and communitarian, whereas relationships among individuals were sharply hierarchical. Status differences governed life, buttressed by divine authority or the dictates of a cosmological state. Figure 2 shows the general structural location of compliance ideologies of this type.

In the West trends favoring continuous structural changes in prevailing forms of compliance had collapsed with the decline and then demise of Roman authority. In their place was a more fragmented economy and social

[28] Etienne Balazs, *Chinese Civilization and Bureaucracy: Variations on a Theme*, trans. H. H. Wright (New Haven, Conn.: Yale University Press, 1964), pp. 7, 16.
[29] Hane, *Peasants*, p. 8.
[30] Ostrogorsky, *Byzantine State*, p. 225.
[31] Hane, *Peasants*, p. 7.
[32] George C. Lodge, *The New American Ideology* (New York: Knopf, 1975), p. 69.

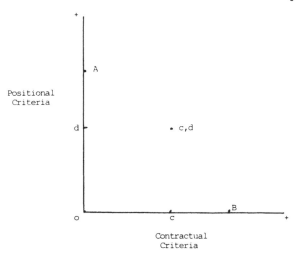

Figure 2. Traditional compliance ideologies.

order. Political thinking through the Middle Ages was characterized by an inability to establish common goals and by a rigid adherence to established social organization. Not until the first mechanical revolutions in windmills and watermills occurred in the eleventh, twelfth, and thirteenth centuries did change begin again. Significant social transformation only truly started with the rise of towns and with the beginning of new ideas about the rational organization of labor.[33]

Commercialization

Change in the traditional pattern of compliance began with individuals seeking in small ways to further family interests. Transformation was gradual, based partly on increased security of travel, which was itself a reflection of growing political stability, and on increases in wealth, found first within the monasteries. These changes constituted a form of enhanced social technology that provided resources for new ventures. What then began to occur was a search for new objects to trade and for new trading channels. The stimulus to find these arose as the growth of trade narrowed profit margins (because, to obtain more from the initial producers, merchants had to offer a higher price, while to sell more they had to dispose of their goods at a lower price).[34]

---

[33] Fernand Braudel, *Civilization and Capitalism: 15th–18th Century.* Volume 1: *The Structures of Everyday Life: The Limits of the Possible* (translated from the French. Revised by Sian Reynolds) (New York: Harper & Row, 1979), pp. 353, 483.

[34] Hicks, *Theory*, p. 45.

The transaction costs associated with trading ventures were affected by institutional restraints. Trading economies could be obtained only in an environment that was socially and politically sympathetic to these activities. These conditions were met in the Renaissance city-state, which in southern Europe first, and later in Flanders and Germany, became the unique seedbed for a way of life separate from the political power of the countryside. The city, in fact, became itself a type of organization that stimulated diversified trade. In a sense one can think of the cities as collectivities of merchants who organized themselves politically (with intense patriotism) to further their own commercial operations. In Florence in the thirteenth century, for example, of the ten "Major Arts," or guilds, that took over the government, seven were in export trades.[35]

Transaction costs steadily declined in Europe between the fourteenth and eighteenth centuries, creating new incentives for altering patterns of economic interaction. Demands for protection of property and security in exchange relationships led to the rise of middlemen as stock holders (i.e., those who kept goods safe for ultimate exchange in the marketplace) and of institutions and institutional forms for diminishing risks (i.e., forms of contract, insurance, hedging, pooling capital, etc.). Jews, the constant target of abuse by nobles and kings, reacted to the mistreatment they received, and to the new opportunities that were available, by inventing the *lettre de change*, or bill of exchange. Manifestly, these developments did not occur because of a conscious desire to change social meanings; they occurred because people, faced with immediate and close problems, sought ways to minimize the costs and risks associated with their daily activities.

The feudal nobles ultimately lost out because they sold their surplus to the growing towns for nonessential consumption items, thus jeopardizing their obligations to their tenants and military followers. The towns of the merchant elites, however, were themselves ultimately crushed by counterrevolution or declined because they were racked by worker dissent. In their place came two new institutions that have proven of lasting viability (although they have changed greatly in form from their beginnings). The first was the civil administration of the new centralized state, whose recruitment and promotion patterns varied sharply from the patrimonial-retainer pattern of the feudal era. Second, trading and financial institutions became increasingly able to choose the areas where they wished, and were able, to operate. Linked inextricably, but nevertheless separate, these two institutions would be crucial for the emerging modern phase of property relations.

Changes in ideas about *how* to do something stimulated changes in ideas about *why* something is done (as well as an interest in ideas as such). This

---

[35] Ibid., p. 40.

stimulus to thinking was not confined solely to areas affected by commerce. There developed a new interest in exploring – and in discussing with others – the relationship among things in general (science), the relationships among people in societies (political philosophy), and the relationship of people to those transcendental forces that up to then had been taken for granted (skepticism and critical inquiry in general). As different ideas about property and self-expression began slowly to percolate in people's visions, there came to be a new frankness about them that was sharply at variance with the communitarian family-oriented appeals of the earlier age. General Ireton (who fought with Cromwell in the English Civil War and who carried the main burden of the fight against the radical Levellers) could say, "All the main thing that I speak for is because I would have an eye to property"; no medieval knight would have spoken in this way.[36] At the same time, the Puritans in general, of which he was one, believed in a new set of business principles that emphasized frugality, self-denial, diligent toil, scrupulous adherence to contract, the absence of cupidity, and reliability in business relationships with everyone.

These changes notwithstanding, family and kinship loyalties remained as the locus of most individual activity even as absolute monarchy (by the sixteenth century) began to overturn locally based feudal constitutionalism and the close-knit community life of the free city-states. In this sense political modernization and social life were nonsynchronous. Economically the family was the source for most capital accumulation, and the fount, as well, for innovations in the introduction of new technical methods and techniques for reducing costs. It was also the locus for investment, and the area of concern as regards the preservation of capital, being the major conduit for intergenerational transfers of property. Social stratification along family lines reflected major differentials of wealth and power. In England, for instance, between 1580 and 1680, gentlemen with their immediate families constituted about 2 percent of the population yet owned about 50 percent of the land, not including the 15 percent owned by the peerage.[37]

Any idea of autonomous entrepreneurs taking charge of development, therefore, is misleading. It was family-linked groups, still characterized by hierarchy and unequal power, that fueled change. There were, however, forces favoring the growth of individualism, especially in England. There, at the lowest levels, in the villages, kinship ties were of nominal significance, being closer to what they are today in modern Britain than to continental peasant societies. Most people did not marry and settle in the parishes of

---

[36] Cited in J. R. Pole, *The Pursuit of Equality in American History* (Berkeley and Los Angeles: University of California Press, 1978) 45.
[37] Keith Wrightson, *English Society 1580–1680* (New Brunswick, N.J.: Rutgers University Press, 1982), p. 24.

their birth.[38] What this suggests is an uncommon degree of mobility and self-determination that would become increasingly important as technological improvements fostered further changes in institutional arrangements.

The Industrial Revolution did not come to England by accident. The cardinal change was the moving of industry from the home to the factory that occurred between 1760 and 1820. When that happened, however, there was already a capital and entrepreneurial surplus, an effective transportation system, an education system that produced talent, internal security under an effective civil administration, and a body of rules and regulations that facilitated commercial activities and that gave entrepreneurial groups the liberty to act. More significant than any of these, however, was a structural change in the compliance ideology that both reflected and underwrote new relationship patterns.

Changes in law

The law always justifies particular interests, statements about its impartiality notwithstanding. Yet it is impartial within the framework of the interests that it protects, and people turn to it on that account for whatever relief it can offer from the stress of mundane conflicts. Changes in compliance ideologies are reflected in the rules that protect interests and mediate conflicts. The form of law, and its purpose, thus gives clues to the phase of development of compliance and to the criteria that inform its content.

In the traditional phase, joint liability by family or community members was considered to be the underpinning of contracts that were entered into by an individual. Entitlements and duties were set forth in particularistic terms. From these circumstances, contractual criteria in a phase of property form slowly began to emerge. They developed from the old idea that to the extent a particular entitlement is "owned" by a group, others, including the state, do not have a right to intrude on the way the group exercises its prerogatives.

A legal order developed in Europe, fitfully and unevenly, from a hodgepodge of disorganized decrees, protected privileges, and dual judicial systems (lay and ecclesiastical); it came into being because existing laws were imperfect for governing and for securing particular interests. Henry II, for instance, reorganized the law codes of England (grouping diverse concrete circumstances into manageable categories, etc.) because he sought to improve the efficiency of government. But no prince, including Henry, was powerful enough to impose "bureaucratic" law on his subjects; European aristocracies, in fact, looked to the legal order to protect themselves from the prince and to ensure the continuity of their entitlements in a situation where the stable feudal hierarchical order was breaking down. The desire to protect

[38] Ibid., pp. 43, 45, 50.

autonomous privilege was also upheld by the crown. James I expressed this desire well in his *True Law of Monarchy* when he asserted that the king's power was above laws.[39] His son Charles, however, was to speak to the generality of the law when his conflict with the Puritan members of Parliament set him face-to-face with death. In his famous words spoken on January 22, 1649, to the High Court of Justice trying him for high treason and high misdemeanors he said, "For if power without law may make laws, may alter the fundamental laws of the kingdom, I do not know what subject he is in England that can be sure of his life or any thing he calls his own."[40] Here, indeed, is the idea, starkly stated, that authority must be constituted on the recognition that all interests are bounded by law. It is, in fact, one of the critical triumphs of the modern phase that a legal order characterized by general principles was able to submerge efforts to use the law for maintaining special privilege.[41]

Against the demands of greedy, and sometimes needy, nobles middle-class groups sought protection, and the legitimation of their status, through a legal system that could enforce contract and protect property. Christian moral sensibility was not deemed to be a sufficient protection in the face of royal privileges and monopolies and the interests of economically powerful families. In the city-states merchant governments had organized customs and excise, public credit, public loans, and gold coinage (reinvented in Genoa in the late twelfth century). These practices, which required legal safeguards, were extended into the new states. Utilizing new forms of business law and new legal tools, interpreted by a growing profession of lawyers, both the new civil administrations and property holders were able to protect their interests against challenges.

What developed was a totally new conception of legality and legal forms. In natural law there was a search for norms that, viewed independently, could legitimate positive law. With regard to positive law itself, there was an impetus, not fully realized in practice, toward a legal order where judges were bound by recognized legal norms rather than by the dictates of the powerful. There was also an emphasis, again superseding the will of the prince or the aristocracy, on rights to private property, ownership, transfer via inheritance, and freedom of use. At the same time, however, in Stuart England, there was much emphasis on the law binding persons to their duties. This was aimed as much at magistrates as at the common subject.[42] In essence what was coming into being was a conception of rights (especially

---

[39] J. Bronowski and Bruce Mazlish, *The Western Intellectual Tradition: From Leonardo to Hegel* (New York: Harper, 1960), p. 153.

[40] Andrew Sharp, *Political Ideas of the English Civil Wars 1641–1649* (New York: Longman, 1983), p. 50.

[41] Unger, *Law in Modern Society*, pp. 75, 87, 134, 164–6.

[42] Ibid., p. 16.

those regarding the possession of fixed and liquid assets) as property to be honored beyond particular considerations of kinship or group affiliation; concomitantly, there was an increasing emphasis on the sanctity of agreements (i.e., obligations) bound not by personal ties or sacred oaths but by law.

Laws regarding property specified the ways owners could prevent the use of their assets by others; this included the right not to sell to those who would not, or could not, meet an asked-for price (i.e., laws whose purpose initially was to protect property against arbitrary seizure). This entitlement became extended later to include the right not to offer employment to those who were unwilling to meet stipulated wage terms. Laws to this effect became a "response to the desires of the interacting persons for adjustment to new benefit-cost possibilities."[43] The benefits, of course, were skewed markedly in the direction of those with resources who could then legally exclude others from their use. Additional laws protected other aspects of property ownership. Formal rules regarding embezzlement, for example, unknown under early English common law, reflected the interests of merchant groups in protecting their property in an increasingly mobile society with its growing reliance on paper money.[44] Rights of inheritance and succession were codified. These were no longer privately enforced but were, as William Blackstone said in his *Commentaries on the Law of England* (1769), "creatures of the civil or municipal laws, and accordingly are in all respects regulated by them."[45]

Around the concept of property there developed ideas about the legitimacy of various groups and the criteria by which they should be judged. In premodern Britain, for example, with the exception of the poor law, scant consideration had been given to any redistribution of national resources. Differences in wealth (and the power of class position) were accepted as given with the consequence that trial procedures, and the court system, essentially denied equal justice for weaker groups. By making it a crime to expropriate the property of others, ideas about equality with regard to enjoying property came into being as a weapon against the arbitrariness of the old order. Equal rights to enjoyment of property then began slowly to underwrite an idea of equality of persons, at least on this dimension. However, because contract law was independent of laws regarding property, the consequence was still unequal treatment, although now for theoretically equal persons (i.e., because social relations were said to derive from free and voluntary associations entered into without coercion by the state, responsibility for any inequality in

---

[43] Harold Demsetz, "Toward a Theory of Property Rights," *American Economic Review* 57, no. 2 (May 1967): 350, 356.

[44] John F. Galliher and John R. Cross, *Morals Legislation Without Morality: The Case of Nevada* (New Brunswick, N.J.: Rutgers University Press, 1983), p. 10.

[45] Ronald Chester, *Inheritance, Wealth, and Society* (Bloomington: Indiana University Press, 1982), p. 19.

property holdings worked by the market was allocated to differences in personal merit).[46]

The new economic system that came into being presupposed unambiguous and systematized laws designed to eliminate capriciousness. The bedrock of the compliance ideology that evolved was a principle of formal legal equality whose two basic supports were the law of contract and the law of property. Two new privileges then came into existence that represented a marked forward step in the structure of meaning of compliance. No longer were individuals to be given consideration solely in terms of their status. Henceforth, they had a formal autonomy that eliminated traditional restrictions on how relations with others were to be governed. However, although the right to form voluntary autonomous relationships required a relaxation of customary restraints, this could be guaranteed only if the individual was protected from interference within the new social environment. These privileges were underwritten by laws that sanctioned an equal right to accumulate property and an equal right to make contracts untrammeled by authority. At the same time, differences in property holdings among those entering into contracts came to play a role in defining yet a new overall pattern of inequality.[47]

New theories for compliance

The traditional phase did not recede in a day. In the process of transition, centuries were to pass, noted in the new laws that came into being but also in new explanations that tugged at accepted understandings of the world as it was. The process of thinking about life occupied the minds of countless individuals whose perceptions and interpretations were at the forefront of the interaction between individual and social constructions of meaning. To single out particular individuals, therefore, is to do an injustice to the process of discourse as a whole. Yet some people stand forth as the founders of important intellectual initiatives.

Abelard in the twelfth century reinvented the idea of nature and the idea that intention is basic to an understanding of morality. It is strange today to think of these contributions as novel and noteworthy. The fact that they were, however, is an indication of the general intellectual level of his time. Perhaps for this reason he was not widely read except by his students. Moreover, there is no indication that his experience was uncommon. For virtually everybody who lived in the predawn of the new era, life was taken as given

---

[46] Peter Gabel and Jay M. Feinman, "Contract Law as Ideology," in *The Politics of Law: A Progressive Critique*, ed. David Kairys (New York: Pantheon, 1982), p. 176.

[47] Wolfgang Friedmann, *Law in a Changing Society* (New York: Columbia University Press, 1972), p. 100.

with its verities explained, beyond the need for interpretation, by sacred revelation.[48] The true and the right were to be found in a sacred law that was beyond the reach of individuals or governments, similar to the view held by fundamentalists today in parts of the world that are dominated by Koranic law.

Five hundred years later the words of particular individuals would shake the foundations of social order. Nowhere is this more noticeable than in the Reformation, when reformers challenged prevailing religious, political, and economic views. Martin Luther (1483–1546), who was no friend of radical political change, nevertheless struck a new note in his contest with Rome when he said, "I wish to be free. I do not wish to become the slave of any authority, whether that of a council or of any other power, or of the University or of the Pope. For I shall proclaim with confidence what I believe to be true, whether it is advanced by a Catholic or a heretic, whether it is authorized or not by I care not what authority."[49] This clear note of autonomy of conscience was carried into the political and economic realms by the followers of John Calvin (1509–64). As a minority in both political and economic life, they became identified with ideas about freedom of association despite their doctrinal tendencies toward intolerance. Their forbiddance of envy (in their "Rule of Equity") pointed the way toward an acceptance of the new manner whereby property was being acquired. In England, Thomas More, who was Lord Chancellor from 1529 to 1532, died for upholding the validity of individual conscience against the authority of government (despite his equally strong belief that an individual should not preach against accepted dogma).[50] In that great time of change names such as these stand out. While speaking the language of their time, they nevertheless sounded the drumbeat for a new way of thinking about social life.

The world of religious controversy spawned by the Reformation was one, like our own, of intense political struggle. Conflict seethed around religious issues, stirred into a pot of discontent that soon brought into question the validity of authority, first the Pope's but then spilling into the secular domain. Economic issues were clearly of great importance, but the solution to questions about property and its distribution seemed to many to be secondary to the proper foundation of a political order and the appropriate distribution of political power. The arguments went well beyond the canonical discourse of the traditional phase. They hearkened to the ancient idea of a natural law that embodies principles transcending those of the social order, and whose existence permits a radical criticism of existing institutional

[48] Radding, *A World Made by Men*, pp. 210, 220.
[49] Bronowski and Mazlish, *Western Intellectual Tradition*, p. 86.
[50] Ibid., pp. 59, 99.

arrangements. Additionally, ideas from new areas of knowledge were incorporated into discourse. The advances in mathematics and celestial mechanics in the century following Machiavelli (1469–1527) suggested that laws of motion could be found for societies as well as for planets and falling bodies.[51] There developed from this a search for laws of human conduct embodying order and causality.

Thomas Hobbes (1588–1679) and John Locke (1632–1704) gave the autonomous individual an important theoretical role in a larger society, although England in their time was far from individualistic. By seeing societies as originating from the actions of separate individuals (i.e., autonomous bodies in motion interacting in a framework of causality), they raised doubts about accepted communitarian ideals. In different ways they suggested that sovereignty in a civil order is the product of an agreement or contract among individuals seeking to adjust conflicting claims. Of these claims the most important are those that relate to property; the primary duty of government, then, is to guarantee a set of minimal entitlements to individuals regarding their claims.

For Hobbes the state acts to mediate the egoistic propensities of its members. Locke, however, formulated an extreme view of natural rights in which government exists to guarantee individual rights. Like Luther, Locke felt compelled to state an equality of freedom in the face of social power. This equality, he said, is "that *equal right* that every man hath, *to his Natural Freedom*, without being subjected to the Will or Authority of any other man."[52] The right to property, too, was a natural one not civilly created but possessed by people in the state of nature. Unequal ownership of assets was justified because it represented the voluntary admixture of personal commitment, these being part of the equal rights that every man possessed, with material substances. Locke, in fact, used the word "property" in its broadest sense to refer to life and liberty and estate, to states of being and social processes as well as physical substances. This formulation was an exceptionally important one in the sense that life and liberty were thus protected because they fell under the rubric of property rights. It is here we see the beginning of structural change in the conceptualization of compliance.

The idea that property is beneficial for mankind received further impetus in the decades following Locke. Montesquieu (1689–1755) believed that commerce would wear away prejudices and animosities, although, as he made clear in his *Persian Letters*, economic ruin awaits those who consult only particular rather than general interests. David Hume (1711–66) also echoed the

---

[51] Albert O. Hirschman, *The Passions and the Interests: Political Arguments for Capitalism Before Its Triumph* (Princeton, N.J.: Princeton University Press, 1977), p. 13.

[52] From John Locke's *Second Treatise of Government*. Cited in Douglas Rae et al., *Equalities* (Cambridge, Mass.: Harvard University Press, 1981), p. 47 (italics in original).

idea that love of gain can have beneficial social consequences.[53] Adam Smith (1723–90) in *The Wealth of Nations* went further by giving the pursuit of self-interest an economic rather than a social justification. Yet, as Smith noted in *The Theory of Moral Sentiments,* before private business is encouraged it is essential that there be a stability and balance of institutions in society in order first to ensure justice and security and the existence of ethical standards in the culture as a whole.[54]

The ethical restraints placed on economic activity by Montesquieu and Smith were never entirely shouldered aside (although contemporary economists in the Western world have largely shied away from such concerns). In the United States, however, the untrammeled right to engage in business and pursue one's own self-interest early became a dominant strain. In his autobiography Benjamin Franklin noted the Bible phrase that his Calvinist father had drummed into him: "Seest thou a man diligent in his business? He shall stand before Kings."[55] As the fifty-first paper of the *Federalist* argued, the good can be most dependably secured by arranging things so "that the private interest of every individual may be a sentinel over the public rights."[56] John Adams, for one, did not believe that any conception of a common human nature should lead to equal shares of property. Said he, "Equal laws are all that can ever be derived from human equality."[57]

Others, however, began to see flaws. They pointed to the harm that can exist when personal-use commodities and production facilities are both subsumed under the rubric of property. In this circumstance the contractual right to sell labor and the contractual right to purchase it may entail vastly unequal bargaining positions. The consequence is that authority in production facilities commands obedience with every bit as much power as any separate structure of formal political authority. Ultimately the two may become complementary.

To Marx and Engels this complementarity was predetermined in the sense that different types of control over property (i.e., control over the means of production) were conceived of as the root of different forms of social and political relationships. As they stated in *The Communist Manifesto* regarding what communists in revolutionary movements should do concerning property: "In all these movements they bring to the front, as the leading question

[53] Hirschman, *Passions,* pp. 60, 66; Bronowski and Mazlish, *Western Intellectual Tradition,* p. 265.

[54] Dipak K. Gupta, "Political Psychology and Neoclassical Theory of Economic Growth: The Possibilities and Implications of an Attempted Resynthesis," *Political Psychology* 8, no. 4 (December 1987): 637.

[55] Cited in Bruce Mazlish, *The Revolutionary Ascetic: Evolution of a Political Type* (New York: McGraw-Hill, 1976), p. 58.

[56] Aaron Wildavsky, *The Politics of the Budgetary Process* (Boston: Little, Brown, 1964), p. 179.

[57] Herbert McCloskey and John Zaller, *The American Ethos: Public Attitudes Toward Capitalism and Democracy* (Cambridge, Mass.: Harvard University Press, 1984), p. 80.

in each, the property question, no matter what its degree of development at the time."[58] Without addressing the issue of property, they said, it would be impossible to foster change. What was truly significant, however, was their acceptance of property itself as the organizing concept of social life.

Transitional compliance ideals

Europe at the close of the traditional phase was largely a place of narrow vision and, sad to say, narrow heart. Villagers looked no farther than their own hamlets; indeed, they did not identify in any significant way with other than local groups. Societies were highly stratified with elites demanding deference and obedience while offering paternalism in return. The Anglican catechism of the seventeenth century sets the appropriate tone in adjuring believers to "honour and obey the King and all that are put in authority under him; to submit myself to all my governors, teachers, spiritual pastors, and masters; to order myself lowly and reverently to all my betters."[59] Braudel points out the consequences of the ferocious indifference that often existed among classes. In Savoy, he notes, at the end of an epidemic, the rich would often install a poor woman in their disinfected homes for a few weeks to ensure that the danger was really over. The attitude of the better-off toward the poor was laced with contempt. The prince of Strongoli, for example, described the hundred thousand poor of eighteenth-century Naples as follows: "They proliferate without families, having no relationship with the state except through the gallows and living in such chaos that only God could get his bearings among them."[60]

The decisive break from this pattern originated not with the lowliest but rather with those from the fledgling middle order who chafed under the customary bonds of their betters. Nowhere was this pattern more pronounced than in England where, after the Revolution of 1688, the idea of individualism, of an autonomous person not subject to the dictates of others, took root. Individualism at that time did not equate with political freedom; it meant that control over behavior and thought, especially in the area of business affairs, was freed from status obligations and from custom, tradition, and consensus. In their place, and integral to the whole of vision of personal autonomy, was a new conception of legality in the form of contracts with standard, impersonal procedures for regulating relationships. There developed the idea that through individual self-control and legality, lusts for power, money, and advantage could be controlled and channeled for the benefit of the community.[61] In its origins, therefore, the ideological break toward the

---

[58] Karl Marx, *Selected Writings*, ed. David McLellan (Oxford: Oxford University Press, 1977), p. 246.

[59] Sharp, *Political Ideas*, p. 27.

[60] Braudel, *Civilization and Capitalism*, pp. 85, 532.

[61] Hirschman, *Passions*, p. 41.

modern phase embodied concepts of freedom from dependence on the will of others and liberty to exchange property among individuals who were equals in law.

The movement toward defining rights as entitlements shared equally by autonomous individuals decisively changed existing ideas about social arrangements. This movement, however, led not to equal privileges but to a different pattern of disregard for others. For as a new structure of moral meanings came into being, so also did there develop new justifications for elite privilege.

In the "contractual" mode of the modern phase status is not determined by transcendental authority. It flows, rather, from an aggressive, confident work style in an environment freed from the intrusion of state power. Ideally, status is determined by self-improvement (manifested by industry and frugality), whose measure is material success. Success, then, is proof of moral merit and justifies assertions of a right to control others; moral merit makes meaningful why subordinates should be submissive and deferential and why they should respect money as a definition of status. In establishing this pattern of compliance, religion, of course, played a role, especially in providing an explanation for the linkage between hard work and moral worth. The message, however, was no longer one of maintaining a transcendentally determined hierarchy in established social relationships but was one of fostering individual self-worth through personal striving and achievement.[62] Thus, although the original religious goal had been to create a pious world fit for salvation, there crept alongside this noble aspiration the idea of accumulation as a necessary condition for a stable social order and of self-interest as the only motive that could truly provide protection against social diminution.

At first, the inequality of condition that accompanied self-interested accumulation was made bearable by a generally held belief that both rich and poor should live frugally. Moreover, equality was largely conceived of as a legal and procedural matter rather than an economic one. It was important, therefore, to press for political equality, for this ensured the right of individuals to participate in decisions regarding social life. The idea that political power should be hedged because social inequalities would otherwise be fostered was more salient at that time than the idea that inequalities in economic distribution could lead to permanent inequalities in power. On the contrary, if wealth is the product of hard work and frugality, these traits are not restricted to those born to high status; hence, acquiring wealth, it was thought, could offer no permanent threat to social equality.

In democratic politics, however, there is one vote per person, whereas in the market power is distributed according to property. The clear discrepancy here in the influence available to individuals was partly resolved by viewing property ownership as simply another natural right among many. As Article

[62] Abercrombie, Hill, and Turner, *Dominant Ideology Thesis*, pp. 101–3.

II of the Rights of Man and the Citizen declared, "The aim of all political association is to preserve the natural and imprescriptable rights of man. These rights are liberty, property, security and resistance to oppression."[63] Yet the world into which these ideas were introduced was still one of private family wealth and inherited social standing. If natural and imprescriptable rights were possessed equally in theory, there was nevertheless still no idea of creating a level economic playing field or of compensating for inequality of endowment. In these circumstances, therefore, the encouragement of individual private gain, even when justified as a contribution to the public weal, could ultimately violate the very idea of equal natural rights. The solution, as it developed, was twofold: (1) to praise a stratification system where privilege is the consequence of individual enterprise and personal effort (while simultaneously condemning laziness and lack of initiative); and (2) at the same time to sponsor social change that creates equality of opportunity. Equality, then, rightly became an honored value in contractual compliance ideologies in the modern phase (in America it, along with liberty, is one of the two most honored values).[64] This equality, however, is basically one of opportunity rather than of results. While most Americans, for example, refuse to endorse clearly inegalitarian views, they remain skeptical about the desirability of state intervention to make social groups or individuals more equal in condition.[65]

Within a period of about ten generations these ideas became writ. In English-speaking countries especially, although with different emphases, the idea of a society of autonomous, striving individuals joined together by contract took a firm hold. By the nineteenth century John Stuart Mill's maxim that "the individual is not accountable to society for his actions in so far as these concern the interests of no person but himself"[66] became widely accepted as the basis for a new type of social order. And, indeed, England late in that century was described as the "most strongly anti-Socialist in the world," while in the United States neither social-democratic attitudes nor a party representing them took root.[67]

The ideal of autonomy has not, however, been universally endorsed. Most societies have not embraced contractual criteria with the same enthusiasm as was manifested by English-speaking peoples. Yet no modern society has entirely escaped the impact of these ideas for none has been able to avoid the

---

[63] Bronowski and Mazlish, *Western Intellectual Tradition*, p. 406.

[64] McClosky and Zaller, *American Ethos*, p. 63.

[65] Ibid., p. 71; Myron Weiner, "The Political Economy of Industrial Growth in India," *World Politics* 38, no. 4 (July 1986): 607.

[66] Cited in Anita L. Allen, *Uneasy Access: Privacy for Women in a Free Society* (Totowa, N.J.: Rowman & Littlefield, 1988), p. 177.

[67] Werner Sombart, *Why Is There No Socialism in the United States*, trans. Patricia M. Hocking and C. T. Husbands (White Plains, N.Y.: International Arts and Sciences Press, 1976) (from the introductory essay by C. T. Husbands, pp. xix, xxxii).

rise to prominence of property as an organizing principle for social meanings. Indeed, the emphasis on property, and its acquisition, is as characteristic of modern socialist states as it is of those termed capitalistic. Whether change is championed in the name of public or private property is clearly not irrelevant, but in either case the measure is property itself.

6

Equality and the technobility

In the transition to the modern phase compliance ideologies assumed different forms. In some societies, such as Germany, a combination of contractual and positional criteria was embraced that, together with potent vestiges from the traditional phase, knit various groups together in a strained combination of conflict and accommodation. In others, including the United States, the Soviet Union, and China, rights and obligations emphasized either contractual or positional criteria. These societies became "strong" exemplars of the two great modern variants of compliance in the modern phase of property relations;[1] in their development they exhibited novel but different forms of institutional life, leadership patterns, and subordinate behavior, ways of life that were logically tied to the past yet had no precedent. Because these strong variants clearly reveal the tragedy of change and the horror that has attended different commitments to new ways of life, they are the focus of this chapter. Alternate paths and the possibilities for further change are discussed in Part IV.

Historically the traditional phase lasted for about two millennia. In many areas of the world, however, its hold on cultures is still powerful, as the present-day force of Islamic fundamentalism reveals. Where such patterns predominate, great disparities of wealth often exist. For example, even as late as 1930, 84 percent of the population of Japan possessed only 50 percent of the nation's household income; 19 families had incomes over 1 million yen while at the bottom 2,232,000 families had yearly incomes of 200 yen or less.[2] Although economic growth tends to be accompanied by an increase in inequality, continued discrepancies are, in part, an extension of older patterns. For

---

[1] I have borrowed the word "strong" from the work of Benjamin R. Barber, *Strong Democracy: Participatory Politics for a New Age* (Berkeley and Los Angeles: University of California Press, 1984). Barber uses the term, of course, in a context different from the one I employ.

[2] Mikiso Hane, *Peasants, Rebels and Outcastes: The Underside of Modern Japan* (New York: Pantheon, 1982), p. 11.

a long period during transition peasants and artisans are held in the grip of fatalistic beliefs about the inevitability of glaring social differences.

With several notable exceptions (e.g., the Chinese and Byzantine civil bureaucracies) the army and church were the basic models of organization in the traditional phase. Directed, respectively, toward securing internal and external security and toward religious instruction designed to achieve conformity with divine will, neither organization was directly concerned with economic development and neither pursued accumulation as a primary objective.

When organizations primarily oriented toward accumulation came into being, they were viewed with mistrust and hostility. Their patterns of rational economizing – however rudimentary in form – violated the ideals of traditional institutions. With the full emergence of a spirit of impartial, functional rationality, the break with tradition accelerated. There arose a distinctive type of social arrangement characterized by impersonality and the need for subordinates to accept the discipline of the clock; what now became required was regularity and predictability, organized around a work flow dominated by machinery. In this milieu craft techniques and a craft mentality had to be subordinated to a requirement for segmented work in which overall productivity depended crucially on authoritative coordination of diverse functions, efficient communication, and a concentration of the work force. New skills were thus required, as well as new standards for merit, and new justifications for authority. As newer institutional patterns proliferated, societies also experienced, concomitantly, an increase in capital accumulation and in the range and variety of fixed capital goods in which investment was embodied.[3] Emanating from the goal of accumulation, therefore, was a transforming aura that slowly choked the power of the old order.

As institutional processes change, normative requirements in different areas of life vary, leading to a sense of formlessness, what Emile Durkheim called anomie and Robert K. Merton, deinstitutionalization.[4] Strictly speaking, what is occurring is a disjunction within and among social domains in moral justifications for rights and obligations. The division is often particularly acute within the newly emergent institutions themselves, with elite preferences founded on a new conception of equal rights and with subordinate constraints justified by an ongoing need for harmonization of unequal relationships.

For new elites the pursuit of purely economic goals is justified by appeal to a novel conception of rights. As elites attempt to justify activities related to

[3] John Hicks, *A Theory of Economic History* (Oxford: Clarendon Press, 1969), p. 143.
[4] Harry Eckstein, "A Culturist Theory of Political Change," *American Political Science Review* 82, no. 3 (September 1988): 796.

profitability and productivity, they champion an end to status restrictions legitimated by traditional principles of hierarchy. The emphasis is always and invariably on equality. Equal rights are asserted as a protection against the domination of traditional elites; in the process these rights become the basis for a new justification of authority. At the same time, however, subordinate expectations remain largely constrained by existing social obligations. In great part this is so because traditional family-type relations are likely to prevail in the workplace in the formative period of new institutions. The consequence is that workers remain tightly controlled by older criteria even as their leaders seek to establish a new pattern of rights and obligations to legitimize their own activities.

Within institutions there is an increasing emphasis on efficiency, on subordinating followers to technical requirements, on living by the clock, and on substituting quantitative for qualitative evaluations of performance. As newer forms of technology are introduced into work procedures, the division of labor becomes ever more minute, requiring greater emphasis on planning, work design, and control over subordinates. Work assignments emphasize repetitive tasks, with any given worker's output constituting but a part of the final product. With this type of division of labor there is a rise in productive efficiency and a decline in costs of innovation (from the accumulation and transferability of skills), realizable to the degree that impersonal control through a system of rules is exercised by "officials" at formally designated hierarchical levels; these officials are responsible, in graded terms, for performance and output. This type of institutional arrangement, usually called a bureaucracy, has from its efficiency become the dominant form of organization in the modern phase.

In bureaucratic societies ownership patterns both determine and are determined by the relative salience of contractual or positional criteria. When the state and economy are separated (i.e., when the ownership of property is vested in individuals or institutions) property rights are set forth in contractual terms that guarantee personal and institutional autonomy. When positional criteria are paramount, property inheres in a collective purpose; it is an aspect of political power per se. Control over property differs, therefore, with positional societies tending toward a pattern of control from the political apex through a tightly interlocked bureaucratic structure while contractual societies leave significant aspects of control free from overt political restraint. Yet even for contractual societies, although less noteworthy than for positional ones, the institutional propensity to assume an ever larger work agenda is matched by the growth of government that takes on increasing responsibility for the overall coordination of institutional activities.[5] These develop-

---

[5] Hicks, *Theory*, p. 99.

ments are independent of whether a society adheres to contractual or positional criteria in that they are a universal phenomenon in the modern phase of property relations.

It is during the period of transition to the modern phase that the pathologies of change are most apparent. Mass participation in political activities is likely to increase, owing, in part, to discrepancies between people's budding aspirations and governmental capabilities for control. Political instability is thus likely.[6] It is also during this period, which many in the world are still going through, that the confrontation between the followers of contractual and positional compliance ideologies is most intense. The adherents of each elevate the moral expectations that have been minimized by the other as justifications for new institutional arrangements. Only when further change reveals the weakness of partial moral justifications does it become possible to ameliorate ideological conflict.

Strong contractual compliance in the modern phase

Defining strong contractual compliance

The contrast between traditional societies and modern ones centers around the importance of economic growth. In traditional societies people primarily oriented themselves toward physical security. Most individuals had a fixed bundle of wants and there was thus an accepted, intuitive ceiling on accumulation (with any excess distributed through ceremonies, etc.). It was these patterns especially that eroded as the modern phase emerged.[7]

The break with the past occurred gradually as a consequence of the rise of the market as a dominant institution. Composed of interacting private groups, the market embodied both an economic mechanism for exchange and a social order in which the drive for wealth was the most significant value. Initially, as formulated in the Puritan ethic, the behavior necessary for accumulation was framed in religious terms as part of an overall demand for self-realization; charity, lack of envy, and group-spiritedness were co-equal with the emphasis on frugality and hard work. This new ethic powerfully disorganized existing status justifications at the same time that the market provided an institutional mechanism for realizing new status aspirations. In effect, the market system devalued the justifications of the traditional order by defining status in terms of success in productive, accumulating activity.

From these beginnings a distinctive pattern of values emerged. These emphasized, variously, the importance of competition in all areas of life, of

---

[6] This argument is developed at length in Samuel P. Huntington, *Political Order in Changing Societies* (New Haven, Conn.: Yale University Press, 1968).

[7] Jules Henry, *Culture Against Man* (New York: Random House, 1963), p. 9.

individual achievement, of a rational mind-set, of political equality and the need to prevent concentrations of political power, and of equal opportunity in the economic realm along with the free right to use the property accruing from personal accomplishment. These values were tightly interlocked. They depended for their realization on a fundamental belief in personal autonomy and the priority of negative rights. Individualism was honored by explicit reference to the importance of unfettered individual activity.

The values of strong contractual compliance unleashed prodigious economic growth. For the successful, enormous latitude was permitted. Inequality of results was morally justified; in the height of nineteenth-century laissez-faire capitalism, inequality was said by Herbert Spencer to be but a Christian restatement of a law of nature that those not energetic enough should die.[8] Subordinates, therefore, were expected to fulfill their duties without complaint. Their obligations, ideally, were conceptualized in terms analogous to positional criteria as defined at the traditional phase (i.e., subordinates should manifest loyalty to the established status hierarchy; status roles should define gradations of responsibility and reward; and inferiors should scrupulously obey their leaders – as outlined in the Table in Chapter 4).

Even today 75 percent of America's economic elite deny that their wealth is in any way the product of exploitation, 90 percent explain it as the consequence of a willingness to take risks, 60 percent deny that poverty is produced to any degree by a failure of industry to provide jobs, and there is a strong tendency to deny that greater equality of results is either just or beneficial.[9] The compliance criteria of strong contractual systems in the modern phase are shown in Figure 3. The implications of this pattern will now be explored in detail.

Strong contractual values

In England in the eighteenth century working-class offenders were executed for crimes as minor as robbing someone of a shilling in a field near a city. A blind boy accused of breaking into a house with intent to steal was condemned to death.[10] The law heavily emphasized ownership rights. In these earlier days legal safeguards for workers or consumers were far less emphasized than the need to protect the interests of the owners of property. The autonomous pursuit of wealth, and the right to be protected in the private use of property, became central concerns of the legal order.

[8] Arthur M. Okun, *Equality and Efficiency: The Big Tradeoff* (Washington: The Brookings Institution, 1975), p. 17.

[9] James R. Kluegel and Eliot R. Smith, *Beliefs About Inequality: Americans' Views of What Is and What Ought to Be* (New York: Aldine De Gruyter, 1986), p. 254.

[10] David C. McClelland, *Power: The Inner Experience* (New York: Irvington Publishers, 1975), p. 321.

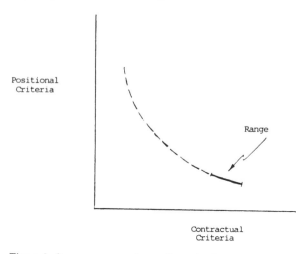

Figure 3. Strong contractual compliance in the modern phase.

In the nineteenth century, as commercial and industrial institutions grew larger and their activities more salient, the law underwent a massive change. With the development of an industrial economy, legal forms designed to foster ventures came into being, through the public incorporation by law of private corporations and by acts whose purpose was to free corporations from legal restrictions vested in those interests associated with land ownership and the like. Indeed, it became a principal function of the law to enlarge the corporation's maneuverability and to restrict regulatory interference by governmental authority. To this end the American Supreme Court defined the corporation as a person within the meaning of the Fourteenth Amendment, extending to it rights associated with personal private property. State legislatures joined with the Supreme Court in proscribing legislation that would limit corporate activities.[11] This overwhelming emphasis on negative rights is nicely revealed in a statement by Andrew Carnegie, one of the great captains of enterprise in the nineteenth century. Said he, "Great inequality of environment, the concentration of business . . . in the hands of a few, and the law of competition between these [are] not only beneficial, but essential for the future progress of the race. . . . It follows that there must be great scope for the exercise of special ability in the merchant and in the manufacturer who has to conduct affairs upon a grand scale."[12]

[11] George C. Lodge, *The New American Ideology* (New York: Knopf, 1975), p. 134.
[12] Cited in Douglas Rae et al., *Equalities* (Cambridge, Mass.: Harvard University Press, 1981), pp. 100–1.

There is, in America at least, strong support for equality of opportunity and the voluntarism that gives it meaning. Voluntarism is associated with liberty, one of the strongest-held American values. Rather than question the harm that may be associated with that value, Americans by a wide margin (72 percent to 20 percent) affirm their belief in liberty over economic equality; for leaders this affirmation is virtually unanimous.[13] Those who have more property are also believed by a wide margin to have more ability. As such, people in general oppose both floors and ceilings on the amount of money a person can obtain. In 1972 it was blue-collar workers who raised a storm of protest over Senator George McGovern's proposal for confiscatory estate taxes.[14] A well-regulated social order, it is thought, must positively permit the pursuit of private self-interest because without such autonomy local self-government will be threatened and personal rights in areas of dress, travel, education, sex life, and so on, imperiled.

Institutional patterns in systems of contractual compliance

From 1880 to 1930 there emerged bureaucratic institutions of extraordinary power and wealth, which slowly came to dominate the values, role concepts, and culture of all Western societies. Their rise to prominence, of course, was due in part to the prior development in England of joint stock companies (created to finance privateering and colonizing activities) and the astonishing growth of capital wealth, in Britain from less than £10,000 in 1560 to approximately £50 million in 1720.[15] The growth of new bureaucratic institutions furthered this trend. By 1930 the two hundred largest nonfinancial corporations in America controlled about 15–25 percent of the total national wealth (45–53 percent of the total nonbanking corporate wealth).[16] By 1961, 10.5 percent of all private firms took in 77.1 percent of private business receipts; of almost two million corporations in existence in the late sixties and early seventies, one-tenth of 1 percent of them controlled 55 percent of all corporate assets.[17] Against these huge, market-oriented, vertically integrated behemoths smaller entities accommodated themselves in what became in-

---

[13] Herbert McClosky and John Zaller, *The American Ethos: Public Attitudes Toward Capitalism and Democracy* (Cambridge, Mass.: Harvard University Press, 1984), pp. 18, 227. Sidney Verba and Gary R. Orren, *Equality in America: The View from the Top* (Cambridge, Mass.: Harvard University Press, 1985), pp. 6, 72.

[14] Okun, *Equality and Efficiency*, p. 49.

[15] Ralph F. De Bedts, *The New Deal's SEC: The Formative Years* (New York: Columbia University Press, 1964), p. 2.

[16] E. Digby Baltzell, *The Protestant Establishment: Aristocracy and Caste in America* (New York: Random House, 1964), p. 207 (citing A. A. Berle and G. C. Means, *The Modern Corporation and Private Property* [New York: Macmillan, 1932]).

[17] Anthony Downs, *Inside Bureaucracy* (Boston: Little, Brown, 1966), p. 255; Herbert J. Gans, *More Equality* (New York: Pantheon, 1973), p. 14.

creasingly a system of centralized control by enormous, semiautonomous economic institutions.

The importance of property as a lever in social relations is derived solely from its control or, more accurately, from the denial of control to others. Legal ownership, therefore, does not in itself constitute effective control, although ownership establishes a presumption of authority over the use of property. Authority may be delegated, however, and this, in fact, is precisely what has happened in societies with strong contractual compliance ideologies. For example, in the period 1950–71, 55 percent of the largest three hundred industrial corporations in America were outside of direct family control;[18] in 1981, Edward Herman found that 64 percent of the two hundred largest nonfinancial corporations were controlled by their managers with another 17 percent controlled by management and an outside board of directors.[19] In effect, power over property has increasingly passed from the owners of property to the managers of it.

The largest institutions in contractual societies possess the characteristics of bureaucracy set forth by Max Weber: sets of offices with clearly delineated responsibilities, the exclusion of particularistic criteria in personnel judgments, clearly demarcated hierarchical relationships, and so on, with a concentration of power and responsibility at the apex in the hands of a small number of managers. Except in cases of outright family ownership, legal possession is distributed among a number of owners through the mechanism of the joint stock company. Effective decision-making within the institution, however, requires a delegation of authority by owners to managers in order to eliminate the prohibitively high negotiating costs that would occur if all owners were continuously involved in management.

Within large institutions there is generally a wide gap between leaders and followers. Control over labor processes, the physical means of production, and the allocation of resources are concentrated in the hands of a few people with only modest beginnings of regularized and nonconfrontational mechanisms for ascertaining subordinate concerns. Although leaders and followers are inextricably bound together and in theory share equal rights in society at large, there is generally a marked lack of autonomy for subordinates. Following the principles of Taylorism, most subordinate work remains highly controlled; design and execution are separated and there is heavy reliance on standardized work procedures. The number of people directly involved in this compliance pattern is not trivial. By 1963, for example, 70 percent of the British labor force was employed by corporations with more than five hun-

[18] Alvin W. Gouldner, *The Future of Intellectuals and the Rise of the New Class* (New York: Seabury Press, 1979), p. 12 (citing work by Maurice Zeitlin and Philip Burch).

[19] Cited in Robert A. Dahl, *Democracy, Liberty, and Equality* (Oslo: Norwegian University Press, 1986), p. 106.

dred employees; by 1980 approximately 90 percent of the U.S. work force were employees and of these, one-half worked in bureaucratic settings characterized by large size, standardized and impersonal settings, hierarchy and dependence, and specialization and standardization.[20]

Political theorists have been slow to recognize that if the democratic process presupposes a unit (city, state, country, etc.), as Robert Dahl suggests,[21] then a crucial arena in our time is the modern bureaucratic institution whose members fit rightfully within it by virtue of their role of responsibilities. Personal power in modern contractual compliance systems begins with high office within bureaucratic institutions. Elite status in society, however, depends on the recognition by government of its limited right to interfere with institutional autonomy. The consequence is that the owners and managers of property, a very small proportion of society, functioning within their own constituencies and insulated from government, exercise relatively unrestricted authority over areas of concern to themselves.[22] As Ralph De Bedts noted of the extreme disregard for the general public by the New York Stock Exchange in its laissez-faire pre–Great Depression heyday, "Any reference to the activities of its members in pursuit of personal gain at the violent expense of the public economic good was effectively forestalled. . . . As SEC commissioner William O. Douglas [later a Supreme Court Justice] described it several years later, the image presented was one of a private club in which the members could do no wrong, so long as their behavior toward each other was governed by club rules."[23]

In America the autonomy of private institutions rests on the recognition of them as being entitled to the common law rights of persons. The fundamental legal safeguard is the Fourteenth Amendment to the Constitution, passed initially with regard to race, which has been interpreted as holding that redistributionist forms of taxation and profit control amount to unequal protection (i.e., the amendment states, in part, "No state shall make or enforce any law which shall abridge the privileges or immunities of citizens of the United States, nor shall any State deprive any person of life, liberty, or property, without due process of law; nor deny to any person within its jurisdiction the equal protection of the laws"). This legal safeguard for property rights, however, is bolstered by advertising that "sells" the importance of free enterprise as essential for the maintenance of liberty (e.g., the tobacco industry has for years touted the importance of autonomy in general in its fight against government regulation; the National Rifle Association has used similar arguments in opposing gun control). Two other factors are also at

---

[20] Graeme Salaman, *Work Organization and Class Structure* (Armonk, N.Y.: M. E. Sharpe, 1981), pp. 114, 117, 242 (citing, in part, work by Robert Presthus).

[21] Dahl, *Democracy*, p. 122.

[22] Grant McConnell, *Private Power and American Democracy* (New York: Vintage Books, 1966), pp. 7, 142, 145, 150, 154, 341.

[23] De Bedts, *New Deal's SEC*, p. 15.

work. First, many of the major institutions in the communication, cultural, and educational areas that directly influence citizen beliefs and values are themselves jealous of their autonomy and no less inclined than their more economically powerful brethren to speak against it. Indeed, the Fourth Estate, for example, believes itself to be the bulwark of liberties and a major source for their extension. Second, in a society increasingly dominated by bureaucratic values, the leaders of institutions are generally accorded the accolade of "expert." For businessmen, this is part of their prestige, which clearly tops that accorded to the leadership of groups such as blacks, feminists, and even intellectuals.[24]

As contractual compliance in the modern phase evolves, property is increasingly dispersed away from families and individuals toward institutions – financial institutions, equity and loan markets, and the like – partly as a consequence of their growing importance in property transactions; more than one-half of all shares traded on the stock exchange, for instance, are now bought and sold by large institutions.[25] With these changes, property as a concept is increasingly divorced from its moorings in the social groups that were of primary importance in the traditional phase and the beginning period of the modern phase. Institutional power thus grows and enlarges of itself.

Elite power in systems of strong contractual compliance in the modern phase

As Philip Burch points out, there has been relatively little good work done in the United States on the relationship between business and government, especially as it affects the policymaking process. Non-Marxist political scientists rarely study the business community, and economists often view the political process as outside their primary area of concern. Sociologists have more aggressively pursued this tack, but the number of works are few in comparison to the importance of the problem.[26]

Granting autonomy to the economic institutions of society does not mean political democratization. The modern large corporation, in fact, exercises disproportionate influence over public policy owing to its significance for the economic well-being of society and because of the numbers of people, both within the corporation and outside it, who are directly and indirectly influenced by its activities. It is not the people themselves whose interests are expressed by the institution, however, for within the corporation internal democratic controls are excluded under the principle of the autonomy of property.

[24] Verba and Orren, *Equality*, pp. 187, 189.
[25] Nicholas Abercrombie, Stephen Hill, and Bryan S. Turner, *The Dominant Ideology Thesis* (London: Allen & Unwin, 1980), pp. 128–9.
[26] Philip H. Burch, Jr., *Elites in American History: The Federalist Years to the Civil War* (New York: Holmes & Meier, 1981), p. 9.

The concerns of institutions, which are of such crucial social and political importance, are brought to government attention through special-interest groups organized for this purpose. These groups aid the democratic process only in the sense that they compete for attention and priority as autonomous units. They are not in themselves elected bodies, however, and they have no formal representation in the legislatures that are. Indeed, to the extent that most of these groups are representative at all, it is to the leadership of the institutions whose interests they articulate. As Stein Rokkan noted, "votes count, but often organizational resources decide."[27]

The leaders of large institutions are in no sense democratically representative of the institution's members, nor is their position dependent on a participatory electoral process. In corporations, stock ownership confers votes (proportional to the number of shares that are owned) and these votes control the choice of directors of the corporation. Only in this very limited way does democratic theory operate. In fact, management frequently appoints the board and the board endorses management, including its personnel decisions, in a manner that is clearly illegitimate from a democratic perspective. This situation is a by-product of the increasingly hazy distinction, as regards the ultimate locus of authority, between owners and managers.

In the modern phase, individuals are equal as regards their property rights, but this equality has in no way impeded the flow of wealth and influence into the hands of those who exercise control over physical capital and over the supervision of the labor force. As a consequence, while the United States has one of the most participatory and open political systems, it is also one of the least egalitarian. Access to enhanced reward is increasingly restricted to a group that can be called a technobility, those who combine educational attainment with bureaucratic skill in order to obtain top managerial positions. The authority that accompanies occupational status is then a potent lever for acquiring rewards from institutional resources and for exercising greater influence in society.[28]

Recognition of autonomy as a basic value carries with it a concomitant recognition of the right to control property. And, of course, it also carries with it a tacit acceptance that those who own, or can purchase access to, TV, radio, newspapers, and so forth, can translate their economic clout into political power. It means also that those who can bring their economic influence to bear can hope for legislation that will be favorable to their own interests (e.g., tenants, whose rents generally cover interest payments on property

---

[27] Dahl, *Democracy*, p. 243.
[28] Verba and Orren, *Equality*, p. 19; also Harold L. Wilensky, *The Welfare State and Equality: Structural and Ideological Roots of Public Expenditures* (Berkeley and Los Angeles: University of California Press, 1975), pp. 61–2 (citing Christopher Jencks).

loans and local taxes, have traditionally had no access to the returns that go to owners from federal tax deductions for these items).

Although some individuals are politically potent, the influence of institutional elites as a whole on public power is primarily through trade and professional associations: the National Association of Manufacturers as well as a variety of policy-planning groups and special-interest organizations. Government bureaucrats and politicians, who have generally the same social background characteristics as institutional elites (e.g., they come largely from the 10 percent of American families with business or professional status),[29] respond to special interests largely to obtain the information essential for the efficient performance of their roles. Some groups, such as the National Rifle Association, are able to bring an extraordinary amount of political influence to bear on individual politicians. In many, if not most, cases, however, this influence is far more diffuse and the overall relationship is more reciprocal. The state plays a pervasive role in support of the economy (e.g., establishing tax incentives and minimum wage levels), while individual institutions jockey for preference in defense contract awards, the rulings of regulatory commissions, and so on. At times, of course, specific institutional interests are favored. For example, in 1971 a most peculiar law was passed by the Nevada state legislature outlawing prostitution in any county with a population of 200,000 or more. As it turned out, the law applied only to Clark County, where Las Vegas is located. A member of the state legislature pointed out how this came to be: "Prostitution in Las Vegas represents competition for casinos. If you have a legal business, it would take away customers and they would spend less time in the casinos. Illegal Las Vegas prostitution in the casinos themselves doesn't do this."[30]

In short, formal political authority is deeply influenced by private individuals and groups. As Grant McConnell noted more than twenty years ago, substantial segments of formal state power are affected by the activities of autonomous institutional elites. These elites, however, do not act cohesively, and the influence they project rarely equates with actual political rulership.[31] Moreover, this influence does not constitute some sinister pattern of ruling-class domination, as some writers aver.[32] It is, in fact, a thoroughly normal aspect of institutional activity in a modern society whose compliance ideology is strongly contractual. These activities are no more to be condemned as sinister than are the acts of a bishop who rigorously suppressed heresy in the traditional phase of encompassing hierarchy.

[29] G. William Domhoff, *The Powers That Be: Processes of Ruling-Class Domination in America* (New York: Random House, 1978), p. 157.
[30] John F. Galliher and John R. Cross, *Morals Legislation Without Morality: The Case of Nevada* (New Brunswick, N.J.: Rutgers University Press, 1983), p. 72.
[31] McConnell, *Private Power*, pp. 162, 339.
[32] See, for example, Domhoff, *Powers That Be*.

Reward patterns under contractual compliance

In societies where contractual criteria are balanced to some degree with positional criteria, there is a degree of acceptance of basic welfare programs and of limitations on the size of the income gap between the best- and worst-off segments of society. Sidney Verba, in his study of the United States, Sweden, and Japan, shows clearly the sharp contrast among them in this regard. America stands out strikingly from Sweden and Japan in the general opposition by all groups to redistributive policies[33] and in the way widely shared values, abetted by special-interest pleading, influence government policies regarding the distribution of rewards. The consequence is that virtually all groups in America affirm the desirability of private property[34] and of equality of opportunity even though structural constraints limit the egalitarian claims embedded in the latter ideal.

Although inequality among groups in America increased in the nineteenth century during the period of early industrial expansion (following the familiar Kuznet's inverted-U formulation regarding development and inequality), it has been suggested that inequality of wealth today is roughly the same as it was on the eve of the Declaration of Independence[35] (in the eighteenth century, before the American Revolution, 500 of Boston's 16,000 residents, approximately 3 percent of the city's population, owned 50 percent of the town's assets, while one of three adult men had no property or even a regular job).[36] In the late nineteenth century the Census Bureau estimated that 9 percent of America's families owned about 71 percent of the nation's wealth.[37] Fifty percent of all families had no property.[38] At the present time the top 10 percent of the population owns 65 percent of all net worth (and 90 percent of all corporate stock), while the bottom half owns a scant 4 percent.[39] The greatest amount of control over property is at the apex of society. The genuine upper class, which is about 0.5 percent of the adult population and constitutes a little more than a million people including adults and children, consistently holds about 22 percent of the personal wealth of society.[40] When the categories are expanded the differences are still sharp. According to a

[33] Sidney Verba et al., *Elites and the Idea of Equality: A Comparison of Japan, Sweden, and the United States* (Cambridge, Mass.: Harvard University Press, 1987), pp. 261–2.
[34] McClosky and Zaller, *American Ethos*, p. 225.
[35] Verba and Orren, *Equality*, p. 50 (citing Jeffrey Williamson and Peter Lindert).
[36] A. J. Langguth, *Patriots: The Men Who Started the American Revolution* (New York: Simon & Schuster, 1988), p. 14.
[37] Baltzell, *Protestant Establishment*, p. 110.
[38] Werner Sombart, *Why Is There No Socialism in the United States*, trans. Patricia M. Hocking and C. T. Husbands (White Plains, N.Y.: International Arts and Sciences Press, 1976), p. 8.
[39] Daniel Patrick Moynihan, "Half the Nation's Children: Born Without a Fair Chance," *New York Times*, September 25, 1988, sec. 4, p. 25; Lester C. Thurow, *The Zero-Sum Society: Distribution and the Possibilities for Economic Change* (New York: Basic Books, 1980), p. 31.
[40] Burch, *Elites*, p. 11; Domhoff, *Powers That Be*, pp. 6–7.

1984 report by Congress's Joint Economic Committee, the share of the national income received by the wealthiest 40 percent of families in the United States was 67.3 percent, while the poorest 40 percent received 15.7 percent.[41] In effect, the distribution is highly skewed, with those at the top having enormously greater access to the rewards that are available.

The senior managers of America's economic institutions receive emoluments in line with this general pattern. In 1986 the average chief executive's salary and bonus was $829,887 according to a study by *Business Week*.[42] This is nearly seven times the average pay for top union leaders ($118,619)[43] and almost thirty times greater than the median family income ($27,735 according to census figures for 1985).[44] Marked differences are also noteworthy between other levels. Lipset reports that wage differentials between skilled and unskilled workers are greater in the United States than in France, Germany, Italy, the Netherlands, and Norway.[45]

Clearly, to be an institutional elite in America is to be well rewarded. Yet the compensation is only a fraction (less than 1 percent) of the national wage bill and, indeed, but a fraction of the total human resources costs for large companies.[46] The wealthiest are in business fields (especially banking, insurance, and real estate), although some professionals (e.g., top corporate attorneys) are also highly compensated. The rich in America do not begrudge themselves their powerful position. Joan Huber and William Form found, in fact, that this group had the highest consensus on who ought to have the most power; 30 percent said people in big business.[47]

In America privilege on one dimension tends to be related to privilege on others. The quality of legal services available to an individual, for example, is clearly distributed according to wealth (as well as race and ethnicity).[48] Individuals are theoretically equal in the rights they possess, but the rich, by being able to buy services qualitatively superior to those available to the average person, in effect enhance their rights vis-à-vis others. Better housing, for instance, may mean better fire and police protection (e.g., private security guards, in some cases). Indeed, for those who own their residences, fed-

[41] Barbara Ehrenreich, "Is the Middle Class Doomed?," *New York Times Magazine*, September 7, 1986, sec. 6, p. 44.

[42] John A. Byrne, "Executive Pay: Who Got What in '86," *International Business Week*, no. 2995-325 (May 4, 1987): 50.

[43] Jonathan Tasini with Jane B. Todaro, "How Much Top Labor Leaders Made in 1986," ibid., p. 69.

[44] Ehrenreich, "Is the Middle Class Doomed?," p. 54.

[45] Seymour Martin Lipset, *The First New Nation: The United States in Historical and Comparative Perspective* (New York: Norton, 1979), p. 182.

[46] Okun, *Equality and Efficiency*, p. 54; Byrne, "Executive Pay," p. 56.

[47] Joan Huber and William H. Form, *Income and Ideology: An Analysis of the American Political Formula* (New York: Free Press, 1973), p. 143.

[48] Jerold S. Auerbach, *Unequal Justice: Lawyers and Social Change in Modern America* (New York: Oxford University Press, 1976), pp. 12, 294-5.

eral subsidies in the form of income tax exemptions for mortgage payments amount to about twice as much as direct subsidies for housing for poor people.[49] Although there are welfare programs in areas of medical care, unemployment, retirement, housing, educational opportunity, and so on, the structure of tax preferences and exemptions amounts to an enormous reverse welfare program that greatly favors the well-off. Allowing interest deductions on federal taxes for home equity loans, for example, provides credit for consumer spending for property owners that is not available to others.

Although inheritance is only a minor source of assets for the American population as a whole (80 percent claim never to have inherited anything), it plays a very large role for the 2.5 percent of the population who own 43 percent of the nation's wealth. For them, inheritance is an important boost in the start one has in life (hardly equality of opportunity) and is also an important factor explaining the persistent inequality in the distribution of wealth that has been noted for well over one hundred years.[50] Although the percentage of big business executives who are sons of wealthy families has declined markedly in this century,[51] it seems reasonable to infer that inheritance as such plays some part in the fact that the sons of families who are from the top quintile of the socioeconomic pyramid have average incomes 75 percent higher than those who come from families in the bottom quintile.[52] The public, nevertheless, is deeply attached to the right of inheritance and views efforts to curtail it as unwarranted governmental intrusion.[53]

Recent data point out how the rich attribute their status to personal factors (being competitive, skillful, etc.).[54] For those who are successful the failure of others is more than reassuring; it makes their own work and status respectable, legitimates the norms that undergird status, ensures that the least desirable jobs will get done, and provides a relatively defenseless group who can be made to absorb the costs for risks that the successful deem are too great to be borne by any particular group of individuals or institutions.

In sum, the drive to accumulate has resulted in large, independent institutions whose surpluses have provided the wherewithal for the dominance of money in social and political life. A new elite, a technobility, the flower of the leadership of these new institutions, has come into being, largely responsive to their own organizations and their own personal needs and aspirations.

---

[49] Huber and Form, *Income and Ideology*, p. 123.
[50] Thomas Osman, "The Role of Intergenerational Wealth Transfers in the Distribution of Wealth over the Life Cycle: A Preliminary Analysis," in *The Distribution of Economic Well-Being*, ed. F. Thomas Juster (Cambridge, Mass.: Ballinger, 1977), pp. 403, 409.
[51] Lipset, *First New Nation*, p. xiii.
[52] Okun, *Equality and Efficiency*, p. 75 (citing Christopher Jencks and Associates).
[53] Ronald Chester, *Inheritance, Wealth, and Society* (Bloomington: Indiana University Press, 1982) pp. 74–5.
[54] Huber and Form, *Income and Ideology*, p. 116.

Using the power available to them, they have been able to influence policies in ways that favor their own interests. What is surprising is not that this is done but that it receives such widespread popular support.

Some consequences of support and neglect

In the nineteenth century Henry Ward Beecher, an extraordinarily influential minister in Brooklyn, denounced strikes as occurring because of the sinfulness of those who were, he said, unwilling to "nobly bear" their "self-induced" poverty.[55] In subsequent years the federal government ignored the pious callousness of people like Beecher and recognized the right of workers to form and join unions. Beyond minimum wage legislation, however, a right to a minimum annual income or some "just" compensation has never been recognized. It is certainly worth asking why the great mass of subordinates in America accepts the income disparities that exist as well as the relative helplessness that goes with them. Indeed, why is there an acceptance in general of obligations to be obedient to those whose status is higher? Clearly it cannot be said that subordinates comply from the threat of whips and chains. Something more powerful is at work; it is to be found, I think, in moral beliefs that both legitimate status differences and sustain solidarity.

Part of the reason subordinates in bureaucratic institutions accept the constraints that go with low status is that their lives in these circumstances are less onerous than the alternatives. In an interesting statement expressing sentiments that were shared by many others, a young Japanese girl from a rural village in Kagoshima prefecture contrasted her work in a textile plant in Osaka in 1930 with her previous life: "Think of weeding . . . in June in the rice field with the burning sun on your back and crawling on all fours in the boiling paddy-field water. Compared to that, indoor [Factory] work is easy."[56] Yet there is ample evidence that not all factory work has been so desirable, especially in the early period of industrialization. Upton Sinclair's journalistic description of life in and around Chicago's stockyards at the turn of the century reveals a savage world.[57] Work in the packing houses can still be a grim, monotonous, and even dangerous affair, with workers sometimes repeating the same motion eight thousand or more times a day. One worker described waking in pain at night, unable to open her fists, after days in which she made 1,900 cuts an hour on hog's heads that passed her station.[58]

It is, perhaps, unsurprising that polls of American business leaders reveal that only 22 percent think it fair to tax the rich to help the poor, only 14

---

[55] Baltzell, *Protestant Establishment*, p. 101.
[56] Hane, *Peasants*, p. 31 (brackets in original).
[57] Upton Sinclair, *The Jungle* (Toronto: Bantam Books, 1981) (first published in 1906).
[58] William Glaberson, "Safety Remains Elusive at Morrell," *New York Times*, August 21, 1988, sec. 3, pp. 1, 8.

percent think the government should reduce income disparities, and but a scant 2 percent believe there should be a top limit on incomes;[59] it is more surprising that 67 percent of *all* people oppose the idea of government guaranteeing a minimum annual income instead of providing relief and welfare.[60] There is, in fact, general opposition to income redistribution as a solution to social problems, along with a general tendency to blame the poor for their condition and to uphold the principle that people deserve the income they get. Although workers would like more in the way of income, they support the values and institutions of contractual compliance with virtually the same enthusiasm as do the wealthy.[61] The social structure is widely supported, by the owners and controllers of property, of course, but also by the bulk of society including, especially, the self-employed, who epitomize the ideal of autonomy and who detest state intervention (and the welfare state in particular).[62] There is, in fact, no lack of support for social forms as they exist, for the focus is not on the dire consequences that befall some people in a system of unassailable private property rights but on the possibilities for individual advancement within that system. Only about 20 percent of low-status people believe they have a worse than average chance to get ahead; with regard to others, most people believe that the poor, blacks, and women have opportunity equal to or better than the average.[63]

Support for contractual compliance, widely shared, predominates even in the face of trends that indicate growing inequality. For instance, although there was a tendency toward income equality during the first half of the twentieth century (e.g., although the average income of the richest fifth of society in 1929 was fifteen and a half times the poorest fifth, this dropped to nine times by 1951), this leveling process ceased by 1950.[64] In the subsequent forty years there has been a progressively more unequal distribution of income, masked somewhat by transfer payments and by female participation in the labor force. The widening of the gap is not dramatic, but the poor have clearly become somewhat poorer and the rich somewhat richer (a number of perceptive articles in the *New York Times* have chronicled increases in poverty, hunger, and homelessness).[65]

The members of modern contractual societies believe strongly in equality of opportunity. Yet because positional criteria are secondary, the needs of the

[59] Verba and Orren, *Equality*, p. 79.
[60] McCloskey and Zaller, *American Ethos*, p. 275.
[61] Ibid., p. 159.
[62] Wilensky, *Welfare State*, pp. 61–2.
[63] Kluegel and Smith, *Beliefs About Inequality*, pp. 49, 68.
[64] Jeffrey G. Williamson and Peter H. Lindert, *American Inequality: A Macroeconomic History* (New York: Academic Press, 1980), pp. 84, 92.
[65] For example, John Herbers, "Poverty of Blacks Spreads in Cities," *New York Times*, January 26, 1987, pp. 1, 27; John Herbers, "Hunger in U.S. Is Widening, Study of 'New Poor' Reports," *New York Times*, April 20, 1986, pp. 1, 28; and Holly Metz, "Who Benefits From Charity," *New York Times*, March 9, 1986, sec. 11, p. 28.

disadvantaged are neglected and opportunities themselves denied. The values of these societies, strongly supported at all levels, do not easily permit the rectification of neglect and the imposition of restraints on those who have used this concept of equality for their own advantage. There are, of course, impulses toward charity that prompt the erection of safeguards against disaster. Yet there is often scant regard for personal tragedy (e.g., catastrophic medical needs) and an institutional inability to provide care outside normal limits.

Recently, in obtaining aid for Ethiopian famine victims, entertainment stars staged a successful benefit to raise funds to purchase food. These supplies could not be obtained from wealthy food corporations. It would be erroneous and mean-spirited to accuse these institutions and their leaders of a deliberate failure to heed the needs of the indigent famine victims, for the institution's goals and its viability in a system of contractual compliance prohibits such altruism. Yet, as Albert Gore, Jr., the American senator from Tennessee, has pointed out, 37,000 children under the age of five die of starvation or preventable diseases every day.[66] To be sure, much of this appalling tragedy is because of crop failures and local politics. But if only 5 percent is due to the structural inability of autonomous contractual institutions to respond to such problems, it means that 6,752,500 little children will perish for this reason in a single decade alone.

Strong positional compliance in the modern phase

Sources of positional compliance

Men shrink from the talons of the greedy. As the values of contractual compliance extended ever more broadly through the social fabric of Western societies, the disadvantaged cried out. The organic, ordained relationships inherited from the traditional phase of encompassing hierarchy were shattered, while the moral justifications for a new world seemed skewed toward a mindless recognition of the rapacious. Indeed, in the nineteenth century, as soon as industrialization became a significant feature of the social landscape, certain groups did suffer an absolute decline in living standards; the rural poor often lived below present-day subsistence levels on potatoes, bread, cheese, and water.[67] Small wonder that peasants increasingly pressed their ancient demand for land. In the rapidly growing cities workers also began to protest and to develop their own savings institutions, friendly societies, trade unions, and reading groups. These institutions gave back to the

[66] Albert Gore, Jr., "An Ecological Kristillnacht. Listen," *New York Times*, March 19, 1989, sec. 4, p. 27.
[67] John D. Montgomery, *Technology and Civic Life: Making and Implementing Development Decisions* (Cambridge, Mass.: MIT Press, 1974), pp. 31, 35.

disadvantaged that sense of community life which many felt had been violently torn from them.

Yet although the disadvantaged clung to the values that had given life much of its meaning in the traditional phase, no society that became strongly contractual in the modern sense has ever turned from that path. There have been, to be sure, powerful political undercurrents to challenge the contractual mode of life (e.g., in left-wing socialist movements). There have also been movements favoring fascism, which rejects the moral arguments of both contractual and positional compliance at the modern phase, substituting for them a brutal secular version of encompassing hierarchy. But no genuine, wholesale turning away has taken place, seemingly because the moral arguments of contractual compliance resonate deeply with psychological needs for individuation. When associated with private property rights, sufficient support has been generated to relegate positional criteria to a subsidiary position. As a consequence, the ascendance of positional criteria to a strong position in the modern phase of property relations has not occurred as a succession to a contractual stage at the same phase; instead, it has invariably taken place in agrarian societies emerging directly from the traditional phase. It is these societies that have attempted to institutionalize accumulation in terms of positional rather than contractual moral criteria.

Clearly, in the early period of change to the modern phase, the existence of legally recognized autonomous groupings (e.g., free towns with their merchant elites) spurred the emergence of a contractually oriented market economy, although other factors (e.g., the general status of the peasantry) were also of crucial importance. Whatever the actual mix of influences, the institutional system that evolved was in no sense planned. The idea that any alternative path of development might be possible only gained strength after the French Revolution and then, for many decades, rather fitfully. It is in the twentieth century that the belief that political authority can guide accumulation has taken hold. What has given this idea particular urgency is that the choice of which moral underpinning is most appropriate for initial development appears to be a once-only opportunity.[68] Change thereafter is incremental along the initial chosen trajectory toward the ultimately more integrative patterns of the emergent phase.

Patterns of contractual compliance deeply affront the morality of the traditional positional ethic. The utilitarian individualistic paradigm appears to those who still live in the world of encompassing hierarchy as self-interest; praise of autonomy is seen as but a pious covering for selfishness. True morality, it is argued, is embedded in social relationships; conduct should ideally be guided less by the need for self-expression and more by a reasonable

---

[68] Ibid., pp. 215, 227.

regard for human feelings. So powerful are these traditional ideals that almost without exception every new developing nation has enshrined them. This is true from their most radical expression in places like Cuba and China to more benign manifestations in India and Israel.

The leaders of new nations wish neither to perpetuate traditional social relationships nor to adopt the individualistic patterns of contractual compliance. Instead, they seek to curtail the influence of autonomous, foreign (largely contractually oriented) enterprises, to break the power of the old landed oligarchy, and to transform the bases of land ownership. As it has turned out, although individualism has been restrained, the assumption of control over property by the leaders of accumulating institutions has not been avoided. This is a general phenomenon in the modern phase. Although the technobility who lead positional institutions justify their status by moral criteria that place greater emphasis on the community than on individuality, the justifications are equally based on a property relations concept.

For both communists and nationalists a monopoly of power has appeared as the most effective way to ensure rational planning and spur accumulation. Although very different perceptions of the government's role have been set forth, authoritarian means (i.e., government intervention) have often seemed necessary in order to maximize growth. Individual interest is then presumed to be a function of community interest. Mao Zedong put this very succinctly when he wrote, "The individual is an element of the collective. When collective interests are increased, personal interests will subsequently be improved."[69]

Unity supersedes individuality. Property inheres in a collective image. There is, in theory, an ideal of simple equality in which rights are the property of the community while the individual achieves personal fulfillment through the performance of duties. Simple equality in this sense does not mean the extinction of natural differences, but it does mean the reduction of inequalities across blocs, especially in terms of class privilege and class distinctions.

The Leninist variant of Marxism, as it was developed under Stalin and others, is perhaps the best example of strong positional compliance in the modern phase. J. R. Talmon described this type of system as "Secular Messianic Monism," a phrase that nicely encapsulates its fervor, its divergence from the traditional phase, and its difference from systems based on pluralism.[70] Marx described the nature of leadership in communist institutions as akin to the authority of an orchestra conductor: "Cooperative labor

[69] Cited in Andrew J. Nathan, "Sources of Chinese Rights Thinking," in R. Randle Edwards, Louis Henkin, and Andrew J. Nathan, *Human Rights in Contemporary China* (New York: Columbia University Press, 1986), p. 141.
[70] J. L. Talmon, *The Origins of Totalitarian Democracy* (New York: Praeger, 1960), p. 10.

requires . . . 'one commanding will.' "[71] Lenin, speaking in 1917 of the planned economy as something analogous to the technical division of labor in a single workshop managed by administrative means, said, "The whole of society will have become a single office and a single factory with equality of work and equality of pay."[72] Yet within this vision there was a dark shadow, a stain carried down from the early socialists, who castigated individual freedom of thought as inherently dangerous in a planned society. As Saint-Simon (1760–1825), the founder of French socialism, said of those who might not obey his proposed planning boards, they would be "treated as cattle."[73] Figure 4 sets forth the compliance criteria of a strong positional system in the modern phase.

Institutional behavior, law, and positional values

In the strongest positional systems (i.e., communist societies) the state reserves for itself power over property while allowing the enjoyment of property to rest in private hands. Although there are limits on the degree to which wealth can be accumulated, the legal concept of private property is thus not significantly different from noncommunist systems. The basic difference lies in the values associated with the conceptualizations of institutional life.[74]

In communist societies, especially in their formative period, unity is a central value. It is usually contrasted with individualism, which is equated with selfishness, unresponsiveness, and irresponsibility. Sectarianism and pleasure seeking are considered evils that are best countered by the authority of the state. Personal selflessness, and its corollary, social egalitarianism, on the other hand, are goals that, if carefully pursued, are said to lead to modesty, prudence, diligence, industriousness, and social harmony and cooperation. Whatever contributes to achieving these ends is considered just, fair, and desirable; again, it is the state that is empowered to ensure their existence. Justice, then, is predicated on a requirement for state intervention. It rests, fundamentally, on the principle of collective control. More narrowly, it rests on the leadership of political institutions and on group responsibility for insuring that individuals manifest correct value orientations.

Within the state, partly as a consequence of the administrative nature of economic planning and institutional coordination, power is highly concentrated. In marked contradistinction to contractual systems, power is not di-

---

[71] Cited in Michael Walzer, *Spheres of Justice: A Defense of Pluralism and Equality* (New York: Basic Books, 1983), p. 299.
[72] Cited in Friederich A. Hayek, *The Road to Serfdom* (Chicago: University of Chicago Press, 1944), p. 119.
[73] Cited in ibid., p. 24.
[74] Wolfgang Friedmann, *Law in a Changing Society* (New York: Columbia University Press, 1972), pp. 106, 107.

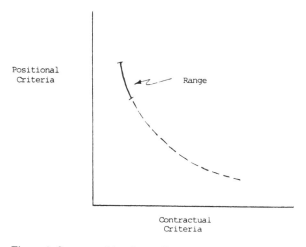

Figure 4. Strong positional compliance in the modern phase.

vided in a pluralistic manner among formal constituencies but remains collective in theory and in its formal facade (but definitely not in practice – cliques abound in violation of ideal requirements). Within this framework, decision making is broadly personal rather than hedged by established, objective legal constraints. The faithful, held in the grip of an elite assumption of their own suprapolitical competence, are goaded to emulate politically defined virtue. Andrew Walder believes, however, that in China it is concrete loyalty to institutional superiors that is of critical importance, and he is undoubtedly correct.[75] Yet he is surely wrong to dismiss the moral quality of relationships as a significant factor because that quality defines the appropriate modes of loyalty both up and down the hierarchical chain.

In China wholehearted participation in social activity is expected but without any prospect that it can influence authoritative decisions. Instead, followers are enjoined to study the moral principles set forth by their leaders in order to conquer any tendency on their part toward weak and confused attitudes. The model of society is an organic one with individuals clearly differentiated from each other positionally but within a web of relationships that is seamless, permitting no autonomous separation among society's constituent elements. Leaders, therefore, must perforce make final decisions on moral and intellectual issues. Because they set forth principles of justice that are required to be followed, they must also have the unquestioned right to interfere continuously with people's lives so these principles will be

[75] Andrew G. Walder, *Communist Neo-Traditionalism: Work and Authority in Chinese Industry* (Berkeley and Los Angeles: University of California Press, 1986), p. 131.

realized.[76] The result is a concentration of power that is deemed to be completely justified. As Stalin said in 1930 in his Political Report of the Central Committee at the Sixteenth Party Congress:

> We are waiting for the withering away of the state. But at the same time we are for the strengthening of the dictatorship of the proletariat, the strongest and mightiest state power that ever existed. The highest development of state power in preparation of the preconditions for the withering away of state power – that is the Marxist formula. Is that 'contradictory'? Yes it is 'contradictory.' But this contradiction is inherent in life and it completely mirrors the Marxist dialectic.[77]

In Chinese law there is no presumption of innocence or of a right to counsel. Courts are responsible to political bodies; social order is given precedence over procedural concerns. Rights against arbitrary treatment (e.g., work or residence assignments or even arrest) are weakly honored, for as long as decisions have been made by proper authority and are in accordance with law, they are not deemed to be unreasonable. In 1988, Yu Shutong – Professor of law, vice-president of the China Law Society, and director of the Department of Education and Bureau of International Judicial Assistance of the People's Republic of China's Ministry of Justice – declared emphatically that the party had no intention of giving up its control over legal matters, nor should it.[78] For much of the history of Communist rule in China jural law (i.e., formal, codified, independent rules) took a distinct second place to law articulated in terms of the party's norms and values. A reliance on codes has lately become more noticeable, but they often contain provisions that are highly substantive in nature (e.g., two offenses noted in the 1979 criminal code dealt with counterrevolution and crimes against the socialist economic order).[79] As might be expected, political rights are especially weakly protected. Nathan points out, for example, that constitutional and criminal provisions against damaging public order, interfering with traffic, disrupting work, harming social morals, and damaging state property have been used to restrict freedom of assembly, association, processions, and demonstrations; at times, as the Tiananmen Square incident of June 3–4, 1989, indicates, such acts have also been authoritatively labeled as counterrevolutionary.[80]

Chinese authorities have been quite explicit that there is no such thing in China as freedom of speech. In 1981, *Red Flag* summarized legal provisions

---

[76] Robert Nozick, *Anarchy, State, and Utopia* (New York: Basic Books, 1974), p. 163.

[77] Cited in Ernst Topitsch, "How Enlightened Is 'Dialectical Reason'?" *Encounter* (May, 1982): 49.

[78] In response to my question at a luncheon on May 10, 1988.

[79] Shao-chuan Leng, "The Chinese Judicial System: A New Direction," in *Organizational Behavior in Chinese Society*, ed. Sidney L. Greenblatt, Richard W. Wilson, and Amy Auerbacher Wilson (New York: Praeger, 1981), p. 121.

[80] Andrew J. Nathan, *Chinese Democracy* (New York: Knopf, 1985), p. 119.

regarding this matter as follows: "A person is free to express any opinion (including erroneous ones) and will be protected by law so long as he stands on the side of the people and safeguards the constitution and the law. [But] no one is allowed to air antiparty and antisocialist views."[81] Nor is one free to express dissent by action. The right to strike, for example, was eliminated from the 1982 constitution as potentially destabilizing. Paternalistic management rather than objective law usually determines the outcome of grievances (as well as important personnel matters). Indeed, in a society that glorifies labor it is no small irony that labor is used as a category of punishment. Repeat minor offenders and political dissidents not charged with felonies can be arbitrarily assigned to a penal work camp by authority without the due process guaranteed by the constitution (i.e., they are not entitled to public trial or legal counsel) for up to three years of "re-education thru labor."[82]

Negative rights, which are of such critical importance in systems of contractual compliance, are always subordinate to the needs of society and the state. Although laws in theory are above individuals and have a rational relationship to commonly accepted social goals, they are, in fact, always subject to meta-legal considerations. Rights in general, therefore, have no universal, abstract, "natural" definition in law. As *Red Flag* put it in 1979,

Human rights are not "heaven-given," they are given and regulated by the state and by law; they are not universal, but have a clear class nature; they are not abstract but concrete; they are not absolute but limited by law and morality; they are not eternally fixed and unchanging but change their nature and proper scope in accordance with changes in the functions and positions of people in the midst of shifting conditions of material production.[83]

Given the variable nature of rights, it is perhaps understandable that citizens are not expected to use legal means to secure them.[84]

Individuals in strong positional systems are politically and economically dependent despite leadership efforts to foster self-reliance. The rights that people possess are constantly subject to reinterpretations in a manner that can decisively affect career and status opportunities. Stalin put it succinctly when he said, "Cadres decide everything."[85] In this environment procedural law is unwanted, for it imposes obligations on authority vis-à-vis ordinary citizens that may restrain the rapid realization of ideologically defined goals.

[81] Cited in Nathan, "Sources of Chinese Rights Thinking," p. 135.
[82] R. Randle Edwards, "Civil and Social Rights: Theory and Practice in Chinese Law Today," in Edwards, Henkin, and Nathan, *Human Rights,* pp. 66, 69.
[83] Cited in Nathan, "Sources of Chinese Rights Thinking," p. 130.
[84] Edwards, "Civil and Social Rights," p. 65.
[85] Cited in Lynn T. White III, "The End of China's Revolution: A Leadership Diversifies," unpublished paper delivered at the Third International Congress of Professors World Peace Academy, Manila, August 24–9, 1987, p. 8.

Small wonder that during the Russian Revolution lawyers were initially banned and were only brought back as employees of the state, organized in "colleges of advocates."[86]

Authority patterns in strong positional compliance systems

"The labor of superintendence" is what Marx called the new style of institutional management that would arise with the collapse of bourgeois capitalism. Originally it was thought that many would be able to play a part in this activity. After the USSR was founded, however, it became clear that those with management and technical skills (experts) must play a major role in institutional life. In theory the party was to formulate the overall goals, policies, and programs with the experts being merely in charge of implementation. As it has turned out, this distinction has blurred with time, although not all party members are experts and not all experts, by any means, are party members. The party, nevertheless, has been extensively involved in implementation to a degree quite beyond historical precedent. In China, for example, during the days of the last imperial dynasty (the Qing) only about 27,000 civil and military officials assisted by several million underlings were required to manage a society with approximately (by its end) 315 million citizens. Today, with a population more than a billion, China is governed by a party of approximately 40 million assisted by an equal or greater number of "superintending" bureaucrats. Not all of these, to be sure, are part of China's technobility, for only a few have a major say over the use of property. All, however, are members of bureaucratic organizations that are linked in the overall drive for accumulation.

Institutions such as the party, the military, state ministries, and so on, are distinct organizations knit together in theory by the party apparatus. For subordinates, however, a particular institution is the focal point for the obligations that must be honored and for the rights to which they are entitled. Through its bureaucracy, an institution provides its members with the goods and services (e.g., housing, recreation facilities, education for children, etc.) that are important determinants of a person's standard of living. The consequence is that an individual's life may become far more deeply meshed with the institution than with the wider community. Status within the institution, determined by bonuses, raises, and promotions, is critical, for there are few other ways to obtain standard-of-living benefits. As a result, the institution's "political" system is extraordinarily significant.

Criticism of superiors tends to be muted, especially in public, although the top elite, *in camera*, do engage in sweeping, critical debate. At lower lev-

---

[86] Friedmann, *Law in a Changing Society*, p. 22.

els the discretion of supervisors vis-à-vis subordinates is relatively unrestrained. Followers are prevented from forming independent associations that can bargain collectively with authority. Instead, dependency is fostered. For themselves, leaders stress (ideally) the positional obligations associated with the modern phase – to protect rights defined in terms of community, to fulfill community needs, to achieve rational ends defined by substantive law, and to uphold solidarity. For subordinates, the obligations of contractual compliance in the traditional phase are emphasized as duties – awareness of the importance of hierarchical ranking, understanding that role responsibilities are defined in terms of status, accepting the importance of ideology in defining and enforcing obligations, and deferring to superiors (see the table in Chapter 4 and Figure 4).

To a degree unknown in contractual compliance systems institutional authority is personal and diffuse. This does not mean a lack of formal bureaucratization. Stephen Andors, for instance, reports that before the Cultural Revolution the Kweichow #9 Chemical Industry Construction Company had no fewer than eight hundred pages of rules covering 755 regulations; in nearly thirty offices and sections one-third of the workers were administrative personnel (a ratio, however, that is still lower than the one prevailing in contemporary America).[87] Leadership style, as would be expected in a positional system, stresses interpersonal relations. For those accustomed to contractual bureaucratic patterns (highly articulated divisions of labor, etc.) organizational interplay appears informal. In Walder's view this represents an amalgam of Weber's patrimonial style with a modern rational-legal form. As he says, "What is notable about this pattern is not that there is a personal and informal side to the organization, but that the entire complex of formal and informal, public and private relationships represents a form of particularism that is at the very core of this type of industrial bureaucracy."[88] In my view, however, the compliance system that we observe is not an amalgam of traits derived from a *unidirectional* theory of change (i.e., patrimonial to rational-legal); it is, rather, the natural form of a strong positional compliance system in the modern phase in which the system as a whole (and elite status in particular) is justified structurally at a modern level, while subordinate duties are demarcated by contractual criteria that are articulated in a manner appropriate for the traditional phase of encompassing hierarchy (the reverse of the conditions that hold in the modern phase for a strong contractual compliance system).

Within Chinese institutions security departments have the right to enact administrative punishments including, although rarely resorted to,

[87] Stephen Andors, *China's Industrial Revolution: Politics, Planning, and Management, 1949 to the Present* (New York: Pantheon, 1977) p. 188.
[88] Walder, *Communist Neo-Traditionalism*, p. 251.

sentencing to a prison or labor reform camp.[89] The institution, therefore, has many all-encompassing social control powers. The dependency that is thus fostered, however, should not be viewed as merely coerced. First, there are many dedicated, technically competent, sensitive, and responsible leaders who encourage limited subordinate participation and who earn the respect of their followers by protecting their interests. Second, and of greater importance, the legitimacy of authority is bolstered by the same moral criteria that serve as the rationale for solidarity. It is interesting in this regard to note the comments about Soviet leadership made by David Kreger, a medical student at Harvard who in 1986 participated in a joint American, Swiss, and Soviet backpacking excursion in the Caucasus:

> The Americans were struck by the degree of authority carried by the leader of the Soviet group. . . . While the Americans accepted the practical need for leadership, they expected that the group leaders would try to minimize the loss of individual independence. They expected the leader to spell out his intentions and ask for their opinions. The Soviets did not share these expectations. Their respect for their leader's ability and judgment was clear. His right to lead was not in question. The Soviets had well-defined roles within their group. . . . For Soviets, leadership status is part of a person's identity.[90]

Characteristics of ideology

Modern positional compliance systems, like those of contractual compliance, are dedicated to accumulation and therefore must do certain things that every society that makes the transition to the modern phase must do. Agriculture must be reorganized to create a food surplus, the surplus must then be transferred to workers, and the workers must then be used to create capital. In this process the number of tillers of the soil are reduced in order to create a capital-producing work force. There must not, however, be any loss of agricultural productivity during this transition (for the same, if not more, mouths must be fed), nor can the peasants who remain on the land be allowed to enjoy the fruits of their productivity.[91] The key problem, of course, is how authoritatively to control the peasantry (and rationally plan food production and consumption) while preventing the rise of an unmanageable level of peasant discontent.

Dependence on the peasantry was eliminated in strong positional systems by smashing the bases of peasant power, first by crushing the former landlord class (and, concomitantly, eliminating the private sector in industry and

---

[89] Ibid., p. 93.
[90] David Kreger, "Leadership Styles in the Wilderness: Bridging the Soviet–American Divide, *Center Review* 2, no. 1 (Winter 1988): 2 (a publication of the Center for Psychological Studies in the Nuclear Age, an affiliate of Harvard Medical School at Cambridge Hospital).
[91] Robert L. Heilbroner, *The Great Ascent* (New York: Harper & Row, 1963), pp. 95–7, 160.

commerce), and, second, by transforming the entire structure of production in the countryside and the mechanisms for the extraction of surplus. Opposition from below was neutralized, in both urban and rural areas, by placing reliable cadres in leading positions as far down as possible into basic work units and by charging these cadres with maintaining strict political control over economic activities.

By eliminating any division between those who controlled property and those who governed (i.e., by vesting ownership of the means of production in the state and concentrating control in the hands of bureaucratically designated planners who function under the direction of a vanguard elite), potentially divisive, alternate sources of authority would, it was thought, be suppressed. By prohibiting bargaining between those who labored and those who controlled property, the distinction between them would, in theory, be reduced at the same time that work conditions and levels and types of remuneration could be authoritatively determined. Labor, then, would take on the aspect of fixed rather than variable capital and could be rationally factored into planning. In the countryside, which was always a critical initial area of concern, the institutionalization of strong positional compliance thus tended, commonly, to have seven basic features (that to a greater or lesser degree also became dominant in other sectors of society): centralized planning; collective ownership; large-scale production; unified distribution; economic, social, and political integration; welfare guarantees; and territorial cellularity (i.e., needs provided by the unit to which one was assigned).[92]

In theory the subjects of this new positional compliance system were equal, and, in fact, considerably greater economic equality did result from the initial forced policies of redistribution. Change took place, however, under conditions of avowed political inequality (Verba noted that Japan and Sweden, both far less positional than communist systems, showed the same pattern of political inequality stimulating economic equality).[93] At first, political inequality was associated with the monopoly of power held by revolutionary organizations and with the rigors of revolutionary terror, involving the neutralization, often elimination, of former elites and their purported allies. Later, and equally significant, it was associated with the rise of a technobility that tended to become, over time, bureaucratically entrenched and immune from popular control. For those who would object to the emergence of this new elite, there was the memory of the millions who died in the process of revolutionary terror to remind them of the virtue of deference.

---

[92] Kathleen Hartford, "Socialist Agriculture Is Dead; Long Live Socialist Agriculture! Organizational Transformations in Rural China," in *The Political Economy of Reform in Post-Mao China*, ed. Elizabeth J. Perry and Christine Wong (Cambridge, Mass.: Council on East Asian Studies, Harvard University, 1985), pp. 32–3.
[93] Verba et al., *Elites*, p. 270.

For the Chinese, far more than was the case in the Soviet Union, social transformation involved a series of experiments in administrative devolution along with continuous efforts to instill in the population new values and behavior patterns that would, presumably, promote disciplined and efficient accumulation. Under Mao Zedong the development of a centralized bureaucracy was opposed as ineffective and unwieldy (although tight control was evident in the financial sector over the size and composition of provincial outlays) and efforts were made to stimulate local organizations to exercise effective leadership (within, of course, an overall politically efficacious context).[94] A determined effort was made to steer a middle and novel course between the Scylla of market socialism (i.e., individual enterprise within a socialist context) and the Charybdis of centralized bureaucratic control.

However, although some administrative responsibilities may be devolved, the decisive quality of strong positional compliance in the modern phase is the refusal to tolerate completely autonomous groups, with special attention in this regard focused on the forces of moneyed capitalism. The general trend was toward statewide organization building and the elimination of potential competitive power centers. These objectives were pursued within a political structure in which the ultimate say regarding goals (and planning to achieve them) was a jealously guarded prerogative. Of course, some institutions did protect ordinary people in their daily lives from intrusive demands, and networks did evolve to coordinate an exchange of mutual benefits.[95] Yet the underlying cement of relationships was vertical loyalty (both personal and impersonal) within a moral framework whose criteria were sanctified by explicit ideological statements. For those who overtly violated these ideological strictures, the elite reserved the right of summary intervention, legitimized by a malleable legal cloak. Small wonder that dissidents who sought reform intensely scrutinized the personalities of leaders rather than relying on objective legal rights.

Economic decision-making was thus moralized and politicized to an extreme. At the same time certain populist values were touted, although their political aspects were truncated by the reality of arbitrary power. Economic performance could be noteworthy, brought about by effective institutional innovations to limit shortcomings and maximize strengths (e.g., generally this occurred in the early periods of transition, but also, in China, in the decade of the 1980s). Import substitution policies fostered industrial development and administrative allocation of resources functioned effectively (again, usually in the early periods of growth) without the spur of domestic or international price competition. Worker performance was often coerced but

---

[94] Carl Riskin, "Maoist Economics in Retrospect," paper presented at the Columbia University Seminar on Modern China, April 10, 1986, pp. 1–4.
[95] Walder, *Communist Neo-Traditionalism*, p. 25.

was also obtained by various efforts to stimulate commitment, not least by providing welfare benefits, bonuses, and the like.[96]

As is now abundantly clear, however, the growth of economic complexity that accompanies development eventually surpasses the coordinating capabilities of centralized planners. When this happens planning institutions begin to take on a rigid and obstructive coloring. Arbitrary power, always there whether devolved or centralized, emerges more clearly, especially when it is employed to restrain justifiable criticisms of institutional efficacy. The consequence is a collapse of morale and a discrediting of the ideology, leading to a systemwide crisis of enormous magnitude.

Patterns of status and reward

In the search for a better society, leadership justified its policies morally in terms of securing the interests of the disadvantaged. That these same policies would lead, simultaneously, to a more hegemonic system of political control than heretofore known was not at first apprehended. There was, after all, a set of ideals, said to be grasped fully only by the elite, which when implemented were to create a more desirable life for all. As the controllers of knowledge, the new elite was to work selflessly for others, their rulership buttressed against counterrevolution by the sinews of power, to be sure, but their true authority deriving from their position as a vanguard leading others toward a more sublime way of life. As it has turned out, the only group set truly free, and then only at the apex, has been the technobility itself. This fact, however, should not obscure social changes that have served to justify the elite morally in their claim to high status.

The attempt (now widely rescinded) to eliminate property-based income markedly reduced income inequality, although wide disparities continue to exist depending on unit efficiency, region, and so on. As important, there were also great gains in health care, education, sanitation, transportation, entertainment opportunities, and the like. A sense of belonging in the new system and an enhancement of self-respect were fostered by permitting limited forms of participation in institutional affairs. These improvements make clear that income increases are not always the best way to measure improvements in social life and living standards. Entitlements to benefits in health and education, and increases in social equality and self-respect, are of great importance and may be masked by income measures used alone.[97] The innovation of social improvements can lead to a marked betterment of the lot of

[96] Thomas G. Rawski, *China's Transition to Industrialism: Producer Goods and Economic Development in the Twentieth Century* (Ann Arbor: University of Michigan Press, 1980), pp. 152–4.
[97] Amartya Sen, "Development: Which Way Now?," in *The Political Economy of Development and Underdevelopment*, ed. Charles K. Wilbur (New York: Random House, 1988), pp. 48–9.

the poor especially and be a source of enthusiasm for a new system. At the same time, however, certain policies, instituted out of regard for the disadvantaged, can seriously impede overall development. In China, for example, policies supporting full employment have meant it is difficult to dismiss redundant workers or to penalize those who are lazy and inefficient.[98]

Work discipline, in fact, takes place within a network of complex, informal, hierarchical ties. As Andrew Walder points out with regard to China, although such ties are by appearances based on political appeals and nonmaterial incentives, they are, in fact, grounded in the concrete allocation of career rewards and opportunities; they are backed by paternalistic institutional policies that provide goods, services, job security, and so on.[99] These networks, which are strongest between a minority of devoted workers and the party and management, circumvent formal channels yet are indispensable for achieving institutional goals. As Walder says, "This complex web of personal loyalty, mutual support, and material interest creates a stable pattern of tacit acceptance and active cooperation for the regime that no amount of political terror, coercion, or indoctrination can even begin to provide."[100]

It is within this general institutional framework that advantages have been secured for the lowly. In what way, however, are elite advantages secured? What precisely are the rewards for leaders within this matrix of clientalist ties and normative appeals? There are, of course, here as elsewhere, prestige rewards, and these are not insignificant. More concretely, however, rewards flow from the power that inheres in the bureaucratic control of property. This control, at the top, ensures higher than average incomes, but what it does especially is to permit access to perquisites of office that can include special stores, special educational opportunities for one's children, the use of limousines, dachas, and special recreational facilities. These rewards are not easily quantified but clearly amount to a privileged life-style. Moreover, not the least significant aspect of the reward system is the opportunity to enjoy privileges in an environment that is relatively unrestrained by law, custom, or the objections of followers.

In theory, of course, tendencies toward the manipulation of position for privilege would be checked by an ideological commitment to work for the welfare of others before fulfilling one's own needs. No one, however, initially foresaw the magnitude of the bureaucracies that would develop. Nor did they clearly perceive that within these institutions a new privileged stratum would be created whose ability to strangle criticism would become a dominant feature of the new system. Trotsky spoke of it, as, later, did Djilas and even Mao

---

[98] William Byrd, et al., *Recent Chinese Economic Reforms: Studies of Two Industrial Enterprises,* World Bank Staff Working Papers no. 652 (Washington, D.C.: World Bank, 1984), p. 27.
[99] Walder, *Communist Neo-Traditionalism,* pp. 246–8.
[100] Ibid., p. 249.

in his own way, but in general there has been a failure in strong positional societies to speculate theoretically on how a vanguard ideologically dedicated to equality could become the world's most entrenched technobility. Surely, they puzzle, dedication to ideological tenets as a requisite for high office should in itself ensure a continuous process of soul-searching. It does not.

Institutional efficiency depends more on technical expertise than it does on ideological knowledge. There is, in all bureaucracies, a built-in tendency for technical ability to be favored, increasingly so as those who possess these skills move in ever larger numbers into positions of authority. In this process there is a point where dedication to equality becomes largely a formula for the lips rather than for the heart. This tendency, of course, is by no means restricted to societies with positional compliance ideologies. As bureaucracies have become entrenched in modern economies generally, the emergence of a self-serving technobility has become a feature of all societies in the modern phase of property relations.

In 1964 the ideas that had been promoted by Khrushchev for more egalitarian education were pushed aside in favor of meritocracy, the selection of the best students for elite schools.[101] Clearly, in the Soviet Union, the stress on technical expertise had become irreversible. What makes this fact of special and ironical interest is that by the late 1950s, 60–70 percent of the students in Moscow's institutes of higher education were from families of former officials or prerevolutionary intellectuals.[102] But why should this be a cause for wonderment? These groups, after all, ideology aside, are but the chrysalis of a new elite based on property.

Constraints in strong positional systems

In the early stages of strong positional compliance in the modern phase a rapid and substantial redistribution of income occurred as a consequence of the forcible nationalization of the assets of former property owners. The wealth thus obtained, however, was not distributed in a way designed to achieve income equality. As Charles Lindblom shows, wage and salary income in the USSR has at times been more unequal than in the United States or Great Britain.[103] Despite an avowed dedication to egalitarianism, therefore, positional societies are far from that ideal in practice. Moreover, the inequality that exists functions as a major mechanism for social control.

[101] Daniel Bell, *The Coming of Post-Industrial Society: A Venture in Social Forecasting* (New York: Basic Books, 1973), p. 104.
[102] Jeremy Azrael, *Managerial Power and Soviet Politics* (Cambridge, Mass.: Harvard University Press, 1966), p. 250 (cited in Andors, *China's Industrial Revolution*, p. 18).
[103] Charles E. Lindblom, *Politics and Markets: The World's Political-Economic Systems* (New York: Basic Books, 1977).

Among communist systems certain aspects of social life are widely shared. These include a stable vertical relationship between leaders and activists (i.e., an officially sponsored clientalist system), a distinction between activists and nonactivists, and a network of instrumental–personal ties through which nonactivists especially seek to influence superiors. This relationship pattern evolved not out of a history of conflict and bargaining among autonomous groups but, rather, in a familistic way with both followers and leaders linked by a web of mutual dependency. As in a family, the linkage does not imply equal power and responsibility. Superiors can and do manipulate need satisfaction with regard to vacations, leaves, and so on, and, critically, with regard to work assignments and income rewards.[104] Differences in income, therefore, through their manipulation within the framework of positional relationships, have played a critical role in constraining behavior.

In theory positional relationships are knitted together by a harmony of interests – among individuals and between the government and the people. Because of the web of interdependence, no need is said to exist for the legal protection of autonomy. Rights, therefore, primarily concern the obligations of the community toward the individual (e.g., to provide an education, to ensure full employment, etc.); those rights that underwrite the claims of individuals are not inalienable; they are, rather, set forth as privileges that can be modified. Individuals who break the bonds of harmony thus appear less worthy of the compassion that ideally informs relationships among community members.

Who would break these bonds? Initially it was presumed, as a matter of faith, that dissenting forces would include recalcitrant former elites from the discredited traditional phase as well as their modern successors, the elites of contractual compliance systems in the modern phase of property relations. Within strong positional societies the remnants of these elites, their offspring, their allies, and their recruits were thought certain to be opponents of the new system. Added to these, over time, would be the deluded and the backsliders. To protect itself against these powerful and malignant forces the new state would have no recourse but to reserve to itself the full right to root out and suppress its internal foes.

In the search for enemies positional societies have murdered not thousands but millions of their citizens. The record of repression is unmatched in its ferocity. So fearful were the consequences that all members of these communities were acutely concerned over the direction of prevailing political winds. Over time, dependency became mute subservience, matched against increasing levels of arbitrary power. As W. H. Chamberlin, an American correspondent in the USSR for twelve years in the early period of Bolshevik rule, said

---

[104] Walder, *Communist Neo-Traditionalism*, pp. 20–2, 164–5.

of the general political climate, that "socialism is certain to prove, in the beginning at least, the road NOT to freedom, but to dictatorship and counter-dictatorships, to civil war of the fiercest kind. Socialism achieved and maintained by democratic means seems definitely to belong to the world of utopias."[105]

In the evolution of strong contractual systems millions suffered. Yet the tragedy that accompanied their neglect is not remotely equal to the intentional slaughter, inflicted without compassion, that was visited upon the enemies of communism. For the leaders of strong positional societies the intimidation and liquidation of enemies was but a necessary aspect of progress that accorded with the historical need to mobilize the state in its drive for accumulation. Dictatorship thus controlled opposition, helped to achieve social transformation, and enforced the legitimacy of the party (and the class that this party claimed to represent) through the period of transition to the realization of ultimate moral ideals. Yet it has never been explained how the use of repressive politics will ever teach those who experience it to trust authority and to believe in dignity and equality in social relationships.

China's constitution confers upon its citizens the right to assemble, to speak, write, and publish freely, and to demonstrate. China's concept of human rights differs from the West's, however. When students demonstrated in December 1986 and early January 1987 (a harbinger of the 1989 Tiananmen demonstrations – and, I believe, of events yet to come) the government cracked down on what was perceived to be a threat to stability. Deng Xiaoping, once hailed as a socialist reformer, had this to say in a December 30, 1986, speech on halting the student demonstrations: "It won't do not to use dictatorial methods. As regards such methods, we must not only talk about them, but we must also use them in times of need."[106] And so they have.

Conclusion

The captains of industry and the fervent ideologues have slipped slowly into history. In their place is an elite never before seen, a technobility who draw their power from the bureaucratic institutions they lead. The central problem these leaders face is productivity and accumulation and how to structure institutions and societies efficiently to achieve these goals. The question facing societies is how to deal with a degree of elite power over resources that has never been seen before.

In the modern phase a central issue is the degree of equality in political and economic life. Leadership of institutions confers control over property,

[105] Cited in Hayek, *Road*, p. 28.
[106] "Deng's New Book Defends Use of Harsh Methods on Dissent," *Korea Herald*, March 21, 1987, p. 4.

which is then converted into elite status and into disproportionate influence within society. In this sense the technobility, albeit in different ways, violates possibilities for equality in both contractual and positional societies. Yet equality, to participate equally in political and social life and to be accorded equal consideration in terms of rewards and self-respect, is a basic moral precept in the modern phase that, when violated, arouses groups and individuals to action. As general prosperity grows, therefore, questions about how to arrange distributive transfers of wealth and power do not abate but take on different forms as excluded groups (e.g., women, religious minorities, political dissidents, etc.) demand their share.

A long umbilical cord, in the mind and in social life, links the past and the future. It is a cord that is never cut, even by revolutions. For modern contractual systems, for example, the initial thrust toward autonomy was against government power, the deadening hand of authority cloaked in the inviolable privileges of an aristocratic order. This dedication to autonomy remains powerful, especially in the form of support for privacy, but has been joined by other beliefs that soften it by arguing for government restriction of unlimited shareholder power and for government responsibility for the poor and hungry (68 percent of Americans now hold this belief).[107] Governments in these systems are increasingly expected to control disease and epidemics, to ensure the sale of pure food and drugs, to back occupational licensing laws, to guarantee fair employment and safe and reasonable conditions of labor, and so forth, all of which clearly violate the theory of a self-regulated, free and autonomous market. Yet the past is still there. In the United States, for example, although new beliefs about fairness have come into being, Americans nevertheless continue to see economic inequality as a source of variety and derive vicarious enjoyment from it.[108] They vigorously support pluralism, even though the extraordinary concentration of economic power in private institutions, closely linked with a highly bureaucratized and regulatory government, hardly fosters it. They do not see that pluralism, autonomy, and privacy are two-edged, providing protection against authority but also serving to justify and strengthen the status of the advantaged.

Strong positional systems are beset by their own incongruities. Although rhetorically dedicated to eliminating social and economic inequality, they have conspicuously failed to achieve this objective. Even in the fervent heyday of communism the Soviet Union was as much a welfare state laggard as was the United States.[109] But it is in the area of political equality that the discrepancies are most glaring. Marx and Engels did not say much about mechanisms of rule and did not foresee the persistence of group conflict in

---

[107] McClosky and Zaller, *American Ethos*, p. 274.
[108] Kluegel and Smith, *Beliefs*, p. 108.
[109] Wilensky, *Welfare State*, p. 102.

communist societies. They apparently saw little need to fashion a political theory that would reveal how equality of participation would arise from a transitional period of dictatorship. Their followers have tended to believe that the solution to this puzzle is to be found in changing people's values. This had led to an emphasis on ideological control, which only results in alienation from the ideology itself. What exists, instead, are highly calculating attitudes about authority, challenges within institutions that are based on hidden, factional loyalty, and mass participation that is voluntaristic only within limits that do not challenge the authority of elites.

Late in Mao Zedong's life, as he himself became increasingly despotic, he began to perceive the outlines of a phenomenon that has overwhelmed strong positional societies, revealing them to be not the revolutionary successors to contractual compliance but a variant with them in the modern phase. As new types of institutions have developed, the dominance of professional and technical classes has become apparent, as has the technobility as a new ruling group. Mao fought against the Chinese technobility, believing that continuously and intentionally destabilizing society would prevent their consolidation of control. He fought in vain for he mistakenly perceived them to be historically doomed adherents to capitalist values, rather than the inheritors of a new system of compliance.

The rise of a technobility and of a spirit of equality have gone hand in hand. Both are the product of the modern phase. For the technobility justifies its very rule by being the provider of equality of opportunity or of results. Change toward the emergent phase occurs, however, when people in the modern phase perceive the truncated nature of the moral obligations that are championed by the technobility. This perception is stimulated by the issue of unfulfilled equality. It is not too much to say, in fact, that in the modern phase the lack of care or autonomy in social life underlies a restless, unceasing quest for change.

IV

Change in compliance ideologies

7

Equality and conflict

In a query that rings with the predicament of the age George Gilder asks, "If socialism is dead, in some sense intellectually bankrupt, morally defunct, as they say, why does the capitalist vision seem to teeter so precariously over the same ash can of history?"[1] Into what far land, indeed, have the visions fled, leaving us with only expectation, surrounded as always by possibilities that lead us forward yet promise nothing?

Strong forms of contractual and positional compliance are grounded in the modern phase of property relations and derive their separate dreams for equality from the meanings of that phase. Yet both are but heralds of truncated ideals for they express powerful tendencies in the search for fulfillment rather than attainment itself. Each stands as a beckoning light, yet each simultaneously veils the full range of possibilities that exist.

Equality and morality

Discussions about the validity of a compliance ideology become intense during a change in phases. The content of social meanings is scrutinized in terms of an emergent evaluative structure. Much of the debate concerns inequality and focuses on the moral standards embodied in institutional rules. Equality as a moral issue comes to the forefront because of new possibilities for "reciprocal reversibility" that, in the Piagetian sense, accompany structural development. Questions about equality focus on the reciprocal quality of exchanges; rules that regulate differences in life-styles and opportunities, therefore, become topics for moral evaluation.

In formulating ideas about reciprocity the fundamental issue, as Douglas Rae has framed it, is not whether equality is desirable but which equality and for whom, for about these questions there is a great deal of argument.[2] Moreover, which inequalities are most unacceptable differs over time and

[1] George Gilder, *Wealth and Poverty* (New York: Basic Books, 1981), p. 3.
[2] Douglas Rae et al., *Equalities* (Cambridge, Mass.: Harvard University Press, 1981), p. 19.

place, as do the individuals or groups who confront each other in the search for solutions. In effect, both the issues and the contestants have changed historically in a manner that is complex and even contradictory.

In the modern world the search for reciprocity in exchange has had three major characteristics. First, there have been demands, not for absolute equality but for a juster distribution of the good things of life. This involves, as Verba found in his three-country study of Sweden, the United States, and Japan, persistent desires to reduce another group's income and influence if they are perceived as "too high."[3] Second, there has been a drive for accumulation. This drive would not enlist widespread support unless it was perceived as the underpinning for broadly shared prosperity. Third, there has been a search to define the meaning of equality and to incorporate that meaning into moral justifications for emergent patterns of compliance. This has involved, crucially, setting forth new legitimations for status hierarchies.

Conflict and the technobility

Although two decades after World War II less than one-sixth of the population of the world was absorbed as workers into modern economies,[4] the tendency to accept accumulation as a goal, to adopt, where possible, bureaucratic administrative styles, and to foster, however minimally, some education, health, and welfare programs, has been virtually universal.

The strength of the modern bureaucratic institution lies in its patterns of work organization. These foster enormous productivity, generating around the world many trillion dollars' worth of goods per year. The basis for this extraordinary, world-girdling power lies in technological development and the rational structuring of work procedures.

Knowledge regarding technology and how to apply it is the ultimate basis of authority (and privilege) within modern bureaucratic institutions. Although some are more specialized in this knowledge than others (staff versus line assignments), all elites are associated with knowledge generation, knowledge utilization, and opportunity generation.[5] What I have termed the technobility, therefore, is that group in modern societies who are at the peak of the technocratic strata that uses knowledge to supervise institutional activities and who, by their positions, control property. They are elite in the same way that others at different periods of history were also elite, by their predominant control over the total flow of economic activity, their ability to

[3] Sidney Verba et al., *Elites and the Idea of Equality: A Comparison of Japan, Sweden, and the United States* (Cambridge, Mass.: Harvard University Press, 1987), p. 221.

[4] John Hicks, *A Theory of Economic History* (Oxford: Clarendon Press, 1969), p. 159.

[5] John D. Montgomery, *Technology and Civic Life: Making and Implementing Development Decisions* (Cambridge, Mass.: MIT Press, 1974), p. 230.

regulate the distribution of rewards, and their influence on the formulation of symbolic justifications for inequality.

If control of institutional property is determined by access to, and use of, knowledge, then those who are less favored in this regard will have less influence and less affluence, in other words, they will be unequal in their ability to control property. In fact, as the technicality of modern economies increases, more rather than less premium is placed on knowledge and on preventing mindless interventions into technical matters by the uninformed. Concomitantly, increases in automation, far from making ordinary work more meaningful, often lead to greater lack of autonomy and feelings of powerlessness for subordinates.[6] Societies in the modern phase of property relations are thus caught in a situation where knowledge is essential for general accumulation but where, at the same time, its conversion into sophisticated technology weaves subtle threads of inequality throughout society.

Knowledge, however, is merely the skill base for the technobility. Its acquisition is required for elite status and for greater access to rewards; it does not, however define the types of rewards available nor the moral justifications for them. Equality questions, therefore, do not focus on knowledge per se. They are concerned instead with legitimations for status differences and with the institutional arrangements and symbolic justifications that support them. In strong contractual societies this has led to questions about the appropriate limits to private property, the ideological criteria that legitimize control of property, and the institutional forms used as mechanisms for elevation to elite status. In strong positional societies the questions have concerned political power, who is a legitimate member of the community, and the acceptable limits for mass participation and dissent.

Different paths of change

At any given time institutional arrangements provide clues to the structure and content of a compliance ideology and its trajectory of change. It is significant, for example, that the compliance ideology that came into being in Germany in the late nineteenth century did not mirror the strong contractual type of Britain's. Although a technobility existed and could be said, in fact, to have achieved a position of de facto predominance by the time of World War I, Germany's political culture was still deeply influenced by patterns from the traditional phase. Following defeat, the search for traditional positional certitudes in the Nazi glorification of hierarchy and race would have disastrous consequences. Strongly communitarian tendencies, albeit evolved, remain robust to this day. German companies, for instance, cannot make

[6] Graeme Salaman, *Work Organization and Class Structure* (Armonk, N.Y.: M. E. Sharpe, 1981), pp. 91–2.

major policy shifts without the approval of a board that includes community and worker representatives.[7] In a strongly contractual society like the United States, restraints on authority of this magnitude and nature are significantly less.

In Japan, as well, change in the modern phase has been on a trajectory that has conserved adherence to positional criteria. Individualism is not highly valued, although there is a growing trend toward concern with personal needs. In industrial employment there have been persistent calls, whose origins date back to World War I, for tripartite participation in the making of rules among employers, employees, and the state. There has also been a belief in the importance of establishing socially desirable minimum living – and working – standards and in providing protections for employees.[8] These allow Japanese workers to enjoy employment privileges that in Britain are restricted to the middle class.[9] Moreover, in comparison to the United States, the earnings gap between the top and bottom 10 percent of the population is a full 50 percent less.[10]

In contrast, the compliance ideologies of Britain and the United States are skewed toward contractual criteria. Britain, however, is less notable than the United States in this regard. From the 1830s on, in fact, the British government, acting against the pure dictates of the market, began to take a substantial interest in the oversight of public health, the regulation of work hours and employment conditions in factories and mines, the provision of housing for the working class, and so forth. At the start of the twentieth century, Britain began a national system of social insurance.[11] In America there has been far less flexibility regarding public welfare and government intervention (although politicians are less dogmatic than the general public in this regard).[12] Even as late (compared to Britain) as the 1930s, health insurance of any sort did not exist, the elderly had no income security to cushion the impact of old age, and hours of work for virtually everyone were long and arduous; a six-day work week was standard and a twelve-hour workday not uncommon.

[7] David Kairys, "Freedom of Speech," in *The Politics of Law: A Progressive Critique*, ed. David Kairys (New York: Pantheon, 1982), p. 167.

[8] Solomon B. Levine, "Management and Labor in the Japanese Economy," in *Tradition and Creativity: Essays on East Asian Civilization*, ed. Ching-I Tu (New Brunswick, N.J.: Transaction Books, 1987), p. 158.

[9] Salaman, *Work Organization*, p. 186.

[10] Lester C. Thurow, *The Zero-Sum Society: Distribution and the Possibilities for Economic Change* (New York: Basic Books, 1980), pp. 7–8.

[11] Keith Thomas, "The United Kingdom," in *Crises of Political Development in Europe and the United States*, ed. Raymond Grew (Princeton, N.J.: Princeton University Press, 1978), p. 77.

[12] Gordon J. Di Renzo, "Politicians and Personality: A Cross-Cultural Perspective," in *A Psychological Examination of Political Leaders*, ed. Margaret G. Herman with Thomas W. Milburn (New York: Free Press, 1977), p. 163.

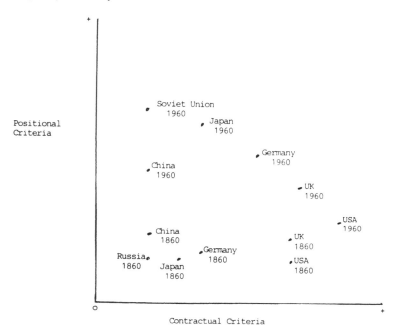

Figure 5. Changes in compliance ideologies over time for selected countries.

Although Marxism stressed the autonomy and free development of individuals, communist societies have been characterized by an extraordinary exaltation of positional criteria. Their path of development involved an attack on traditional values carried out with ruthless enthusiasm; in this process, however, a romantic nostalgia for the unity of encompassing hierarchy continued into the modern phase in the form of a relentless suppression of individualism and an equally unbending emphasis on communitarianism. This process of forced development is only slowly abating, noted by efforts in a number of former communist countries to eliminate party influence and increase individual legal security.[13]

The ways that the compliance ideologies of selected countries have changed is shown in Figure 5. The positions given are, of course, hypothetical, based on my own best judgment. Of more importance than precise location is the general direction of change and the comparative differences among societies.

[13] Richard Lowenthal, "Development vs. Utopia in Communist Policy," in *Change in Communist Systems,* ed. Chalmers Johnson (Stanford, Calif.: Stanford University Press, 1970), pp. 112–13.

Obstructing transvaluation

Although change in the compliance ideologies of societies has been marked in the modern world, it does not take place without stress and conflict. Indeed, as in ancient Greece, warfare has been endemic and civil strife a brutal reality (in 1988 alone, thirty-two wars were in progress around the globe).[14] Edward Buehrig estimates that in the thirty years following the greatest cataclysm of all, World War II, there have been 265 major domestic and international conflicts with a death toll probably greater than the 15 million battle deaths of that war. The number of people displaced as refugees has also been estimated at 15 million.[15] Taken together, these figures are larger than the entire population of virtually any member state of the United Nations. The United States, whose citizens think of themselves as peaceful, has been no outsider in this process. According to two observers, there were 215 occasions during the same thirty-year period when Americans resorted to military "force without war."[16]

In the process of change to the modern phase, markedly conflictual political economies came into being. Polities developed that encouraged universal participation without, however, granting equality of influence; this inequality was related to a drive for accumulation that placed a premium on extraction of resources from the agricultural sector and its partial redistribution (some being retained for investment purposes) to a developing urban industrial sector. In societies that emphasized contractual criteria, there was economic inequality in the form of a highly pyramidal income and wealth distribution. In societies that emphasized positional criteria, the effort to reduce economic inequality led to a sharply pyramidal distribution of political power.

In both cases there have been efforts to redress inequality by shifting to a new balance between positional and contractual criteria. Intense opposition to such change is generated, however, by two forces. On the one hand, there are those who self-consciously participate in the political or economic exploitation of others and who perceive change as a threat to their own privileges. These defensive reactions are sometimes nakedly self-interested. On the other hand, compliance ideologies justify inequalities (i.e., status differences) in terms of moral criteria that also serve as the bases of solidarity. Hence, many who are least well served, as well as elites, are susceptible to mobilization to conservative political activity by claims that change is immoral.

---

[14] Arthur Schlesinger, Jr., "The Opening of the American Mind," *New York Times*, sec. 7, July 23, 1989, p. 26 (citing a report by the Santa Barbara Peace Resource Center).

[15] Edward H. Buehrig, *The Perversity of Politics* (London: Croom Helm, 1986), p. 7.

[16] Joshua Cohen and Joel Rogers, *On Democracy: Toward a Transformation of American Society* (New York: Penguin Books, 1983), p. 37.

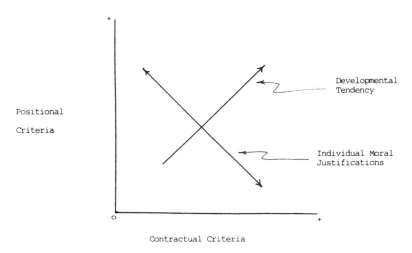

Figure 6. Schematic of the force vectors prompting transvaluation.

There are forces in every society, however, that seek to change the prevailing balance between contractual and positional criteria. In the long view, these efforts have resulted in redefinitions of social relationships toward greater equality. In the shorter view, however, a time span that can be several centuries in length, change has been contested, often violently, by conservative forces of great strength. The contest pits society against society and group against group (defined by class, religion, ethnicity, region, etc.), often in bloody encounters of horrifying magnitude. A highly schematic rendition of the forces prompting change is given in Figure 6.

"Deep seated preferences," said Justice Holmes, "cannot be argued about."[17] The debate about change takes place in an environment charged with mistrust about motives. There is a persistent belief, more powerful, it has been suggested, in the political than in the economic realm, that someone's gain is sure to be someone else's loss.[18] In the women's liberation movement, for example, many believe that an increment for women is automatically a decrement for men, even though no evidence from the actual history of the movement supports such a view.[19] Positional and contractual criteria are often counterpoised despite the fact that an advance on one

[17] Schlesinger, "Opening of the American Mind," p. 27.
[18] Sidney Verba and Gary R. Orren, "Political and Economic Equality: A Theoretical and Empirical Comparison," in *Global Dilemmas*, ed. Samuel P. Huntington and Joseph S. Nye, Jr. (Boston: Center for International Affairs, Harvard University, and University Press of America, 1985), pp. 80, 82.
[19] Nancy Datan, "Male and Female: The Search for Synthesis," in *Dialectic: Humanistic Rationale for Behavior and Development*, ed. J. F. Rychlak (Basel: S. Karger, 1976), pp. 49–50.

dimension need not occur at the expense of the other. That such a possibility is not widely apprehended is probably because justifications for *elite* status are pegged to a particular distribution of meanings at the social level. An effort to shift these meanings is thus likely to be perceived as a direct violation of the "appropriate" moral underpinning of a status hierarchy.[20]

The search to redefine compliance ideologies is thus challenged by what Friedman calls the "zone of deep defense."[21] Normative reinterpretations are matched by calls for normative unity. In the United States, for example, the private property system and the hegemony of individualism stand guard at the gates of America's compliance system. There is, as it were, a constant tug-of-war between those Americans who feel that change has gone too far and those who feel it has not gone far enough.

In the sections that follow, this pattern of confrontation is mapped for strong contractual and strong positional compliance systems in the modern phase of property relations. Ideas and practices that are congruent with "strong" beliefs are contrasted with those that are dissonant and the possibilities for change analyzed. It will be left to the final chapter to discuss the resolution of these contending forces. At that time it will be pointed out how the only way to avoid continuous confrontation is for the opposing sides to coordinate their objectives by redefining the moral bases of institutional life.[22]

Values and institutions in American society

The shibboleths that support strong contractual compliance do not stand up well to scrutiny. The belief that wealth is the product of personal merit and achievement is belied by the exceptionally weak probability (only .00002) that any single individual below the magic top 1 percent of wealth holders will ever be able to move into that group.[23] Despite a historical record of unparalleled success in accumulation, relative inequality in America today is not far different than it was two hundred years ago (although it was worse at other times in between).[24] Indeed, the lowest one-fifth of the American population receives a smaller percentage of after-tax income than the same quin-

---

[20] Lawrence M. Friedman, *Law and Society: An Introduction* (Englewood Cliffs, N.J.: Prentice-Hall, 1977), p. 102.

[21] Ibid., p. 167.

[22] Fred Hirsch, *Social Limits to Growth* (Cambridge, Mass.: Harvard University Press, 1976), p. 10.

[23] Ronald Chester, *Inheritance, Wealth, and Society* (Bloomington: Indiana University Press, 1982), p. 8.

[24] Jeffrey G. Williamson and Peter H. Lindert, *American Inequality: A Macroeconomic History* (New York: Academic Press, 1980), p. 5.

tile in Japan, Sweden, Norway, Canada, Germany, the Netherlands, the United Kingdom, and France.[25] Taxes to reduce inequality are said to reduce incentives to achieve; in fact, they don't do so at all. When taxes go up, some people still work very hard and some don't.[26]

Although the record on income equality is poor compared to other industrial nations, it would be even worse without direct transfer payments (amounting by the late 1970s to more than $224 billion or 10 percent of the gross national product).[27] This means that the private institutions of American society have not shown great regard for reducing distributional gaps. Were it not for government-supported direct income transfers since World War II, earnings would have become much more unequal.[28] It speaks to the strength of the American commitment to their compliance ideology, therefore, that there is consistent opposition to a guaranteed minimum income (President Nixon proposed this in 1970 and was turned down) and to any ceiling on incomes (this is combined, however, with support across all levels for guaranteeing jobs in order that people may *earn* a minimum income).[29]

As might be expected, however, there is wide disagreement about the appropriate size of distribution gaps (if not about inequality in general) and persistent beliefs that all is not well with the stratification order or with the workings of equality of opportunity.[30] There is an inchoate sense that the principle of limitation as set forth by John Stuart Mill is being violated (i.e., that private interests should not be pursued to the point where they invade the rights and liberties of others).[31] Many believe that corporations and the rich really run the country, that the rich don't pay their fair share of taxes, and that the laws mostly favor the well-to-do. Fully 82 percent believe that big business has too much power.[32] In 1976 a Harris survey revealed that 63 percent agreed with the statement that "most people with power try to take advantage of people such as myself."[33] The defenseless are not hard to find. In Boston, not a large city, it is estimated that more than seven thousand men, women, and children are homeless and live on the streets.[34]

---

[25] Cohen and Rogers, *On Democracy*, p. 30.   [26] Thurow, *Zero-Sum Society*, p. 168.
[27] Chester, *Inheritance, Wealth, and Society*, p. 168.
[28] Thurow, *Zero-Sum Society*, pp. 159, 166.
[29] Sidney Verba and Gary R. Orren, *Equality in America: The View from the Top* (Cambridge, Mass.: Harvard University Press, 1985), p. 80.
[30] James R. Kluegel and Eliot R. Smith, *Beliefs About Inequality: Americans' Views of What Is and What Ought to Be* (New York: Aldine De Gruyter, 1986), p. 291.
[31] Louis O. Kelso and Mortimer J. Adler, *The Capitalist Manifesto* (New York: Random House, 1958), p. 85.
[32] Herbert McClosky and John Zaller, *The American Ethos: Public Attitudes Toward Capitalism and Democracy* (Cambridge, Mass.: Harvard University Press, 1984), pp. 177, 178.
[33] Cited in Michael Parenti, *Democracy for the Few* (New York: St. Martin's, 1977), p. 43.
[34] John Maddock, "Homeless Stage Holiday Protest," *Boston Globe*, July 5, 1986, p. 58.

Although historically Americans have rejected state intervention, there have been important bursts of regulatory activity, fueled in the first part of this century by intense dislike of big business and a growing feeling that only the government could balance business influence. This occurred with the antitrust laws at the turn of the century, with support for unions, for increases in social welfare spending, for agricultural price supports in the 1930s, and with the education, environment, and race-and-gender-equality laws that were passed in the post–World War II period. Some notable leaders were in the forefront of the effort to use government power to further social ends. Woodrow Wilson was one. Far more famous, however, was Franklin D. Roosevelt; as early as 1913 he fought on the floor of the New York State Senate for government control of the state's water resources and its hydro-electric potential.[35]

Over time, government intervention has shown a persistent, steady increase at all levels, bolstered by public sentiments that favor establishing minimum standards of personal well-being and the correction of social and economic injustices.[36] Consumer protection, for example, is provided by occupational licensing laws (for lawyers, embalmers, barbers, doctors, plumbers, etc.). The government regulates activity in numerous areas through such agencies as the Tennessee Valley Authority, the Port of New York Authority, the Federal Reserve System, the Federal Communications Commission, and the Postal Service, among others. In fact, sixteen federal regulatory agencies were created from 1930 to 1945, ten more were added in the next twenty years, and twenty-nine more were added in the following decade.[37] Although those in public employment in America, as a percentage of the total working population, are fewer than in the major European societies (U.S. 18.8 percent, Germany 25.8 percent, France 29.1 percent, and Britain 31.7 percent), the federal government nevertheless employed three million civilians by the middle of the post–World War II period and accounted for more than one-fifth of the gross national product.[38]

Some regulatory activity was born of a need to support business activities (e.g., trade regulations). Other activity, however, clearly springs from a genuine desire to alleviate pain and suffering and to check what are perceived to be flagrant abuses. Benefits for the aged, work safety legislation, minimum wages, unemployment compensation, promotion of full employment, bans

---

[35] Ralph F. De Bedts, *The New Deal's SEC: The Formative Years* (New York: Columbia University Press, 1964), p. 194.

[36] McClosky and Zaller, *American Ethos*, p. 302.

[37] Cohen and Rogers, *On Democracy*, p. 113.

[38] Edward C. Page, *Political Authority and Bureaucratic Power: A Comparative Analysis* (Knoxville: University of Tennessee Press, 1985), p. 14; Louis Galambos (with the assistance of Barbara Barrow Spence), *The Public Image of Big Business in America, 1880–1940: A Quantitative Study in Social Change* (Baltimore: Johns Hopkins University Press, 1975), p. 4.

on child labor, and controls on the stock exchange all give evidence of altruistic concern for the disadvantaged. Although the super-rich have legal mechanisms at their disposal for maintaining their children's privileged economic status (inheritance transfers), formal class barriers have been anathema since the abolition of slavery (indeed, less than one-half of upper-middle-class children will, as adults, be part of the affluent upper one-fifth).[39] Public attitudes have increasingly supported racial equality and freedom of speech;[40] there has also been a general willingness on the part of the working population to support sharp increases in social security deductions for the benefit of the aged. Needs defined as public interest are being articulated by a new type of special-interest group; these include Common Cause and Ralph Nader's public interest research organization, as well as universities.

Redefinitions of the status of women in American life are indicative of trends toward greater concern for others. Data indicate that over time both men and women have come to reject a priori limitations on women's opportunity.[41] Gains have been achieved largely by persistent persuasion backed by moral arguments against inequality. These arguments have been double-barreled. On the one hand, there has been a call to redefine positional criteria such that gender in itself is not the basis for being excluded from full participation in community life. On the other hand, there has been a demand for a redefinition of contractual criteria to permit greater respect for the private rights of women in areas such as family planning, sexual harassment, rape, pornography, and so on.

Clearly claims by disadvantaged groups for full equality have become increasingly acceptable. The idea that property ownership in itself should largely define status and privilege is slowly giving way to a conception of status based on personal integrity in a community that is without particularistic requirements for membership; the trend is indicated by data showing that the young, in contrast to their elders, especially support both political equality and welfare measures.[42] There is an increased perception of the need for government programs, especially as they relate to removing barriers to participation and opportunity. Moreover, fully 60 percent of those questioned in a recent poll (including 49 percent Republicans) said they would support increased spending for social programs even if it meant paying more in taxes.[43]

There is no support, however, for socialism as such. The ideal remains going into business for oneself, using one's own ideas, and keeping what one

[39] Christopher Jencks et al., *Inequality: A Reassessment of the Effect of Family and Schooling in America* (New York: Basic Books, 1972), p. 216.

[40] McClosky and Zaller, *American Ethos*, p. 298.

[41] Kluegel and Smith, *Beliefs*, p. 232.   [42] McClosky and Zaller, *American Ethos*, pp. 192, 297.

[43] Lance Morrow, "A Change in the Weather," *Time* 129, no. 13 (March 30, 1987): 27 (poll of 1,014 people taken for *Time* by Yankelovich Clancy Shulman).

makes for oneself. Even when workers are in worker-owned and worker-managed enterprises, no affinity develops for broader socialistic relationships or a more egalitarian and cooperative society. Indeed, there is no evidence that the workers want these institutions run democratically from top to bottom. Attitudes about egalitarianism, such as they are, do not extend beyond the enterprise to include other persons and institutions. While informal cooperative arrangements do develop, and attitudes of mutuality and group responsibility do emerge to an "impressive degree," the self-managed enterprise is still thought of as appropriately located within a system of market capitalism.[44]

Something has happened, however, to the dream of going it alone. The small-scale, self-run enterprise continues in America, but it has been superseded in influence by the powerful bureaucratic organization. Still, the belief continues that somehow the old life is redeemable and can be shared by all. Advertising and popular mythology alike tout the virtues of, and the rewards for being, the self-made person. Yet the environment is not the same as it once was, and the frustration of those who cannot share in the dream is increasing. Especially among the young there is a growing feeling that opportunity in general is less prevalent.[45] These feelings, to the extent that they grow and persist, will clearly become a major factor in how equality is perceived in the future.

Changing patterns of law and regulation in America

Laws and regulations are the formal expression of a compliance ideology. From them important themes that underly social meanings can be extracted. They also reveal the contradictions that afflict compliance ideologies as they are transformed. In this regard, change can be noted in two ways: by legal or regulatory arrangements that establish a new way of doing something; and by actions that block or undo some established arrangement.[46] Frequently, of course, the two go hand in hand.

For the citizens of contractual societies the ideal is one of free private persons who have equal political rights, are equal subjects of civil law, and have equality of opportunity to acquire and control property. As this ideal came to be fulfilled, however, there developed oligarchic structures within the economic institutions of society *alongside* extensive participation in political life by adult white males only. Equality for others was long denied. For example,

---

[44] Joseph Raphael Blasi, *Employee Ownership Through ESOPs: Implications for the Public Corporation* (New York: Pergamon Press, 1987), p. 34; Edward S. Greenberg, "Industrial Self-Management and Political Attitudes," *American Political Science Review* 75, no. 1 (March 1981): 31, 33, 35, 38, 41.

[45] Kluegel and Smith, *Beliefs*, p. 51. [46] Friedman, *Law and Society*, p. 162.

although the Women's Rights Convention of 1845 approved a Declaration of Sentiments that stated it is "self-evident that all men and women are created equal," serious impediments to equality continued to exist for many decades for women as well as for blacks and other minorities.[47]

Yet as oligarchic power grew in scope in the second half of the nineteenth century, so also did attempts to restrain it, fueled by popular dislike and mistrust of concentrations of power, and by criticisms of business power that have been a persistent theme in American history. As early as 1877 property rights came into question in a legal case involving the right of the State of Illinois to regulate the rates charged by a private warehouse. In *Munn v. Illinois*, Chief Justice Morrison R. Waite found that property "affected with a public interest" ceases to be purely private.[48] In the Progressive Era, from 1900–1916, a sizable body of regulations was introduced (sometimes, to be sure, at the behest of the largest corporations, who wanted them in order to weaken competitors) covering food and drugs, banking, meat packing, and so on. The ostensible intent of such regulations was to protect consumers from harmful business practices. The first major restriction on individual control over property was imposed by a constitutional amendment in 1913 permitting a progressive income tax (income taxes as such, however, had been first levied, temporarily, during the Civil War).

Economic collapse in 1929 accelerated trends toward regulation. Although Congress had, for three decades, dismissed efforts to harness the power of financial and corporate interests on the nation's exchanges, regulation was finally instituted by the establishment of the SEC (Securities and Exchange Commission). As might be expected, the motives for doing this were mixed. Joseph Kennedy, the first chairman of the SEC, felt government regulation was needed to prevent uncontrolled economic individualism from wrecking the capitalist system.[49] At the same time that individual and corporate financial power was being restrained, an unprecedented attempt was being made by government to intervene in the "natural" ebb and flow of the economy. A National Recovery Act was passed in 1933 but was struck down (largely unlamented) by the Supreme Court in May 1935. More successful was the effort to make labor the equal of capital. Under the aegis of the National Labor Relations Board union membership more than doubled between 1935 and 1947 (although it later declined when many members, with their rights in the larger society secured, sought release from what they perceived to be an overemphasis on union-dictated positional criteria).[50]

These trends have accelerated in the post–World War II period and, despite retrenchments, are not likely to abate. The thrust of change follows two

[47] Verba and Orren, *Equality*, p. 30.
[48] George C. Lodge, *The New American Ideology* (New York: Knopf, 1975), p. 199.
[49] De Bedts, *New Deal's SEC*, pp. 99, 203–4.   [50] Verba and Orren, *Equality*, p. 42.

directions. On the one hand, there is an assault on autonomous power groups in the name of an expanded definition of community rights. On the other hand, there is a reassertion (and redefinition) of contractual criteria in the area of privacy rights. Both these movements have significantly modified strong contractual compliance.

Disadvantaged groups in America have increasingly challenged the justifications for their lower status. On May 17, 1954, in *Brown v. Board of Education*, the Supreme Court overthrew the doctrine of "separate but equal." From this point on, separate facilities deliberately based on race were judged to be inherently unequal. The civil rights movement in the 1960s brought further attention to substantive and procedural issues that denied equality. In the realm of politics, passage of the Voting Rights Act of 1965 was a major factor in stimulating blacks to engage in political activity. In the area of gender, although physical differences between the sexes have been consistently held by the courts as an appropriate basis for differential treatment (e.g., military combat roles), there has been an effort to reduce purely gender-based discrimination. Justice Potter Stewart emphasized this point in his concurring opinion, given in 1981, in *Michael M. v. Sonoma County* (a decision upholding California's statutory rape law). Said he, in part, "Gender-based classifications may not be based upon administrative convenience or upon archaic assumptions about the proper role of the sexes."[51]

Other groups have also had their status as full citizens affirmed. Congress, for example, recently recognized that anti-Japanese sentiment in 1941 had resulted in a severe violation of the constitutional rights of Americans of Japanese ancestry. In fact, there has, in general, been a redefinition of what constitutes treason and sedition. Over the last quarter-century both Congress and the Courts have largely concurred that ideological dissent and disloyalty are not to be automatically paired. There are current efforts in the House of Representatives to repeal the ideological provisions of the 1952 McCarran-Walter Immigration Act.[52]

Many laws no longer safeguard a system of strong contractual compliance. Autonomous institutions are increasingly hedged by government restrictions on their activities, often prompted by citizen initiative. When Ralph Nader wrote *Unsafe at Any Speed* one result was the National Highway Safety Act of 1965. Many decry the litigiousness of American society, yet class action suits, about discrimination, air and water pollution, and the like, are ways ordinary people obtain an increased role in dispute resolution and a lever for moving a political system that often seems slow and indifferent. Within gov-

---

[51] Nadine Taub and Elizabeth M. Schneider, "Perspectives on Women's Subordination and the Role of Law" in Kairys, ed., *Politics of Law*, pp. 125, 131, 133.

[52] John A. Scanlan, "Why the McCarran–Walter Act Must Be Amended," *Acadame* 73, no. 5 (September–October 1987): 5.

ernment itself special task forces and political action committees (PACs – which have grown tremendously as a consequence of legislation in 1974) have spurred responsiveness. In 1973, for example, a task force on land use headed by Laurance S. Rockefeller (whose extraordinary inherited wealth was derived from a system of unrestricted property rights), advised President Nixon that development rights on private property should rest with the community rather than with property owners.[53]

As the law has groped toward a redefinition of compliance criteria, there have been efforts to redefine the appropriate limits for autonomy. On the one hand, this has involved restricting the definition of constitutional protection of individual liberty. Regulations regarding noise, smoking, and drunken driving all concern a definition of limits. So also do codes of ethical behavior adopted by professional groups. The Supreme Court has addressed issues of this nature that concern freedom of expression (*Tinker v. Des Moines Independent School District*) and freedom of the press (*New York Times v. The United States* – also known as the Pentagon Papers case). Constitutional issues regarding liberty have been especially tested in the area of unreasonable searches and seizures, presumptively prevented by the Bill of Rights. Supreme Court cases involving this issue include *Mapp v. Ohio* and *TLO v. State of New Jersey*. Nowhere is this issue more lively than in questions concerning seizures sponsored by prohibition and drug laws. In May 1988, for example, the Court decided 6 to 2 that the police have a right to search through a person's garbage for evidence in drug-related cases.

Such searches touch on privacy rights, a major area of concern regarding autonomy. This problem is new in the sense that common law precedents do not recognize a legal right to privacy. Yet since 1890, when Louis D. Brandeis and his partner, Samuel D. Warren, outraged by sensational accounts of the wedding of a prominent senator's daughter, wrote an article for the *Harvard Law Review* entitled, "The Right to Privacy," it has become a major issue.[54] In 1905 the Supreme Court of Georgia was the first to recognize a right to privacy, followed by most other states. This culminated in the federal Privacy Act of 1974, which, as approved, applied only to federal agencies and private organizations doing business with the government. Concomitant efforts, part of the overall private rights issue, involve forcing government to allow public access to information that it holds. Sunshine laws, beginning with an 1898 Utah statute, have now become a fixed and universal feature of the judicial landscape.

Concern about privacy has increased hand in hand with the government's regulatory power (not least of all with regard to the Internal Revenue Ser-

---

[53] Lodge, *New American Ideology*, p. 201.
[54] Stephen Labaton, "Privacy: A Definition Is Evolving Case by Case," *New York Times*, June 5, 1988, sec. 4, p. 32.

vice). It has also risen as a consequence of computer-related technological improvements that appear infinitely capable of monitoring the social characteristics, opinions, and activities of citizens.[55] The consequence has been a legitimate fear of harm done by insensitive and powerful bureaucrats; these feelings reflect a centuries-old fear of governmental power. Senator Sam Erwin surely echoed these sentiments when speaking of the Privacy Act, which he, and the Constitutional Rights subcommittee he chaired, had labored to pass. Said he, "The Privacy Act, if enforced, would be a pretty good thing. But the government doesn't like it. Government has an insatiable appetite for power, and it will not stop usurping power unless it is restrained by laws they cannot repeal or nullify. There are mighty few laws they cannot nullify."[56]

Elite responses in American society

By and large most elites in America would subscribe to the ideal set forth by Theodore Roosevelt that "no matter what his occupation, his race, or his religious belief, [a man] is entitled to be treated on his worth as a man, and neither favored nor discriminated against because of an accident in his position."[57] Virtually all support democratic values and most the values of the welfare state as well.[58] In their work many have strived to humanize management patterns and to create better working conditions and relations. Notwithstanding, income inequality has increased since World War II (and in Britain, France, Germany, and Japan as well),[59] and there are sharp differences among leadership groups regarding government responsibility for helping the poor, enforcing affirmative employment, and so on (e.g., among elites, business, Republican, and farm leaders are the least egalitarian). [60]

Not everything about government, of course, is disliked. Companies involved with defense contracts have often been quite enthusiastic about that aspect of government spending. Yet although some specific programs and regulations are favored, business elites in general support the virtues associated with strong contractual compliance and are suspicious of programs that threaten them. A belief that the government should help those in distress, for

[55] David Burnham, *The Rise of the Computer State* (New York: Random House, 1980, 1982, 1983), pp. 88, 108, 196–7, 205; Arthur R. Miller, *The Assault on Privacy: Computers, Data Banks, and Dossiers* (Ann Arbor: University of Michigan Press, 1971), pp. 26, 32, 172.

[56] Burnham, *Rise of the Computer State*, pp. 196, 224.

[57] J. R. Pole, *The Pursuit of Equality in American History* (Berkeley and Los Angeles: University of California Press, 1978), p. 218.

[58] McClosky and Zaller, *American Ethos*, pp. 294–5, 300.

[59] Manus I. Midlarsky, "Scarcity and Inequality: Prologue to the Onset of Mass Revolution," *Journal of Conflict Resolution* 26, no. 1 (March 1982): 33.

[60] Verba and Orren, *Equality*, pp. 105, 134.

example, declines in the face of reminders about individualism and self-reliance. Only a minority (9 percent) see poverty as the fault of the economic system (versus 76 percent of feminist leaders and 86 percent of black leaders).[61] Oddly, business elites are also the least likely to acknowledge that they have powerful political influence.[62] Truly, as the Chinese proverb says, the fish are the last to discover the water.

The best work on elite ideas about equality has been done by Sidney Verba and Gary R. Orren. Their work shows that leadership groups in general tend to deny their own influence (this is as true of labor as it is of business), and all would like to see a considerable rearrangement of the perceived influence hierarchy. But how this should be done is another question. Business leaders, for example, believe their status should go up and labor's down, but labor leaders feel exactly the opposite. Regarding income disparities there is somewhat less confusion and emotion; all would leave the income hierarchy intact, although with modifications in the distribution gaps.[63]

A general feeling shared by elite groups is that incomes should reflect differences in talent and effort and that business executives should be at the top of the income hierarchy. Business leaders, however, are the only group stating that the income gap between themselves and others should be greater than what they believe exists. The size of the gap, in fact, is a matter of some dispute. Big-business leaders in America believe that a proper earning ratio between top and bottom should be 26 to 1 (in Sweden the comparable group says 4.7 to 1).[64] Only 34 percent of low-income respondents, however, believe the pay for manual workers is "about right, considering the amount of skill involved" (versus 69 percent of high-income respondents).[65] By and large the great majority feel those at the top should get less. Lee A. Iacocca's remuneration in 1986 of $20.5 million was clearly in a class by itself, being $8 million higher than the next highest and way ahead of the average compensation for top executives of $1,019,226 (counting in bonuses and long-term incentive compensation). Still, Owen F. Bieber, president of the United Auto Workers, when speaking of Iacocca's earnings, undoubtedly spoke for many Americans in their general sentiments about executive pay. Said he, "No one individual can possibly be wòrth that much money to a corporation. Compensation like this sends the wrong message, a message of greed and complacency."[66]

[61] Ibid., pp. 73, 75.   [62] Verba, et al., *Elites*, p. 264.
[63] Verba and Orren, *Equality*, pp. 177, 190–3, 204; Verba and Orren, "Political and Economic Equality," in Huntington and Nye, *Global Dilemmas*, pp. 90, 97, 102.
[64] Verba and Orren, *Equality*, pp. 159, 165, 256.
[65] McClosky and Zaller, *American Ethos*, p. 154.
[66] John A. Byrne, "Executive Pay: Who Got What in '86," *International Business Week* 2995–325 (May 4, 1987): 51, 53. For an interesting tabulation of incomes, see David Harrop, *America's Paychecks: Who Makes What* (New York: Facts on File, 1980).

Conservatism in contractual compliance

Disputes about the moral quality of compliance ideologies center on the pre-vailing justifications for the distribution of influence and affluence. As tech-nology drives institutional change, there is pressure to reassess long-cherished goals and procedures. The questions are stimulated by a gnawing doubt that what has been touted as just, substantively and procedurally, is not so. Yet questions are often raised in a context of fierce opposition that undermines any assurance of a predetermined outcome.

In the United States powerful groups support the values that undergird private property over those that pertain to democracy (in fact, the relation-ship between the two sets of values is unequivocally inverse).[67] In a number of states, courses designed to instill support for the free enterprise system are required in high schools; in these courses capitalism and political freedom are explicitly equated. Open criticism of "free enterprise" is often not well received despite overwhelming support in theory for freedom of speech. For many, indeed, free speech really means freedom to speak in support of ma-jority views. It is, after all, William H. Rehnquist, Chief Justice of the Supreme Court, who, as an assistant attorney general in the Nixon admin-istration, rejected the contention that the right to free speech was stifled be-cause a person's political activities were placed under surveillance.[68]

Although greater income equality is desired by some groups, there is nev-ertheless strong majority opposition to redistributive policies, including di-rect income transfers and welfare. There is simply no strong support for the government's making incomes more equal or, indeed, limiting the amount of money an individual should be allowed to earn. Absolutely nothing suggests that people want increased government regulation of the economy or that they believe socialism would be better than the system that exists. There is, in short, deep-seated conservatism toward any major economic reform. In-stead, Americans wholeheartedly endorse the idea that reward should be geared to the quality and scarcity of economic skills and that competing with others is a good thing because it keeps a person on his toes.[69] Hence, lower-status minority groups have only themselves to blame because the system it-self functions quite adequately.

The government should intervene, it is thought, only if the system fails to give groups an equal chance. Thus, welfare programs, hiring quotas, and guaranteed minimum incomes are opposed while antidiscrimination laws and minority job-training programs are not. What this means is that there is little sentiment for a direct assault on things as they are. Kluegel and Smith,

---

[67] McClosky and Zaller, *American Ethos*, p. 162.
[68] Ibid., pp. 36, 41; Burnham, *Rise of the Computer State*, p. 37.
[69] McClosky and Zaller, *American Ethos*, pp. 110, 120, 135, 151.

from their data, note "a pattern of majority support for programs that involve changing individuals to fit the existing stratification order and majority opposition to programs that appear to call for change in the stratification order itself."[70]

At present the opponents of economic inequality seem unable to stir up the kind of sentiment that animated the country in the 1890s and the 1930s. The media give little serious and sustained attention to income and wealth inequalities and to measures that would decrease them. How many Americans have even heard of a net worth tax, which many European democracies impose (and which would yield approximately $40 billion)?[71] Relatively unrestricted inheritance has been an issue since the days when it was attacked by Theodore Roosevelt and Andrew Carnegie, but it isn't one that generates heated concern. Indeed, the Economic Recovery Tax Act of 1981 went in the other direction by providing for a massive decrease in estates subject to tax. There is simply no popular constituency in this area.[72] Tax reform itself, of course, has been an issue, and reforms were instituted in 1986. Yet as far as incomes are concerned the wealthy were hardly penalized. For those earning between $70,000 and $150,000 the tax rate was 33 percent, versus 28 percent for those whose income was below $70,000; if more than $150,000 was earned, however, the rate reverted to 28 percent. Efforts in 1990 to change this provision were successful but only in the sense that those earning more than $70,000 would all be taxed at the same percentage rate (31 percent). Progressiveness in the tax rate was clearly rejected.

Political awareness does not necessarily lead to greater support for change. For those who are comfortable with order and stability the possibility of change may, in fact, stimulate resistance.[73] Indeed, among families that enjoy a substantial discretionary income, paying more for social programs (e.g., welfare) may seem an unwarranted attachment of fairly earned reward. People with such incomes now constitute a majority of the population.[74] These sentiments often go hand in hand with a perception of government as overly bureaucratic and a destroyer of individual initiative. Interestingly, these feelings may be most intense among workers who see the dream of working for themselves slowly slipping from their grasp.

Positional values and institutions

Since their beginnings as revolutionary movements (e.g., from the time of Lenin's "What Is to Be Done?" in 1902), there has been an internal political

[70] Kluegel and Smith, *Beliefs*, p. 212.   [71] Chester, *Inheritance*, p. 7.
[72] Ibid., pp. 60, 171.   [73] McClosky and Zaller, *American Ethos*, p. 284.
[74] Burdett A. Loomis and Allan J. Cigler, "Introduction: The Changing Nature of Interest Group Politics," in *Interest Group Politics*, 2nd ed., ed. Allan J. Cigler and Burdett A. Loomis (Washington, D.C.: Congressional Quarterly Press, 1986), p. 15.

debate in Communist Parties about the appropriate balance between discipline and unity, on the one hand, and free participation and openness on the other. In the economic realm the debate has centered on plan versus market, on the desirability of centralized decision-making regarding resource allocation, production targets, and so on, versus some variant of market socialism involving pricing, savings, wages and the like.

In Communist societies governments, directed traditionally by the party, establish trade-offs among such factors as economic stability and growth, energy supply, production priorities, and citizens' standard of living. Problems in directing the economy center around obtaining adequate information and spurring technical innovation. The bureaucratization of central planning, for example, has had a critical negative effect on innovation, in that information feedback from customers through a marketing process is retarded. Small firms that can innovate and introduce new products are also missing; failure to innovate is aggravated by political controls within research institutions (e.g., universities) and by limited rewards for individual inventors.

As the tempo and scale of economic development has proceeded, planning bureaucracies have had difficulty coping with increasingly complex and interdependent economic activities. In order to overcome this difficulty, some relaxation of central control is an obvious policy solution. Doing this, it is hoped, will spur innovative solutions at lower levels and improve information flows. In the process, however, the door is open to demands for greater participation in decision making (i.e., for greater political equality). The need to solve economic inefficiency, therefore, collides with concerns about a loss of unity and discipline.[75]

In China these alternate tendencies have long been recognized. Much of the dynamic of the Chinese political process revolves around the tension between these forces. As early as the mid-1950s, Mao was concerned about how the concentration of political and economic authority at the center would foster bureaucratism, a privileged elite, and a loss of revolutionary idealism while simultaneously stifling mass initiative and innovation. Much of his effort at that time, in the Hundred Flowers campaign and the Great Leap Forward (and also, of course, later during the Cultural Revolution), went into combating bureaucratism within the party and devising ways to give lower levels more responsibility for their own economic activities. As he said (in a most contradictory manner) in 1962 to a conference of seven thousand cadres, "Without democracy, you have no understanding of what is down below . . . you will be unable to collect sufficient opinions . . . thus you will find it difficult to avoid being a subjectivist; it will be impossible to achieve unity of understanding and unity of action, and impossible to achieve true

[75] R. V. Burks, "Technology and Political Change in Eastern Europe" in Chalmers Johnson, ed., *Change in Communist Systems*, pp. 272, 277–9, 285, 287.

centralism."[76] This ambiguity was reflected throughout the decade of the 1970s when China went back and forth between centralization and the delegation of authority from higher to lower administrative levels. Yet, as Dorothy J. Solinger has pointed out, movement away from centralized planning has spawned much disorder (and corruption), whereas reliance on bureaucratic solutions has enhanced the power of those at the center, thereby exacerbating political inequality.[77]

Efforts at economic reform in China in the late 1970s and the 1980s involved a significant devolution of authority to regions and enterprises and encouragement of initiative at the lowest levels. Although not all local officials have been equally enthusiastic (some feel that central authority has simply been replaced by provincial authority), there has been general support for reforms that have permitted increased local control over fiscal revenues, material supplies, depreciation funds, and the retention of a share of profits, tax revenues, and foreign exchange.[78] In the agricultural area, especially, there has been a movement from reliance on centralized team planning to the awarding of contracts to individual households on a long-term basis.[79]

It is the question of who owns property that lies at the heart of the debate about plan versus market. According to Ramon H. Myers, there are now four types of enterprise ownership in China: state-owned, collective-owned, privately owned, and some combination of the first three types. However, although the state owns only 20 percent of the total number of enterprises, these account for nearly 75 percent of industrial output value. This sector above all is characterized by poor efficiency, brought about by subsidies ("everybody eating from the same big pot"), by the absence of lateral connections between firms to facilitate transactions, by stockpiling of production items and high inventories of finished goods, and by inefficient use of capital and labor brought about, in part, by the failure of central planners to close inefficient enterprises and their discouragement of innovation and multiproduct production.[80]

---

[76] Cited in Amartya Sen, "Development: Which Way Now?", in *The Political Economy of Development and Underdevelopment*, ed. Charles K. Wilbur (New York: Random House, 1988), p. 51.

[77] Dorothy J. Solinger, *Chinese Business Under Socialism: The Politics of Domestic Commerce, 1949–1980* (Berkeley: University of California Press, 1984), p. 298.

[78] Susan L. Shirk, "The Politics of Industrial Reform," in *The Political Economy of Reform in Post-Mao China*, ed. Elizabeth J. Perry and Christine Wong (Cambridge, Mass.: Council on East Asian Studies, Harvard University, 1985), p. 218.

[79] Kathleen Hartford, "Socialist Agriculture Is Dead; Long Live Socialist Agriculture! Organizational Transformations in Rural China," in ibid., pp. 35–6.

[80] Ramon H. Myers, "Property Rights, Economic Organizations and Economic Modernization During the Economic Reforms," paper presented at the conference on "China in a New Era: Continuity and Change," Third International Congress of Professors World Peace Academy, Manila, August 24–9, 1987, pp. 5–6, 11.

Worker attitudes are also part of the reason for lack of efficiency. Experiments with piece-rate wage systems to raise productivity have been terminated after worker objections; such moves are considered to violate existing norms of egalitarianism.[81] Another cause of inefficiency lies in the designation of innovators as rule violators. At times, in fact, this is literally true. In order to remedy shortages of supply, bottlenecks in delivery, and so forth, enterprise officials innovate extralegal procedures and manipulate personal ties. Such activities, usually involving the exchange of gifts and favors (i.e., bribes), are a form of corruption that is inevitable under existing institutional arrangements. Although these practices favor efficiency in the short run, however, the labeling of them as corruption means increased enforcement costs for government and a loss of political legitimacy to the extent that corruption cannot be stemmed.

Combating deviant tendencies was traditionally achieved largely through intimidation. Yet the continued use of arbitrary coercion, following the initial suppression of revolutionary enemies, has fostered a calculating and self-interested stance with regard to the collectivity. Although the greatest criticism is not of the justice of socialism as an ideal but of the failure to bring socialism to reality, there is barely disguised cynicism at political attempts to deepen ideological purity and commitment. As a consequence, the fate of an economy in which many enterprises run at a loss is taken personally only when political authority impacts coercively on the individual. Yet freeing enterprises from political control leads to a severe loss of party power. No easy solution to this problem has ever been found.

Changing aspects of law in strong positional societies

Since the death of Mao Zedong and the fall of the Gang of Four, change in China has been spurred by revulsion against the widespread use of arbitrary terror (approximately one-tenth of the population, or 100 million people, had to be rehabilitated following the Cultural Revolution) and by the need to increase economic efficiency. These two features are closely related, in the sense that the economic reforms designed to increase efficiency represent policy positions that were earlier the basis for coercive stigmatization. Articulating a new relationship between the citizen and political power, therefore, is a task that has been assigned to the law. There is, however, a deeply embedded traditional aversion to the use of legal procedures for conflict resolution. Most Chinese continue to believe that justice is truly secured not by appeal to law but by the actions of upright officials.

[81] William Byrd et al., *Recent Chinese Economic Reforms: Studies of Two Industrial Enterprises*, World Bank Staff Working Papers No. 652 (Washington: World Bank, 1984), p. 28.

Efforts to give law a more central position in Chinese life have led to a new emphasis on codifying and publishing applicable law in order to set forth clearly the rights of citizens and the restraints on officials.[82] As of 1984 there were thirty-six law institutes and fourteen times as many law students as in 1978. Including all categories of legal personnel, about a quarter of a million people now work in the legal system supplemented by 5.5 million people's mediators. These people handle about 8 million civil disputes each year[83] which, as a percentage of all court cases, rose dramatically from 53 percent in 1977 to 76.1 percent in 1982.[84]

In 1984, Peng Zhen, a prominent Cultural Revolution victim (he had been mayor of Beijing) but rehabilitated to become chairman of the Standing Committee of the National People's Congress, said, "we must gradually make the transition from relying on policy in managing affairs, to establishing and strengthening the legal system and relying not only on policy but also on law to manage affairs."[85] Two years later, on December 2, 1986, at the Sixth National People's Congress Standing Committee Meeting a trial Enterprise Law was introduced that was designed to improve enterprise accountability.[86] A year later, in 1987, Vice Premier Qiao Shi told China's first national conference on improving the legal system that economic reforms could be adversely affected "if the previous practice of not enforcing laws and regulations and government institutions getting directly involved in economic activities through administrative channels is not corrected."[87] The object of all this attention was a series of reforms in agriculture and industry that amounted to virtually a total repudiation of Maoist policies and radical communitarian aspirations.

In December 1978, at the Third Plenum of the Eleventh Congress of the Chinese Communist Party, the organization of production and distribution in the countryside was changed by promulgation of a new production responsibility system. In 1979 the ten-year modernization program adopted a year earlier (in 1978) was scrapped owing to deficiencies in central planning. In April 1981, state-owned enterprises (80 percent by year's end) shifted from a

---

[82] See, for example, the two translated volumes *The Law of the People's Republic Of China* for 1979–82 and 1983–6 compiled by the Legislative Affairs Commission of the Standing Committee of the National People's Congress (Beijing: Foreign Languages Press, 1987).

[83] "China Trains More Judicial Personnel," *Beijing Review* 27, no. 37 (September 10, 1984): 9.

[84] Zhang Zhiye, "How China Handles Civil Disputes," *Beijing Review* 27, no. 7 (February 13, 1984): 22.

[85] Andrew J. Nathan, "Sources of Chinese Rights Thinking," in *Human Rights in Contemporary China*, ed. R. Randle Edwards, Louis Henkin, and Andrew J. Nathan (New York: Columbia University Press, 1986), pp. 132–3.

[86] Myers, "Property Rights," p. 12.

[87] "China Must Improve Legal System to Streamline Bureaucracy: Qiao," *Korea Herald*, August 30, 1987, p. 4.

profit-sharing to a profit-contract system (annual profit-remittance quotas to be negotiated, with enterprises retaining most or all of above-quota profits). Further reforms were initiated in areas of bank loans, limited use of flexible prices, a tax-for-profit scheme, and so on.[88]

These changes are dramatic evidence of a will to improve the efficiency of production enterprises. Correspondingly, the reforms permit modest enterprise autonomy in ways that represent a significant shift from the earlier mode of authoritative control by party decision-making bodies. They thus constitute, in fledgling form, an evolutionary wedge into the prevailing compliance ideology that is of long-run significance. Indeed, to the extent that the reforms attempt in a formal, legal way to limit the involvement of the party in economic decisions, they represent a modest shift toward contractual compliance and toward a reduction of political inequality.

Laws and rights

During much of the history of rule by the Communist Party in China, individual rights were flagrantly disregarded, despite general constitutional guarantees of the inviolability of individuals and their homes. In the constitution adopted in 1982 a very specific provision was added (Article 38) stating that the personal dignity of citizens is inviolable. This followed general efforts, put in motion in 1978, to establish a comprehensive, formal legal system with codes, lawyers, and public trials.[89] As important, however, has been the effort to change public perceptions regarding the law. In 1986 five years were authorized in which to educate the public in the nation's laws and legal system, aimed first and foremost at the young and at cadres. Such education is necessary, it was said, because "cadres should recognize it is their duty and responsibility to abide by the law. Both Party and administrative cadres should keep their actions well within the limits of China's constitution and laws."[90] In a later injunction it was further noted that "all cadres, including the leading cadres at all levels, only have the power to act according to the law, and they do not have special rights allowing them to ride roughshod over the state laws. . . . From the Central Committee down to the grass roots, all party organizations and members must, without exception, strictly obey the law."[91]

---

[88] Elizabeth J. Perry and Christine Wong, "Introduction: The Political Economy of Reform in Post-Mao China: Causes, Content, and Consequences," in Perry and Wong, *Political Economy of Reform*, pp. 1, 8–12.

[89] R. Randle Edwards, "Civil and Social Rights: Theory and Practice in Chinese Law Today," in Edwards, Henkin, and Nathan, ed., *Human Rights*, pp. 41, 62.

[90] "Cadres Lead in Learning Law," *Beijing Review* 29, no. 4 (January 27, 1986): 28.

[91] "Leading Cadres Urged to Obey, Uphold Laws," *FBIS*, March 3, 1986, pp. K1–2 (from Beijing *Zhongguo Xinwen She*, March 1, 1986).

In a formal sense these attempts to establish new "contractual" criteria for social relationships were not violated in the bloody suppression of student activity in June 1989 (the Tiananmen Incident), for the government was at pains to declare a state of martial law before using violent force. Few, however, except perhaps the authorities, would view what happened as anything less than riding roughshod over the law and the bodies of their opponents. Clearly, the conservative party faction honored the constitution in name only, while arbitrarily labeling a number of the demonstrators as counter-revolutionaries. We must therefore look elsewhere in the Communist world for signs of a genuine redefinition of political participation.

Recent events in the Soviet Union and in Eastern Europe suggest a start is being made in redefining political dissidence. Beginning in Poland, and spreading from there to other countries, the stage has been set for a significant redefinition of positional criteria by the party's grudging willingness to permit nonparty individuals and groups that had formerly (and formally) been banned to participate in political activity. Poland's economic crisis, of course, had much to do with the initial formation of the Solidarity Union, whose activities – strikes, demonstrations, publications – were viewed at the time as unacceptable political activity, which led to the union's being outlawed. Solidarity, however, continued to exist because it served as the focus for deep resentment about economic conditions and the political repression that silenced those seeking to restructure economic life. In June 1989, the very month when the Chinese Communist Party was crushing its student opponents, Solidarity, now legalized, soundly defeated Communist candidates for the Polish parliament. Then, on August 19, 1989, following the inability of the Communists to form a government, the Communist president, Wojciech Jaruzelski, requested Tadeusz Mazowiecki, a senior Solidarity official, to be the first non-Communist prime minister of Poland since the early post–World War II years. That act signaled a momentous change in Poland's compliance ideology and was the spark for subsequent and equally momentous changes in East Germany, Hungary, Czechoslovakia, Bulgaria, Romania, and, indeed, in the Soviet Union itself.

The views of elites in strong positional societies

With the partial exception of Czechoslovakia and East Germany, strong positional societies were plagued in the early years by a shortage of college graduates and trained technical staff. Even when such staff were available, the party cadres assigned to units often had only a low educational level. The negative effect this had on enterprise efficiency was exacerbated by conflicts among leadership types (e.g., Solinger notes three ideal types in China – radicals, bureaucrats, and marketeers, each associated with different policy positions)[92] and by a sluggish supervisory administrative apparatus that often ground out plan targets year after year with little change in the way the targets were determined. The problem of supply not meeting demand became chronic in virtually all these societies. Difficulties related to low cadre competence, leadership conflict, and lack of initiative, however, pale in comparison to the problems posed by overlapping and contradictory jurisdictions. For example, for the Qingdao Forging Machinery Plant in China, production targets were assigned by the municipality and county, supply was shared among central ministry, province, municipality, and county (depending on the category of goods and the location of the supplying agency), sales were handled mostly by the enterprise, but export sales were handled by the Ministry of Machine Building and the Provincial Export Corporation. Given this system, balancing production, supply, and sales was virtually impossible, to say nothing of coordinating these activities with demand factors.[93]

Marshal Tito once exclaimed that "bureaucracy is the cancer of socialism."[94] Although a bitter opponent of Tito, Mao clearly shared with him a fear of the long-term influence of bureaucratism. He worried especially about those cadres lodged interstitially in the maze of bureaucratic life who had a vested interest in maintaining a privileged position. So also, but on a far less exalted level, did many ordinary citizens, who chafed under the petty control and tutelage of bureaucratic officials.

The central problem posed by government bureaucracy as a dominant institutional form is that it limits the policy initiatives of those occupying formal positions of political power. In effect, much of what bureaucrats do (and how they do it) is in response to purely institutional pressures. A bureaucratic system is not necessarily arbitrary or self-interested, but there is a tendency for its operations increasingly to take place beyond the bounds of public control. When that happens, political authority is the loser, usually with ramifications for systemwide institutional efficiency. When Mao perceived this problem in China, he sought to thwart it by unleashing a radical attack on the bureaucrats themselves. Little did he gauge the strength and resilience of a bureaucratic system or of its central position in modern life. The reform movement of the last decade in China has been more effective in curtailing bureaucracy, not because it has challenged bureaucrats as Mao did, but because it has removed from central bureaucratic purview significant decision powers. These reforms have touched virtually every aspect of Chinese life (e.g., agricultural production, health care, education, industrial

---

[92] Solinger, *Chinese Business*, p. 60.
[93] Byrd et al., *Recent Chinese Economic Reforms*, pp. 25, 77, 90.
[94] Cited in John N. Hazard, "China and Socialist Models," keynote address, conference on "China in a New Era: Continuity and Change," Third International Congress of Professors World Peace Academy, Manilla, August 24–9, 1987, p. 4.

organization, the legal system, etc.), and they are not likely to be undone even by recent conservative reaction.

Yet there is, clearly, a powerful opposition to reform. It has been fueled not just by those who feel morally threatened by challenges to the prevailing dominance ideology but more significantly by those, including especially cadres who are uneducated and inefficient, who fear for their niche of power and privilege in institutional life. One main reason why those implementing changes in China wanted their reforms backed by law was because party branch secretaries, many of whom are strong on ideology but short on education, were refusing to surrender control to trained managers. The same problem, of course, exists with implementing *perestroika* in the Soviet Union. There the *apparatchiki*, often not well educated, seek to block changes they believe will lower the prestige of the party. On a more personal level, they fear, quite rightly, for their jobs and a future where new jobs will be difficult to find.[95] No doubt those top leaders who led the unsuccessful coup attempt against President Mikhail S. Gorbachev in August 1991 hoped to tap these sentiments, among others, for support.

General comments on constraints on change in strong positional societies

The basic obstacle to innovation in strong positional societies is to be found in the institution of authoritative central planning. Although this institutional arrangement has proven to be rigid and unresponsive in dealing with changing economic conditions, it is a keystone in the institutional arch of the Stalinist–Leninist party state. As such, its maintenance is a focal point for all those who seek to retain their hard-won positions of privilege. Reformers are thus faced constantly with a coalition of conservative forces from the military, heavy industry, favored regional party committees, and the members of the central bureaucracy itself.

Conservatives have not been slow to point out the dangers of change. In China problems associated with localism, called "cooking in separate kitchens," are widely publicized.[96] Senior leaders have also made public note of the threat they perceive to socialist ideology and of the heavy responsibility borne by subordinates to defend the party's position. Chen Yun, for instance, in a speech on September 24, 1985, to the Sixth Plenary Session of the Central Commission for Discipline Inspection, spoke as follows: "If the unhealthy tendencies that endanger socialism and corrupt the Party's style of work and social values are ignored and go unchecked, then the blame must

[95] Burks, "Technology," p. 297.
[96] Shirk, "Politics of Industrial Reform," p. 221.

not only be placed on the evildoers, but also on the Party committee of that unit or region."[97]

In a budget speech in March 1987, Finance Minister Wang Bingqian said, regarding the performance of state firms in 1986, "Economic efficiency . . . was unsatisfactory as production costs went up and losses increased," necessitating subsidies of nearly $9.7 billion, a figure that was 14.5 percent over subsidies in 1986 and that represented more than 15 percent of national revenue for the year.[98] This staggering outlay represents part of the dilemma of central planners. A knowledge of costs and prices required to achieve an efficient allocation of resources can be acquired only by the operation of some type of market process. But the heads of big state factories are virtually all party members subject, ultimately, to the party secretaries in factory party meetings. Enterprise success or failure is always subject to modification depending on ideological considerations dictated by the party from the center. Efforts to spur innovation and competition by moving to a contract system (thus, presumably, breaking management's "big pot" or guaranteed subsidies, and labor's "iron rice bowl" or lifetime job security) have not, at the same time, minimized the need for party secretaries to enforce ideological discipline and maintain control.

In short, enterprise managers in China still function with the mind-set of central planning, ignoring comparative advantage, appropriate commercial relations, bonuses geared to worker performance, and so forth. They do so largely because the reforms have not, in fact, abandoned subsidies and central control over the allocation of labor and prices.[99] Yet were central authorities genuinely to relinquish these powers, they would, at the same time, relinquish a significant portion of power. This they are unwilling to do. No doubt Gorbachev was confirming this view, and fueling the suspicions of reformers about his commitment to genuine change, when he described the advantages of a centrally planned economy to auto workers in May 1987: "Comrades, we will even have to strengthen the principle of centralization, where necessary."[100]

As is so often the case, insufficient change can lead to problems fully as intractable as those for which remedies are sought. In China the increases in income inequality attending recent changes have been deeply unsettling for many people. So also has been the dramatic increase in corruption (e.g.,

---

[97] Chen Yun, "Combating Corrosive Ideology," *Beijing Review* 28, no. 41 (October 14, 1985): 16.
[98] Mark O'Neill, "State Firms Major Obstacle to China's Economic Reforms," *Korea Herald*, May 8, 1987, p. 4 (from Reuters).
[99] Richard A. Smith, "Class Structure and Economic Rationality: Problems of Industrial Reform in China," paper presented at the Columbia University Seminar on Modern China, February 12, 1987, pp. 1–6.
[100] Gary Lee, "G'chev's Reform Drive Faces Deep Internal Resistance," *Korea Herald*, April 12, 1987, p. 8 (Washington Post service).

bribery, buying materials illegally to sell at a profit, excessive bonuses, etc.), especially on the part of leaders who are well placed to manipulate the easing of central controls for their own private advantage.[101] In the second half of 1988, for example, more than twenty-four thousand party and government officials, including seventeen at ministerial and provincial levels, were reported for committing crimes.[102] Conservatives have not been slow to attribute these and other failings to the reform process. Price increases, inflation, huge trade and budget deficits, and "capitalist tendencies" from private businesses and free markets have all been named in the "indictment" against change.

For conservatives reform has nothing to do with permitting open opposition or with diluting the party's power. Rather, reform is a process of making the government more efficient. To this end purely personal interests should be subordinated to the interests of the nation as a whole. In fact, there is evidence of widespread support for this vision. In a survey of 4,032 undergraduates by the *Beijing Evening News* (*Beijing Wanbao*), 40 percent indicated confidence in the realization of communism and 39.7 percent stated they believed in the correctness of communist theory but doubted its realization (together these responses equal almost 81 percent). In terms of interpreting dissent there is no reason to disbelieve these results. For two-thirds of these students (66.9 percent) also think the socialist system is superior to capitalism, although still much to be perfected.[103] It is precisely here, however, that I believe we see the germ of opposition, not in treason but in loyalty to an ideal seen as unfulfilled. It is a loyalty that is fanned to open resentment by knowledge of official corruption. For just as reform sets loose practices (i.e., excessive bonuses, etc.) that raise the ire of conservatives, so also do these same practices inflame those who associate them with officialdom in general.

Westerners sometimes speak of demonstrations, especially by students, as if these were unalloyed calls for parliamentary democracy and a capitalist economy. There are, to be sure, some who hold these aspirations, just as there are also some who are animated by a tense, pure hatred of authority. But to a great extent the call for democracy, law, press freedom, and freedom of speech is for a more moral society with greater political equality and an end to the abuses associated with authoritarian control. Underlying the dynamic of change, therefore, in China as elsewhere, is the aspiration for equality, to be realized by some new form of socialist democracy.

[101] James T. Myers, "China: Modernization and Unhealthy Tendencies," *Comparative Politics* 21, no. 2 (January 1989): 195–6.

[102] "24,000 Officials Reported for Irregularities," *Beijing Review* 32, no. 5 (January 30–February 5, 1989): 9.

[103] "University Students Have High Ideals," ibid. 28, no. 3 (January 21, 1985): 27.

For those conservative leaders who oppose dissidence, however, the turmoil of political opposition is a threat to production and social order, stability and unity. In their view change is valid only as a spur to efficiency, for, it is thought, with efficiency will also come justice. Thus, those who oppose central control are thought to be truly counterrevolutionary. No sense of moral failing, therefore, is experienced for suppressing, even bloodily, those who protest (e.g., in China in December 1986 and January 1987, and again, more dramatically, in June 1989). In keeping with this vision Chinese conservatives have attempted to direct change down paths that will leave intact the structure of strong positional compliance.

In Eastern Europe, however, the reverse has been the case. There the floodgates, finally fully opened, proved impossible to close. The vision that now animates the citizens of these societies is of a new order of equality. In these countries the possibility for a shift in the fundamental quality of compliance is now more than just the dream of reformers.

Conclusion

At the end of World War II, two concepts of social life appropriate for the modern phase of property relations had come to dominate thinking about a just world. The effort through fascism to create a modern world without either had failed. Henceforth, the problems of modernization would involve a contest over whether property relations should be contractual, negotiated among separate individuals and groups, or positional, based within the community as a whole. The first is the world of autonomous institutions knit in bonds of solidarity by procedural laws that regulate the interactions among them. The second is the world of nested institutions knit in equal bonds of solidarity by substantive law that establishes the framework for the achievement of an ultimate purpose. Between the two lies another world of combination. In each of these worlds there exists an impulse, grounded in the search for equality, toward the realization of a more moral social order. In all modern societies this strain tugs at individual sensibilities and institutional arrangements.

How to resolve the tension between the two strong visions is the greatest political question of this age. It is political because it involves not simply a change in individual moral perceptions but also a related shift in institutional forms and the norms that govern institutional arrangements. Inherent in this change is a shift from viewing equality as an aspect of property relations to viewing equality as an aspect of the inherent integrity of individuals within a community that recognizes integrity as an ultimate end. How to construct institutional arrangements that reflect this consideration is the most difficult political task that has ever been set.

The laws that govern private property have given people some limited freedom from authority. Yet, at the same time, differences in property holdings, of both a relative and an absolute nature, have led to questions about the relationship between political power and the ownership and control of property.[104] Increasingly, many have come to feel that the emphasis on property as such (i.e., a social hierarchy structured around the control of property) has seriously limited the positive rights of people to participate equally in the life of the community.

An earlier answer to this problem was to eliminate private property or, more accurately, to abolish the free market from which property is derived. The dilemma has been that with the market's demise so also have gone those laws of contract that protected individual autonomy. In their place a new evil has arisen, an encompassing bureaucratic web designed to provide public control of production (i.e., of accumulation of property), which, at the same time, subjects the individual to a pervasive administrative control that stifles individual spontaneity and free expression. Increasingly, many who live in these societies ask how forms of pluralism can be created to weaken hegemonic political power.

Internal pressures to reevaluate systems of compliance go hand in hand, as always, with technological development and institutional change. In all compliance systems at the modern phase there has been an increase in institutional size, in the numbers of institutions, and in the interactions among them. Regulating these interactions has become the major function of governments, necessitating the increasing involvement of government in institutional (and individual) affairs. This process, which Daniel Bell has likened to the growth of a "public household,"[105] has been the cause for a profound reexamination of rights. What, for example, is the appropriate definition of individual privacy in the face of governmental intrusiveness and increases in computer efficiency? Or, given the exponential growth in the emission of man-made heat and in the production of pollutants, both as a cause and a consequence of industrial growth, what are the rights of individuals vis-á-vis those who control property (e.g., following the Chernobyl and Bhopal disasters)? Of equal importance have been redefinitions of community and the place an individual or group has within it. Improvements in the technology of medicine, for example, have led to extraordinary increases in population that strain world food resources and raise questions about the appropriate political form for coping with this problem. Surely, many feel, the world itself, not the village or nation, is the community that must be considered for a problem such as this. In a somewhat analogous manner, improvements in

---

[104] Amartya Sen, *Resources, Values and Development* (Cambridge Mass.: Harvard University Press, 1984), p. 324.
[105] Daniel Bell, *The Cultural Contradictions of Capitalism* (New York: Basic Books, 1976) 226.

the technology of killing have led to restraints on national governments (e.g., nuclear arms agreements). New and more inclusive definitions of humanity itself have come to the fore as a consequence of horrendous incidents of genocide.

Clearly, many existing private and public institutions are incapable of responding to the challenge posed by new technologies. Yet unless new institutional arrangements evolve along with a change in social values, the outlook is bleak. Where, however, can models be found? – for the problems that are faced are truly unique.

The likelihood is that government intervention in economic and social affairs will increase as solutions are sought for ever more complex problems in areas of urbanization, transportation, pollution, birth control, and the like. The interventions will take place at both the national and global levels. They may be narrow in scope, as in the cooperation between neighboring countries on environmental issues, or they may be very broad, as in the activities of the World Bank, the International Monetary Fund, and the International Labor Organization.[106] Whatever the scope, new definitions of personhood and of society will be called for. For in order to survive in a world where institutional size and capability have grown ever greater and more inclusive, the need to redefine personal liberty and social responsibility must grow apace.

Richard F. Hixson has analyzed the historical yearning both for privacy and for what William M. Sullivan called "inclusion in a community of mutual concern."[107] In Hixson's view, too great an emphasis on privacy allows one to escape from the obligations of public life and thus threatens collective survival.[108] Interestingly, there is evidence of a generational shift in conceptions of the self and community. Ronald Inglehart notes a growing commitment on the part of Western youth both to self-realization and to the quality of community life. We see this commitment in the women's movement, the consumer advocacy movement, the environmental movement, and the antinuclear movement, all of which redefine community and the individual's place within it.[109]

Equality is a complex concept and no simple or single policy will suffice for its realization. Yet in all its formulations it challenges people who live in the modern phase of property relations, summoning them to defend their value premises in a process of interactive dialogue that transforms both individual and social constructions of meaning. In this process the rights

---

[106] Wolfgang Friedmann, *Law in a Changing Society* (New York: Columbia University Press, 1972), pp. 469, 523.

[107] Richard F. Hixson, *Privacy in a Public Society: Human Rights in Conflict* (New York: Oxford University Press, 1987), p. 217.

[108] Ibid., p. 93.

[109] Ronald Inglehart, "Post-Materialism in an Environment of Insecurity," *American Political Science Review* 75, no. 4 (December 1981): 895.

regulating the control of property become better understood; with understanding comes the knowledge of how to protect the weak and less favored and how to check the aggrandizing urges of the mighty. The first step, as Benjamin R. Barber points out, is the realization that "community without participation merely rationalizes collectivism, giving it an aura of legitimacy [while] participation without community merely rationalizes individualism, giving it the aura of democracy."[110] Ultimately, as Barber goes on to explain, "The road to autonomy leads through not around commonality. . . . As Aristotle noted long ago, the civic bond is in fact the one bond that orders and governs all others – the bond that creates the public structure within which other, more personal and private social relationships can flourish."[111]

[110] Benjamin R. Barber, *Strong Democracy: Participatory Politics for a New Age* (Berkeley and Los Angeles: University of California Press, 1984), p. 155.
[111] Ibid., p. 217.

8

Utopian visions

Political culture is a concept that derives its meaning from the interaction of economic and psychological variables. In terms of economics it is related to the institutional rules that minimize transaction costs. These rules embody property rights that establish the moral justification for commitment to hierarchical social arrangements. Property rights, however, are part of the general rights and obligations that regulate relationships within a society. This context is psychological in that rights and obligations contain social meanings with Piagetian characteristics – they have *structure*, which defines how social interaction is conceived, and *content*, which reflects the historical framework of beliefs about appropriate social orientations.

A shift in the structure of social meanings involves changes in the abstractness and inclusiveness of conceptions of social relationships. Change is brought about by interactions among individuals who seek, through dialogue, to understand the moral justifications for institutional arrangements. On the one hand, interaction is pattern maintaining, providing the basis for ongoing coherence and stability in social life; on the other hand, it is transformative, changing meanings in incremental and evolutionary ways.[1]

Interactive discourse involves choices that have political consequences. Thus, in the United States, liberals and conservatives engage in a continuous debate about the alternate merits of democracy and capitalism.[2] This debate concerns patterns of ownership, the distribution of rewards, and the relationship of political authority to private property. A persistent question concerns whether citizens can be truly equal politically if income and wealth are distributed unequally and, conversely, whether political liberty can exist if government restricts ownership and property-use rights.[3] Other related

[1] Harry Eckstein, "A Culturist Theory of Political Change," *American Political Science Review* 87, no. 3 (September 1988): 795.

[2] Herbert McClosky and John Zaller, *The American Ethos: Public Attitudes Toward Capitalism and Democracy* (Cambridge, Mass.: Harvard University Press, 1984).

[3] Robert A. Dahl, *Democracy, Liberty, and Equality* (Oslo: Norwegian University Press, 1986), pp. 10–11.

questions concern participation in social and political life (race and gender issues) and acceptable limits on privacy (abortion and drug issues).

In other societies, such as the Chinese, the concern about autonomy that underlies debate in American life is less noteworthy; more emphasis is placed on group goals, communal activities, and collective interests. Critiques of society come largely from leadership and community members articulating a different vision of collective purpose. Yet questions about the appropriate balance between autonomy and community are everywhere raised. They concern especially the appropriate role of political authority and the ways this authority has arbitrarily established definitions of property rights and status rules.[4]

Whether economic or political equality has primary consideration has to do with the content of the compliance ideology. When contractual criteria are stressed, debate focuses on economic issues related to individual control of property. Where positional criteria are stressed, the focus is on the monopoly of decision making that is held by those with political authority; the issue is then one of political equality.

Embedded in both these debates is a question about the nature of reciprocity. Before the modern phase, reciprocal behavior was defined by role, status, group membership, and situational context. Relationships were unequal in the sense that social expectations always weighed more heavily on some than on others. Typically, younger people owed duties to elders, females to males, out-groups to in-groups, and, overall, those of lower status to those of higher status. The pattern was relatively invariant and often ritualistic in the sense that specific situations and role relationships required particular forms of reciprocity.

As cultural meanings became conceptually more comprehensive there was movement toward greater abstractness and inclusiveness in conceptions of reciprocity. The emphasis shifted from reciprocity defined by situational and status criteria to reciprocity defined by qualifications that inhere in individuals equally. There was, first, a movement toward a conception of reciprocity based on rights understood as property. Because rights in the modern phase are, in theory, owned equally, questions about inequality in reciprocity became dominant. Struggle ensued over the institutional rules that sanctioned inequality leading gradually to a redefinition of the meaning of rights. Thus, finally, at the most comprehensive level of conceptualization (the emergent phase), reciprocity is increasingly conceived of in terms of rights that are an aspect of the humanity of all persons; the idea of equal inherent rights then obliges the elimination, to the extent that it is possible, of all inequalities in the giving of care and the fostering of autonomy.

[4] Alex Inkeles, *Exploring Individual Modernity* (New York: Columbia University Press, 1983), pp. 303–5, 312.

The goal is not radical equality, which, as Douglas Rae et al. point out, "flies in the face of society's established structure and complexity" and whose achievement would be "a daunting prospect."[5] Rather, it is to create institutional patterns based on laws that are the repository of ideals regarding fairness, impartiality, and individual self-respect. For this to happen the extremes of both individualism and collectivism must be rejected. The law then becomes the mechanism for ensuring that people have the same opportunities regardless of their initial position in society, that they enter the search for a place in society with a rough equality of resources, and that they are treated in social interaction with a measure of approximate equality.[6]

At the emergent phase assuring equality in reciprocity becomes "a rule of procedure, a method of assessing the proportions that actually exist in relation to the proportions that would satisfy so far as is ever humanly possible the combined needs of individual aspirations and social aims."[7] Underlying this rule of procedure is a structure of thought that animates individual minds and infuses social discourse. As institutional change proceeds, it becomes a way of thinking that expands to cover ever more extensive domains of social life.

Changing patterns of institutional arrangements

The Romans in the days of the Republic had a proverb about the most powerful political organization in their society, "Senatores omnes boni viri, senatus romanus mala bestia" (The senators are all good men, the Roman Senate is an evil beast).[8] Many have deplored the sentiment expressed in this statement, for men need organization because of the power it lends to human activity, but that same power, especially in the modern technological world, can also be the source of the most far-reaching oppression.

The forms of modern institutions are not, however, immutable. As conceptions of reciprocity have changed, so also has the nature of institutional arrangements, toward cooperation and mutuality and away from hierarchy and control.[9] This shift, incremental and evolutionary in nature, is both inter- and intraorganizational. Although manifested in different ways in different societies, it has tended in all cases to underlie a new definition of relationships.

In contractual societies relief from abuse by autonomous institutions is more and more sought by appeal to the lawmaking power of government. Po-

---

[5] Douglas Rae et al., *Equalities* (Cambridge, Mass.: Harvard University Press, 1981), p. 149.

[6] Herbert J. Gans, *More Equality* (New York: Pantheon, 1973), pp. 24, 64.

[7] J. R. Pole, *The Pursuit of Equality in American History* (Berkeley and Los Angeles: University of California Press, 1978), 357.

[8] Cited in Serge Moscovici, *Social Influence and Social Change*, trans. Carol Sherrard and Greta Heinz (London: Academic Press, 1976), p. 14.

[9] Daniel Bell, *The Cultural Contradictions of Capitalism* (New York: Basic Books, 1976), pp. 147–8.

litical authority is increasingly tasked with preventing any particular subgroup from submerging the interests of other groups, with protecting individual rights to autonomy, with assuring that all in society receive a fair share of available rewards, and, critically, with establishing legal safeguards to protect others against the potential arbitrariness of its own authority. In all modern societies that are evolving toward the emergent phase, the state has everywhere imposed far-reaching restrictions both on itself and on interests whose unfettered expression would enlarge inequality (e.g, the state has established regulatory commissions, enacted fair trade and antitrust laws, established an independent judiciary, etc.).[10]

Changes are taking place within institutions as well. Outside groups, such as community representatives, are increasingly considered in crucial management decisions, often through the auspices of government. It is in relations with subordinates, however, where the most far-reaching changes are occurring. The traditional attitude that workers have neither the ability, nor the time, nor the inclination to understand and participate in decisions regarding organizational activities is giving way to new ideas about teamwork and worker involvement. In the process, worker alienation is slowly giving way to feelings of worth and self-respect.

In American society these changes have taken place along two independent paths involving, first, efforts to improve labor–management cooperation and, second, plans that make possible employee ownership of institutions. The first of these has involved a number of innovations, all related ultimately to improving transactional efficiency by implementing procedures that encourage workers to participate in, and share responsibility for, the governance of a joint activity. To this end there have been efforts to restructure work groups into teams that have wide responsibility for their own activities, to involve workers or their representatives on corporate boards, and to institutionalize bargaining procedures that are oriented toward concession rather than confrontation.[11]

Of equal significance for the system of private property rights, however, is the second path. Although workers over time have won benefits for themselves (e.g., retirement benefits, paid vacations, company-paid health care programs) that were formerly the sole perquisites of management, ways are now being sought to eliminate the large discrepancies in rewards that still exist between workers and executives. In May 1988, for example, the workers at Chrysler Corporation secured an unusual agreement that would prohibit executives from receiving cash or stock bonuses in any year when the workers themselves did not receive payments under the company's profit-sharing

[10] Wolfgang Friedmann, *Law in a Changing Society* (New York: Columbia University Press, 1972), pp. 496, 512, 525.
[11] Thomas A. Kochan, "Accepting Labor as a Legitimate Partner," *New York Times*, July 26, 1987, sec. 3, p. 2.

plan.[12] Only a decade ago such a restriction on management would have been unthinkable.

Employee stock ownership plans (ESOPs) have also increased in number, totaling seven- to eight thousand in 1986 with eleven to thirteen million workers and $25 to $30 billion in assets (as compared to four thousand ESOPs with seven million workers in 1983).[13] In 1991 the number of ESOPs topped ten thousand. Admittedly, these are still insignificant figures in the total context of American institutional life. Nevertheless, the formation of ESOPs is supported by government; since the late 1970s, in fact, Congress has made available, through more than a dozen laws, a number of incentives to sponsor employee ownership.[14] Banks and commercial lenders, for example, can exclude 50 percent of their interest income on loans to ESOPs from their own taxable income. Some notable organizations are now involved in these plans, although the degree of employee ownership (and control) varies, as do the ways in which ownership is structured. Publicly held corporations with more than 20 percent employee ownership include in their ranks Ashland Oil, Continental Steel, FMC Corporation, Kaiser Aluminum, Lowe's Companies, and US Sugar. Within the 10–49 percent range of employee ownership are Pacific Southwest Airlines, Crown Zellerbach, Rohm & Haas, Western Union, Pam Am, and Kay Corporation.[15]

Although most studies of American firms show that employee-owned enterprises perform well on a number of financial variables, increases in productivity and work quality are not directly related to either employee ownership or worker participation in decision making.[16] What raises productivity is a reduction in worker alienation, which leads, in turn, to less absenteeism, turnover, and poor-quality work. As might be expected, reducing alienation is crucially related to an active environment of labor–management cooperation in which management reveals a clear commitment to change the provisions of financial benefits and the degree of worker involvement in decision making.[17] Where such innovations are introduced, the evidence points toward marked increases in productivity and in the quality of work.[18]

---

[12] John Holusha, "A Union Pact to Restrict Executive Privilege," *New York Times*, May 15, 1988, sec. 4, p. 4.

[13] Joseph Raphael Blasi, *Employee Ownership Through ESOPs: Implications for the Public Corporation* (New York: Pergamon Press, 1987), p. 13.

[14] Ibid., p. 9.   [15] Ibid., p. 18.

[16] Ibid., pp. 29, 43; Sar A. Levitan and Diane Werneke, "Worker Participation and Productivity Change," *Monthly Labor Review* 107, no. 9 (September 1984): 28; Corey Rosen, Katherine J. Klein, and Karen M. Young, "When Employees Share the Profits," *Psychology Today,* January 1986, pp. 30–6.

[17] Blasi, *Employee Ownership*, pp. 33, 41; Levitan and Werneke, "Worker Participation," p. 28.

[18] Claudia H. Deutsch, "U.S. Industry's Unfinished Struggle," *New York Times*, February 21, 1988, sec. 3, p. 7; Ronald Chester, *Inheritance, Wealth, and Society* (Bloomington: Indiana University Press, 1982), p. 88 (citing the sociologist Melvin Tumin).

These possibilities notwithstanding, most American firms still define their mission in terms of property ownership (i.e., maximizing shareholder interests). This is distinctly different from the practices of German and Japanese companies, where collective bargaining, joint consultation, and legislative enactment all serve to favor the interests of workers, lenders, and, especially in Japan, society in general. Japanese institutional practices, in fact, emphasize employee interests by encouraging democratic participation in the making of key decisions. Matters considered appropriate for joint consultation include the general economic outlook, long-range production plans, technological change, and the impact of all of these on needs for labor training, labor deployment, and so on. Combined with a policy to avoid, by every means, layoffs and discharges, an environment of trust and acceptance has developed that is markedly different from prewar relationships. Among the consequences has been a sharing by virtually all Japanese in the prosperity that has flowed from economic growth and the elimination of many inequitable differences among the strata of society.[19]

Across all societies at the modern phase, discourse is taking place regarding appropriate patterns of social organization and the normative criteria that should structure relationships. This discourse builds outward toward defining the context for interinstitutional coordination; it also builds inward toward constructing a place for individuality within a framework of community concern. In societies that are evolving to the emergent phase new patterns of autonomy must exist in the context of a new largeness of group life. The problem involves recognizing the appropriate realms for personal responsibility and institutional pluralism while fostering the empathy that reaches past individual concerns and specific group interests to include the needs of the community as a whole.

Nature of the problems

Modern life is increasingly pan-national and paninstitutional as the context of the problems that must be addressed expands beyond the borders of any particular society. Questions about breatheable air and potable water, the greenhouse effect, population pressures on food supplies, the weapons of mass destruction, and the like are problems that require a conception of community not limited by national borders. These issues are unsolvable in the context of a single community, much less a single person; they require a new definition of mankind and of one's place in a community of all persons. Above all, they require a recognition of the reciprocal needs of others as

---

[19] Solomon B. Levine, "Management and Labor in the Japanese Economy," in *Tradition and Creativity: Essays on East Asian Civilization*, ed. Ching-I Tu (New Brunswick, N.J.: Transaction Books, 1987), pp. 165–7, 171–2, 174.

a fundamental ethical proposition. For no sense of concern about the air that is breathed, or the amount of food that is available, can be translated into effective long-term policy without an empathic awareness of the needs of others.

Problems that pertain to inequality of reward especially require an elevation of concern. The disparity in per capita income between the presently developed and the presently less-developed countries, for example, was negligible in 1750, about 4 to 1 around 1930, and 7 to 1 in 1980.[20] Moreover, the economic condition of the poor in less-developed societies has worsened significantly in recent decades. Except where radical land redistribution has taken place, inequality in rural areas has in most cases increased.[21] Yet to the degree that political strivings to end inequality result in instability, the result is a downward slide in an economy. Such retrogression is the major retarding force acting against income-generating factors (savings, investments, export earnings, investments in human capital – health, education, nutrition, etc.). Without asserting political power, however, how can a society accelerate the slow process of a trickle-down of benefits or free itself from dependency on rich countries?[22]

Whether the focus is national or international conflict over equality can have a severely retarding effect on the development of ethical consideration. When, for example, common success goals are extolled for everyone, but where the possibility of achieving these goals is effectively denied to some, the consequence is likely to be deviant behavior that, if widespread, can seriously affect social and political stability. Or, when sizable numbers of people are denied certain benefits (e.g., health care, adequate nutrition, police protection) that are enjoyed by others, questions of fairness may quickly surface. There are, obviously, many reasons for criminality, alienation, and rebellious behavior, but one surely is the imbalance between aspirations for equality and actual patterns of influence and affluence.

There are clearly two directions that can be followed in confronting these problems. One is to reduce the threat of instability by vesting control in the hands of a new hegemonic elite. In a sense this solution mirrors the pattern often chosen in the past. There is, however, another path, one that leads to increasing participation in decision making by all members of a community and in which diversity and pluralism are honored. In this vision the gap be-

---

[20] Robert L. Heilbroner, "The Coming Meltdown of Traditional Capitalism," *Ethics and International Affairs* 2 (1988): 69.

[21] Dipak K. Gupta, "Political Psychology and Neoclassical Theory of Economic Growth: The Possibilities and Implications of an Attempted Resynthesis," *Political Psychology* 8, no. 4 (December 1987): 655; Keith Griffin, with the assistance of Ajit Kumar Ghose, "Growth and Impoverishment in the Rural Areas of Asia," in *The Political Economy of Development and Underdevelopment*, ed. Charles K. Wilbur (New York: Random House, 1988), p. 337.

[22] Gupta, ibid., pp. 652–4.

tween ordinary people and elites is narrowed rather than widened. Individuals, in their places of work, are encouraged by education and the availability of opportunities to seek ways to participate in organizational activities. While the need for leadership cannot be denied, bureaucracies, and society as a whole, become more communal through policies that ensure the provision of essential services, guarantee employment, provide for a reduction in income differentials, and foster participation in decision making at all levels.

Outside the boundaries of the bureaucratic institution other changes are possible that would both reflect and prompt the greater democratization of work practices. Material deprivation, the greatest enemy of participation in the life of the community, is reduced by focusing on ways to minimize wealth differentials, especially by taxes on consumption, net worth, and inheritance. Ways are sought to sponsor public control of investment, subject to review by a democratic political process, particularly those kinds of investments that enhance human resources assets, growth, and equality. National economic planning that coordinates public and private (i.e., market) activities is encouraged (in fact, for more than half a century economic models have existed that show how efficient allocation of resources, consumer sovereignty, and free worker choice can all be attained within the framework of national economic planning).[23] Such planning would have to ensure that the greater fairness achieved is equally matched by the autonomy of an open and competitive political environment and by institutional pluralism. In such a system rights are multiplied and transformed. On the one hand, the rights of the weak become translated into "claims of the community."[24] On the other hand, the right to autonomy becomes translated into service within and for the community. In this process the values that inform rights change to a form synonymous with consideration for humanity in both its smallest particular and its largest possibility.

Groups sponsoring change

As the modern phase of property relations slowly supplanted the traditional phase of encompassing hierarchy the impulse toward democracy was a powerful solvent eroding the powers of the old landed elite. Later, in communities composed of free farmers and small-shop owners, the local arena was the focus for political activity and the place where property questions were most directly debated. Community politics was a vibrant and essential aspect of life, encompassing issues affecting individual lives and the welfare of the local

[23] Arthur M. Okun, *Equality and Efficacy: The Big Tradeoff* (Washington, D.C.: The Brookings Institution, 1975), pp. 56–7.

[24] Daniel Bell, *The Coming of Post-Industrial Society: A Venture in Social Forecasting* (New York: Basic Books, 1973), p. 159.

district. In essence, the politics of the village meeting was the politics that really mattered for most people.

The emergence of enormously powerful bureaucratic institutions has enlarged the dimensions of property control. At the same time, the rise of problems that are personally immediate but transnational in scope (e.g., environmental pollution) has elevated the meaning of community far beyond the local perimeter. Local politics remain important, but for many people the most pressing problems can no longer be debated and solved in that context. Yet it is within local communities that people learn the art of participation, and it is there that they acquire ideas about fairness, individual integrity, and the appropriate limits of authority. Thus, although government as a whole has become vastly larger in societies in the modern phase (government absorbs more than 30 percent of gross national product in the United States),[25] this increase in size has not invalidated the necessity for citizens in their local communities to learn the art of political discourse.

Yet political discourse, to be effective in a modern society, must go beyond the local milieu. In modern societies large and diverse bureaucracies with different interests must constantly interact to explore areas where there is the possibility of mutual benefit.[26] In this regard government, through its own trained permanent officials, plays a crucial role in facilitating information sharing. If democracy is not to be eroded, therefore, public interest organizations (e.g., national news media) must monitor those who have positions of power in bureaucratic organizations, including government officials. In addition, special-interest groups, dedicated to environmental protection, nuclear disarmament, and so on, must help focus the attention of a broad range of concerned citizens on matters of transnational concern. Occasionally, as formal political parties (e.g., the Greens), such groups may seek to achieve a predominant voice in the political decision-making process. Revolutionary parties, of course, often seek the same. Yet, as is now abundantly clear, revolutionary activity without a prior evolution of individual and social meanings, leads only to the imposition of strong positional controls and the eventual eruption of further social and political turbulence.

Attitudes about social arrangements, of course, reflect the structural development of compliance criteria. As would be expected, there is no uniformity among societies in this regard. According to Sidney Verba et al., Swedish elites support a level of equality that would be considered radically egalitarian in the United States and Japan.[27] In other societies elite groups

[25] Lester C. Thurow, *The Zero-Sum Society: Distribution and the Possibilities for Economic Change* (New York: Basic Books, 1980), p. 7.
[26] Ezra F. Vogel, "Japan: Adaptive Communitarianism," in *Ideology and National Competitiveness: An Analysis of Nine Countries*, ed. George C. Lodge and Ezra F. Vogel (Boston: Harvard Business School Press, 1987), p. 161.
[27] Sidney Verba et al., *Elites and the Idea of Equality: A Comparison of Japan, Sweden, and the United States* (Cambridge, Mass.: Harvard University Press, 1987), p. 266.

may seek to strengthen their position at the expense of others. The Business Roundtable, for example, an American organization representing some two hundred major corporations, successfully lobbied to defeat provisions of a new federal criminal code that would have criminalized violations of certain environmental and safety laws (directed at corporate decisions that "knowingly place a person in imminent danger of death or serious bodily injury"). Not only did the Roundtable have this sanction deleted, it succeeded, as well, in having included other provisions that would undermine the rights of workers, dissidents, and those accused of crime.[28]

In contractual societies the egoism of the wealthy, while prompting accumulation, has also generated instabilities arising from poverty, unemployment, anger over the flaunting of hedonistic life-styles, and so on. Measures such as tax reform on incomes barely scratch a system of inequality still based primarily on differences in wealth (i.e., differences in the ownership of capital). Even the promising introduction of ESOPs has been seen more as a capital-structuring innovation than as one that reframes labor–management relations.[29] In America, at least, the myth remains powerful that government activities are a necessary evil and that inequalities among individuals are a prerequisite for economic growth – despite the fact that German and Japanese governments are both more intrusive, both societies are more productive, and there is far less inequality in both than in America.[30]

Ultimately, structural changes in compliance ideologies are brought about by social dialogue. Paradoxically, one measure of change toward the emergent phase is the acceptance of the legitimacy of active controversy. The understanding that dissidence is not treason, and that participation, not control, is the route to consensus, is the only true pathway to higher structures of meaning. But these caveats apply most crucially precisely where equality is most at issue. In the Soviet Union and other societies with positional compliance systems, it means opening the door ever further to independent parliamentary factions and to opportunities for free expression. In the United States and other societies with contractual compliance systems, it means supporting democracy in economic as well as political domains. In every modern society the truly central question is the degree to which the technobility will tolerate participation in the realm where they exercise control over property.

Shifting to the emergent phase

At the emergent phase the tense dialectical interaction of the past gives way to a type of change that enlarges possibilities from within. It proceeds from the premise that all people are, or can become, ethically responsible and that

---

[28] David Rudovsky, "The Criminal Justice System and the Role of the Police," in *The Politics of Law: A Progressive Critique*, ed. David Kairys (New York: Pantheon, 1982), p. 243.
[29] Blasi, *Employee Ownership*, p. 32.   [30] Chester, *Inheritance*, p. 167.

social conditions can be constructed to maximize this potential by minimizing artificial inequalities. The goal is to perfect, not create, a social life based on democratic participation in all aspects of the life of the community by individuals who cherish both personal integrity and community well-being.

Paul Samuelson defined a public good as something "which all enjoy in common in the sense that each individual's consumption of such a good leads to no subtraction from any other individual's consumption of that good."[31] The right to be let alone, which some believe is the essence of freedom, is such a good when the use made of being left alone does not deprive others either of this good or of other goods that may be needed to share in the life of the community. In the modern phase the recognition of the effect on community life of economic and political inequality begins the process of change. It takes shape in equity-sharing plans, modifications of inheritance laws, the legitimation of opposition political groups, new institutional patterns based on membership participation in decision making, and the prevention of concentrations of property control.[32] In contractual compliance systems in the modern phase it begins with the understanding that economic inequality destroys the community life that gives meaning to the right to make individual choices; for the guardians of positional ideologies it begins by recognizing that only by abolishing their own preeminence can coercive state power be eliminated and political equality achieved. Only in the recognition that diversity is not the antithesis of community can a true community be constructed.[33]

In short, in the development of ethical consideration there is a recognition of the validity of both collectivist and individualist sentiments. Joshua Cohen and Joel Rogers put this well. They point out that if the principle of individual liberty is violated, then individuals no longer retain their status as participants in an order of equal freedom. The same is true for distributional equity, for its violation also negates an individual's status in a community of equal persons.[34] Genuine ethical consideration, therefore, demands a moral concern for both autonomy and community. As a compliance ideology, this pattern is shown in Figure 7.

As the emergent phase comes fully into being the criteria that defined contractual and positional compliance in the modern phase merge and are struc-

[31] Cited in Albert Breton, *The Economic Theory of Representative Government* (Chicago: Aldine, 1974), p. 37.

[32] Louis O. Kelso and Mortimer J. Adler, *The Capitalist Manifesto* (New York: Random House, 1958), pp. 169–70, 191.

[33] Mao Zedong, for one, in his own way, saw this quite well. See quotations cited in John Bryan Starr, *Continuing the Revolution: The Political Thought of Mao* (Princeton, N.J.: Princeton University Press, 1979), p. 43; and Stephen Andors, *China's Industrial Revolution: Politics, Planning and Management, 1949 to the Present* (New York: Pantheon, 1977), p. 46.

[34] Joshua Cohen and Joel Rogers, *On Democracy: Toward a Transformation of American Society* (New York: Penguin Books, 1983), p. 160.

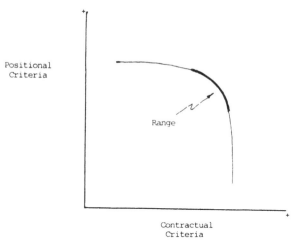

Figure 7. Range of compliance criteria at the emergent phase.

turally transfigured. They increasingly acquire characteristics that have been termed postmodern or postmaterial.[35] Yet the result is not convergence in the sense set forth by Isaac Deutscher and others.[36] Rather than similarity, what develops are systems rich with their own cultural particularity, which share a fundamental belief in the importance of ethical consideration. The heart of this vision is the embrace of diversity in a new and more powerful image of community.

A new kind of compliance

If the principles set forth in this book about individual and social development are valid, then clearly movement toward forms of compliance that embody greater degrees of justice than are currently available is entirely feasible. When that happens the history of mankind will enter a new phase, free of exploitation and war, and based instead on the fulfillment of utopian vision. The goal, of course, will never be fully attained, but it will be approximated in more and more areas of global life.

In positional societies in the modern phase there will be a turning away from the forms of mass politics that deny autonomy to individuals and groups. The rejection of pluralism in the hope of preventing exploitation will give way to the acceptance of diversity as a healthy aspect of communal life.

[35] Ronald Inglehart, "Post-Materialism in an Environment of Insecurity," *American Political Science Review* 75, no. 4 (December 1981): 898.

[36] Alfred G. Meyer, "Theories of Convergence," in *Change in Communist Systems,* ed. Chalmers Johnson (Stanford, Calif.: Stanford University Press, 1970), pp. 320, 322–3, 340.

With the transformation of community values, of the concept of community itself, will come the ability to synthesize communal values with those of a liberal individualistic nature. The signs of this happening are clearly abroad, and no less so than in the former communist world.

In contractual societies there is also a powerful movement toward a redefinition of values. While recognizing the enormous historical contribution of the individual entrepreneur, the thrust will be toward extending the principles of democracy into all areas of institutional life. Such changes will bring questions about the distribution of economic power within the purview of democratic consideration. Some specific changes will signal the beginning of this process. The government, for example, will increasingly be seen as having a major role to play in capital accumulation involving some degree of actual public control of investment; consideration will be given to chartering the largest publicly held corporations, those whose operations affect the life of the entire community, in order to ensure that they fulfill their functions and are open to public inspection.[37] Within institutions, at the workshop level, worker participation in decision making will be further encouraged. Already in the United States many firms now share some form of ownership with their employees. The workers in these firms report satisfaction with the financially rewarding aspects of such plans and with the greater degree of supportive and participative management practices.[38] This experience will become increasingly available to others.

Social and individual constructions of meaning that are appropriate for the modern phase remain overwhelmingly powerful. They are, however, giving way incrementally in Western societies as younger generations espouse the emergent ideals of ethical consideration.[39] Clearly the possibilities for human freedom are not at an end, for social life changes toward ethical consideration as people's conceptions of social relationships expand and develop. In this process no level of society is unaffected. As control is decentralized from the top, permitting pluralistic endeavor in political, economic, and social areas, smaller groups are organized from the bottom to plan in detail how to implement policies agreed upon democratically within the larger community. When this happens, the government is brought closer to the people, while the people are able more effectively to influence government.

There is no point ignoring the obvious, that institutions are imperfect, people are variable in terms of their motives and interests, and the problems to be faced are of enormous magnitude. Conflict is not likely to go away, although one can reasonably hope for its management by law rather than by

---

[37] George C. Lodge, *The New American Ideology* (New York: Knopf, 1975), p. 291.
[38] Rosen, Klein, and Young, "When Employees Share the Profits," pp. 30–6.
[39] Ronald Inglehart, *The Silent Revolution: Changing Values and Political Styles Among Western Publics* (Princeton, N.J.: Princeton University Press, 1977), p. 83.

intimidation and force. Control of lethal technology, alliances among hostile states, security fears, and special-interest concerns are all fertile seedbeds, among others, for continuing contestations. Nor will the technobility simply fade away, replaced by some moral meritocracy that has not and never can exist. Yet it is also not too much to hope that compliance, the use by some of others for their own benefit, can be constrained into patterns that favor mutual benefit and advantage.

What is the pattern of the future? It is one where individuals are free to choose their associates, where the basic protections of life (health care, environmental safeguards, etc.) are provided, where there is both a minimum and a maximum income and a steep inheritance tax to prevent the intergenerational accumulation of power, where participation in group life is assured, and where groups, especially productive units, make decisions affecting social life that are based on equal participation. It is a pattern where there are two, linked tiers of democratic process, within small groups and within the community at large. It is a society in which social life is cultivated in order to enrich the individual but where individuals have the autonomous responsibility to ensure the processes whereby community life fulfills individual needs and expectations. By accepting responsibility for themselves and their community, people come to understand that the outcomes of social processes are just only to the degree that they flow from fair procedures, carried out within a broadly understood framework of substantive justice.[40] For in the end all constraints against justice will fail unless there is a great body of people who are dedicated to upholding principles of ethical consideration. Bringing these people everywhere into the mainstream of social life is the greatest challenge of the modern world.

[40] David Lyons, *Ethics and the Rule of Law* (Cambridge: Cambridge University Press, 1984), p. 138.

Selected bibliography

The books and articles listed represent only a portion of the relevant literature. I have not included here all of the footnote citations and have deliberately excluded chapters in edited volumes, citing instead the complete work.

Abel, Richard L., ed. *The Politics of Informal Justice*, vol. 1. New York: Academic Press, 1982.

Abercrombie, Nicholas, Stephen Hill, and Bryan S. Turner. *The Dominant Ideology Thesis*. London: Allen & Unwin, 1980.

Adorno, T. W., Else Frenkel-Bruswick, Daniel J. Levinson, and R. Nevitt Sanford. *The Authoritarian Personality*, pt. 1. New York: Wiley, 1964.

Ahn, Byung-joon. *Chinese Politics and the Cultural Revolution*. Seattle: University of Washington Press, 1976.

Allen, Anita L. *Uneasy Access: Privacy for Women in a Free Society*. Totowa, N.J.: Rowman & Littlefield, 1988.

Alvesson, Mats. *Organization Theory and Technocratic Consciousness: Rationality, Ideology, and Quality of Work*. New York: Walter de Gruyter, 1987.

Anderson, Terry L., and P. J. Hill. "The Evolution of Property Rights: A Study of the American West." *The Journal of Law and Economics* 18, no. 1 (April 1975): 163–79.

Andors, Stephen. *China's Industrial Revolution: Politics, Planning, and Management, 1949 to the Present*. New York: Pantheon, 1977.

Aronoff, Joel. *Psychological Needs and Cultural Systems: A Case Study*. New York: Van Nostrand Reinhold, 1967.

Aronoff, Joel. "Psychological Needs as a Determinant in the Formation of Economic Structures: A Confirmation." *Human Relations* 23, no. 2 (April 1970): 123–38.

Arrow, Kenneth J. *The Limits of Organization*. New York: Norton, 1974.

Auerbach, Jerold S. *Unequal Justice: Lawyers and Social Change in Modern America*. New York: Oxford University Press, 1976.

Axelrod, Robert, and Robert O. Keohane. "Achieving Cooperation Under Anarchy: Strategies and Institutions," *World Politics* 38, no. 1 (October 1985): 226–54.

Balazs, Etienne. *Chinese Civilization and Bureaucracy: Variations on a Theme*. Trans. H. M. Wright. New Haven, Conn.: Yale University Press, 1964.

Balbus, Isaac D. *The Dialectics of Legal Repression: Black Rebels before the American Criminal Courts*. New York: Russell Sage Foundation, 1973.

Baltzell, E. Digby. *The Protestant Establishment: Aristocracy and Caste in America*. New York: Random House, 1964.

Barber, Benjamin R. *Strong Democracy: Participatory Politics for a New Age*. Berkeley: University of California Press, 1984.

Bates, Robert H. "Lessons from History or the Perfidy of English Exceptionalism and the Significance of Historical France." *World Politics* 40, no. 4 (July 1988): 499–516.

Becker, Gary S. *The Economic Approach to Human Behavior.* Chicago: University of Chicago Press, 1976.

Bell, Daniel. *The Coming of Post-Industrial Society: A Venture in Social Forecasting.* New York: Basic Books, 1973.

Bell, Daniel. *The Cultural Contradictions of Capitalism.* New York: Basic Books, 1976.

Bellah, Robert M. et al. *Habits of the Heart.* Berkeley: University of California Press, 1985.

Bennett, W. Lance. "Imitation, Ambiguity, and Drama in Political Life: Civil Religion and the Dilemmas of Public Morality." *Journal of Politics* 41, no. 1 (February 1979): 106–33.

Berger, Peter L. *Pyramids of Sacrifice: Political Ethics and Social Change.* New York: Basic Books, 1974.

Blasi, Joseph Raphael. *Employee Ownership Through ESOPs: Implications for the Public Corporation.* New York: Pergamon Press, 1987.

Blau, Peter M. *Bureaucracy in Modern Society.* New York: Random House, 1956.

Boocock, Sarane Spence. "Social Treasure: Changing Definitions of Childhood in Japan and the United States." Paper presented at the Columbia University East Asian Seminar on Modern Japan, April 8, 1988.

Bracher, Karl Dietrich. *The Age of Ideologies: A History of Political Thought in the Twentieth Century.* New York: St. Martin's, 1982.

Braudel, Fernand. *Civilization and Capitalism: 15th–18th Century.* Vol. 1: *The Structures of Everyday Life: The Limits of the Possible.* Translated from the French. Revised by Sian Reynolds. New York: Harper & Row, 1979.

Breton, Albert. *The Economic Theory of Representative Government.* Chicago: Aldine, 1974.

Bronowski, J. *Science and Human Values.* New York: Harper & Row, 1956.

Bronowski, J., and Bruce Mazlish. *The Western Intellectual Tradition: From Leonardo to Hegel.* New York: Harper, 1960.

Buehrig, Edward H. *The Perversity of Politics.* London: Croom Helm, 1986.

Burch, Philip H., Jr. *Elites in American History: The Federalist Years to the Civil War.* New York: Holmes & Meier, 1981.

Burnham, David. *The Rise of the Computer State.* New York: Random House, 1980, 1982, 1983.

Burns, James MacGregor. *Leadership.* New York: Harper & Row, 1978.

Byrd, William, et al. *Recent Chinese Economic Reforms: Studies of Two Industrial Enterprises.* World Bank Staff Working Papers No. 652. Washington, D.C.: World Bank, 1984.

Carnoy, Martin, and Derek Shearer. *Economic Democracy: The Challenge of the 1980's.* Armonk, N.Y.: M. E. Sharpe, 1980.

Cash, John D. "Taking Ideology Seriously: The Analysis of Unionist Ideology in Northern Ireland." Paper presented at the eleventh annual scientific meeting of the International Society of Political Psychology, July 1–5, 1988.

Cath, Stanley H. "Caesar and His Barren Relationship with Rome." *Psychohistory Review* 16, no. 2 (Winter 1988): 259–82.

Chasseguet-Smirgel, Janine, et al. *Female Sexuality: New Psychoanalytic Views.* Ann Arbor: University of Michigan Press, 1970.

Chester, Ronald. *Inheritance, Wealth, and Society.* Bloomington: Indiana University Press, 1982.

Chilton, Stephen. *Defining Political Development.* Boulder, Colo.: Lynne Rienner, 1988.

Cigler, Allan J., and Burdett A. Loomis, eds. *Interest Group Politics.* 2nd ed. Washington, D.C.: Congressional Quarterly Press, 1986.

Cirillo, Leonard, and Seymour Wapner, eds. *Value Presuppositions in Theories of Human Development.* Hillsdale, N.J.: Erlbaum, 1986.

Clarke, Donald C. "Political Power and Authority in Recent Chinese Literature." *China Quarterly*, no. 102 (June 1985): 234–52.

Cohen, Joshua, and Joel Rogers. *On Democracy: Toward A Transformation of American Society*. New York: Penguin Books, 1983.

Cohen, Ronald, and Elman R. Service, eds. *Origins of the State: An Anthropology of Political Evolution*. Philadelphia: Institute for the Study of Human Issues, 1978.

Dahl, Robert A. *Democracy, Liberty, and Equality*. Oslo: Norwegian University Press, 1986.

Davies, James C. *Human Nature in Politics: The Dynamics of Political Behavior*. New York: Wiley, 1963.

Davies, James C. "Political Violence: The Dominance–Submission Nexus." In *Violence as Politics*, ed. H. Hirsch and D. C. Perry, pp. 52–71. New York: Harper & Row, 1973.

Davies, James C. "The Priority of Human Needs and the Stages of Political Development." In *Human Nature in Politics*, ed. J. R. Pennock and J. W. Chapman, pp. 157–96. New York: New York University Press, 1977.

De Bedts, Ralph F. *The New Deal's SEC: The Formative Years*. New York: Columbia University Press, 1964.

Demsetz, Harold. "Toward a Theory of Property Rights." *American Economic Review* 57, no. 2 (May 1967): 347–59.

Dennis, Jack. "Political Independence in America, Part II: Towards a Theory." *British Journal of Political Science* 18, pt. 2 (April 1988): 197–219.

Deutsch, Karl W., and William G. Madow. "A Note on the Appearance of Wisdom in Large Bureaucratic Organizations." *Behavioral Science* 6 (1961): 72–8.

Domhoff, G. William. *The Powers That Be: Processes of Ruling-Class Domination in America*. New York: Random House, 1978.

Downs, Anthony. *Inside Bureaucracy*. Boston: Little, Brown, 1966.

Durkheim, Emile. *The Division of Labor in Society*. Trans. George Simpson. Glencoe, Ill.: Free Press, 1933.

Eckstein, Harry. "A Culturist Theory of Political Change." *American Political Science Review* 82, no. 3 (September 1988): 789–804.

Edwards, R. Randle, Louis Henkin, and Andrew J. Nathan. *Human Rights in Contemporary China*. New York: Columbia University Press, 1986.

Eisenstadt, S. N., ed. *The Origins and Diversity of Axial Age Civilizations*. Albany: State University of New York Press, 1986.

Elkin, Stephen L. "Market and Politics in Liberal Democracy." *Ethics* 92, no. 4 (July 1982): 720–32.

Ellul, Jacques. *The Technological Society*. Trans. John Wilkinson. New York: Knopf, 1967.

Emler, Nicholas, Stanley Renwick, and Bernadette Malone. "The Relationship Between Moral Reasoning and Political Orientation." *Journal of Personality and Social Psychology* 45, no. 5 (1983): 1073–1080.

Etzioni, Amitai. *Complex Organizations: A Sociological Reader*. New York: Holt, Rinehart & Winston, 1961.

Etzioni, Amitai. *The Moral Dimension: Toward a New Economics*. New York: Free Press, 1988.

Falk, Richard A. *Future Worlds. Headline Series* No. 229 (February, 1976).

Freud, Sigmund. *Civilization and Its Discontents*. Trans. and ed. James Strachey. New York: Norton, 1961.

Friedman, Edward. "Einstein and Mao: Metaphors of Revolution." *China Quarterly* 93 (March 1983): 51–75.

Friedman, Lawrence M. *Contract Law in America: A Social and Economic Case Study*. Madison: University of Wisconsin Press, 1965.

Friedman, Lawrence M. *Law and Society: An Introduction.* Englewood Cliffs, N.J.: Prentice-Hall, 1977.

Friedman, Lawrence M., and Stewart Macaulay, eds. *Law and the Behavioral Sciences.* Indianapolis: Bobbs-Merrill, 1969.

Friedman, Milton. *Capitalism and Freedom.* Chicago: University of Chicago Press, 1962.

Friedmann, Wolfgang. *Law in a Changing Society.* New York: Columbia University Press, 1972.

Fuks, Alexander. *Social Conflict in Ancient Greece.* Jerusalem: Magnes Press, 1984.

Gaenslen, Fritz. "Culture and Decision Making in China, Japan, Russia, and the United States." *World Politics* 39, no. 1 (October 1986): 78–103.

Galambos, Louis (with the assistance of Barbara Barrow Spence). *The Public Image of Big Business in America, 1880–1940: A Quantitative Study in Social Change.* (Baltimore: Johns Hopkins University Press, 1975.)

Galliher, John F., and John R. Cross. *Morals Legislation Without Morality: The Case of Nevada.* (New Brunswick, N.J.: Rutgers University Press, 1983.)

Gans, Herbert J. *More Equality.* New York: Pantheon, 1973.

Geertz, Clifford. *The Interpretation of Culture.* New York: Basic Books, 1973.

Gilder, George. *Wealth and Poverty.* New York: Basic Books, 1981.

Gilligan, Carol. *In a Different Voice: Psychological Theory and Women's Development.* (Cambridge, Mass.: Harvard University Press, 1982.)

Gluckman, Max. *Custom and Conflict in Africa.* Oxford: Basil Blackwell, 1966.

Gluckman, Max. *Politics, Law and Ritual in Tribal Society.* Oxford: Basil Blackwell, 1967.

Gold, Thomas B. "After Comradeship: Personal Relations in China Since the Cultural Revolution." *China Quarterly* 104 (December 1985): 655–75.

Goodwin, Doris Kearns. *The Fitzgeralds and the Kennedys.* New York: Simon & Schuster, 1987.

Gouldner, Alvin W. *The Future of Intellectuals and the Rise of the New Class.* (New York: Seabury Press, 1979.)

Greenberg, Edward S. "Industrial Self-Management and Political Attitudes." *American Political Science Review* 75, no. 1 (March 1981): 29–42.

Greenblatt, Sidney L., Richard W. Wilson, and Amy Auerbacher Wilson, eds. *Organizational Behavior in Chinese Society.* New York: Praeger, 1981.

Greiff, Thomas E. "The Principle of Human Rights in Nationalist China: John C. H. Wu and the Ideological Origins of the 1946 Constitution." *China Quarterly* 103 (September 1985): 441–61.

Grew, Raymond, ed. *Crises of Political Development in Europe and the United States.* Princeton, N.J.:, Princeton University Press, 1978.

Gupta, Dipak K. "Political Psychology and Neoclassical Theory of Economic Growth: The Possibilities and Implications of an Attempted Resynthesis." *Political Psychology* 8, no. 4 (December 1987): 637–65.

Habermas, Jürgen. *Communication and the Evolution of Society.* Trans. Thomas McCarthy. Boston: Beacon Press, 1979.

Hallpike, C. R. *The Foundations of Primitive Thought.* Oxford: Clarendon Press, 1979.

Hane, Mikiso. *Peasants, Rebels and Outcastes: The Underside of Modern Japan.* New York: Pantheon, 1982.

Harding, Harry. "Competing Models of the Chinese Communist Policy Process: Toward a Sorting and Evaluation." *Issues and Studies* 20, no. 2 (February 1984): 13–36.

Harrop, David. *America's Paychecks: Who Makes What.* New York: Facts on File, 1980.

Hartley, Jean F. "Ideology and Organizational Behavior." *International Studies of Management and Organization* 13, no. 3 (Fall 1983): 7–34.

The Harvard Nuclear Study Group. *Living With Nuclear Weapons.* Toronto: Bantam Books, 1983.

Hayek, Friedrich A. *The Road to Serfdom*. Chicago: University of Chicago Press, 1944.

Hayek, Friedrich A. *The Constitution of Liberty*. Chicago: University of Chicago Press, 1960.

Hazard, John N. "China and Socialist Models." Keynote address, Third International Congress of Professors World Peace Academy, Manila, August 25, 1987.

Heclo, Hugh. *A Government of Strangers: Executive Politics in Washington*. Washington, D.C.: The Brookings Institution, 1977.

Heilbroner, Robert L. *The Great Ascent*. New York: Harper & Row, 1963.

Heilbroner, Robert L. *An Inquiry into the Human Prospect*. New York: Norton, 1974.

Heilbroner, Robert L. *The Nature and Logic of Capitalism*. New York: Norton, 1985.

Heilbroner, Robert L. "The Coming Meltdown of Traditional Capitalism." In *Ethics and International Affairs* 2 (1988): 63–77 (special reprint).

Hellerstein, David. "Plotting a Theory of the Brain." *New York Times Magazine*, May 22, 1988, sec. 6, pp. 17–19, 27–8, 55, 61, 64.

Henry, Jules. *Culture Against Man*. New York: Random House, 1963.

Herman, Margaret C., with Thomas W. Milburn, ed. *A Psychological Examination of Political Leaders*. New York: Free Press, 1977.

Hicks, John. *A Theory of Economic History*. Oxford: Clarendon Press, 1969.

Hirsch, Fred. *Social Limits to Growth*. Cambridge, Mass.: Harvard University Press, 1976.

Hirschman, Albert O. *The Passions and the Interests: Political Arguments for Capitalism Before Its Triumph*. Princeton, N.J.: Princeton University Press, 1977.

Hixson, Richard F. *Privacy in a Public Society: Human Rights in Conflict*. New York: Oxford University Press, 1987.

Hobhouse, L. T. *Morals in Evolution: A Study in Comparative Ethics*. London: Chapman & Hall, 1915.

Huber, Joan, and William H. Form. *Income and Ideology: An Analysis of the American Political Formula*. New York: Free Press, 1973.

Huntington, Samuel P., and Joseph S. Nye, Jr., eds. *Global Dilemmas*. Boston: Center for International Affairs, Harvard University, and University Press of America, 1985.

Inglehart, Ronald. *The Silent Revolution: Changing Values and Political Styles Among Western Publics*. Princeton, N.J.: Princeton University Press, 1977.

Inglehart, Ronald. "Post-Materialism in an Environment of Insecurity." *American Political Science Review* 75, no. 4 (December 1981): 880–900.

Inkeles, Alex. *Exploring Individual Modernity*. New York: Columbia University Press, 1983.

Jacob, Philip. *Values and the Active Community*. The International Studies of Values in Politics. New York: Free Press, 1971.

Jaspers, Karl. *Vom Ursprung und Ziel der Geschichte*. Munich: Piper Verlag, 1949.

Jaynes, Julian. *The Origin of Consciousness in the Breakdown of the Bicameral Mind*. Boston: Houghton Mifflin, 1976.

Jencks, Christopher, et al. *Inequality: A Reassessment of the Effect of Family and Schooling in America*. New York: Basic Books, 1972.

Jensen, U. J., and R. Harre, eds. *The Philosophy of Evolution*. New York: St. Martin's, 1981.

Johnson, Chalmers. *Revolutionary Change*. 2nd ed. Stanford, Calif.: Stanford University Press, 1982.

Johnson, Chalmers, ed. *Change in Communist Systems*. Stanford, Calif.: Stanford University Press, 1970.

Johnson, David G. *The Medieval Chinese Oligarchy*. Boulder, Colo: Westview Press, 1977.

Juster, F. Thomas, ed. *The Distribution of Economic Well-Being*. Cambridge, Mass.: Ballinger, 1977.

Kairys, David, ed. *The Politics of Law: A Progressive Critique*. New York: Pantheon, 1982.

Kelso, Louis O., and Mortimer J. Adler. *The Capitalist Manifesto.* New York: Random House, 1958.

Keohane, Robert O. *After Hegemony: Cooperation and Discord in the World Political Economy.* Princeton, N.J.: Princeton University Press, 1984.

Kerlinger, Fred N. *Liberalism and Conservatism: The Nature and Structure of Social Attitudes.* Hillsdale, N.J.: Erlbaum, 1984.

Kluegel, James R., and Eliot R. Smith. *Beliefs About Inequality: Americans' Views of What Is and What Ought to Be.* New York: Aldine De Gruyter, 1986.

Kohlberg, Lawrence. *The Philosophy of Moral Development: Moral Stages and the Idea of Justice.* Volume 1 of *Essays on Moral Development.* San Francisco: Harper & Row, 1981.

Kohlberg, Lawrence. *The Psychology of Moral Development: The Nature and Validity of Moral Stages.* Volume 2 of *Essays on Moral Development.* San Francisco: Harper & Row, 1984.

Kolakowski, Leszek, and Stuart Hampshire, eds. *The Socialist Idea: A Reappraisal.* London: Weidenfeld & Nicolson, 1974.

Kuczynski, Jürgen. *The Rise of the Working Class.* Translated from the German by C.T.A. Ray. New York: McGraw-Hill, 1967.

Kuhn, Thomas S. *The Structure of Scientific Revolutions.* 2nd ed. Chicago: University of Chicago Press, 1970.

Kurtines, William M., and Jacob L. Gewirtz, eds. *Morality, Moral Behavior and Moral Development.* New York: Wiley, 1984.

La Palombara, Joseph, ed. *Bureaucracy and Political Development.* Princeton, N.J.: Princeton University Press, 1963.

La Porte, Todd R., ed. *Organized Social Complexity: Challenge to Politics and Policy.* Princeton, N.J.: Princeton University Press, 1975.

Lampton, David M. (with the assistance of Yeung Sai-cheung). *Paths to Power: Elite Mobility in Contemporary China.* Ann Arbor: Center for Chinese Studies, University of Michigan, 1986.

Lane, Robert E. "The Fear of Equality." *American Political Science Review* 53, no. 1 (March 1959): 35–51.

Lane, Robert E. *Political Ideology: Why the American Common Man Believes What He Does.* New York: Free Press, 1962.

Langguth, A. J. *Patriots: The Men Who Started the American Revolution.* New York: Simon & Schuster, 1988.

Larson, Magali Sarfatti. *The Rise of Professionalism: A Sociological Analysis.* Berkeley and Los Angeles: University of California Press, 1977.

Lee, Hong Yung. *The Politics of the Cultural Revolution.* Berkeley and Los Angeles: University of California Press, 1978.

Levitan, Sar A., and Diane Werneke. "Worker Participation and Productivity Change." *Monthly Labor Review* 107, no. 9 (September 1984): 28–33.

Levy, Marion J., Jr. "Contrasting Factors in the Modernization of China and Japan, Reviewed." Conference on "China in a New Era: Continuity and Change," Third International Congress of Professors World Peace Academy, Manila, August 24–9, 1987.

Lieberthal, Kenneth, and Michel Oksenberg. *Policy Making in China: Leaders, Structures, and Processes.* Princeton, N.J.: Princeton University Press, 1988.

Lifton, Robert Jay. *The Nazi Doctors: Medical Killing and the Psychology of Genocide.* New York: Basic Books, 1986.

Lin, Justin Yifu. "An Economic Theory of Institutional Change: Induced and Imposed Change." Center Discussion Paper No. 537. Economic Growth Center, Yale University, June 1987.

Lindblom, Charles E. *Politics and Markets: The World's Political-Economic Systems.* New York: Basic Books, 1977.

Lipset, Seymour Martin. *The First New Nation: The United States in Historical and Comparative Perspective.* New York: Norton, 1979.

Lodge, George C. *The New American Ideology.* New York: Knopf, 1975.

Lodge, George C., and Ezra F. Vogel, eds. *Ideology and National Competitiveness: An Analysis of Nine Countries.* Boston: Harvard Business School Press, 1987.

Losco, Joseph. "Understanding Altruism: A Critique and Proposal for Integrating Various Approaches." *Political Psychology* 7, no. 2 (June 1986): 323–48.

Luebbert, Gregory M. "Social Foundations of Political Order in Interwar Europe." *World Politics* 39, no. 4 (July 1987): 449–78.

Lyons, David. *Ethics and the Rule of Law.* Cambridge: Cambridge University Press, 1984.

Madsen, Richard. *Morality and Power in a Chinese Village.* Berkeley and Los Angeles: University of California Press, 1984.

Mannheim, Karl. *Ideology and Utopia.* London: Routledge & Kegan Paul, 1936.

Marcuse, Herbert. *Eros and Civilization: A Philosophical Inquiry into Freud.* Boston: Beacon Press, 1955.

Marx, Karl. *Selected Writings.* Ed. David McLellan. Oxford: Oxford University Press, 1977.

Mason, Henry L. "Implementing the Final Solution: The Ordinary Regulating of the Extraordinary." *World Politics* 40, no. 4 (July 1988): 542–69.

Mazlish, Bruce. *The Revolutionary Ascetic: Evolution of a Political Type.* New York: McGraw-Hill, 1976.

Mazrui, Ali A. "A Third World Perspective." In Volume 1 of *Ethics and International Affairs.* New York: Carnegie Council on Ethics and International Affairs, 1987, pp. 9–21.

McClelland, David C. *The Achieving Society.* Princeton, N.J.: Van Nostrand, 1961.

McClelland, David C. *Power: The Inner Experience.* New York: Irvington Publishers, 1975.

McClosky, Herbert, and John Zaller. *The American Ethos: Public Attitudes Toward Capitalism and Democracy.* Cambridge, Mass.: Harvard University Press, 1984.

McConnell, Grant. *Private Power and American Democracy.* New York: Vintage Books, 1966.

McWilliams, Wilson Carey. *The Idea of Fraternity in America.* Berkeley and Los Angeles: University of California Press, 1973.

Meeks, Wayne A. *The First Urban Christians: The Social World of the Apostle Paul.* New Haven, Conn.: Yale University Press, 1983.

Michels, Robert. *Political Parties.* New York: Free Press, 1962.

Midlarsky, Manus I. "Scarcity and Inequality: Prologue to the Onset of Mass Revolution." *Journal of Conflict Resolution* 26, no. 1 (March 1982): 3–38.

Miller, Arthur R. *The Assault on Privacy: Computers, Data Banks, and Dossiers.* Ann Arbor: University of Michigan Press, 1971.

Mitchell, Neil J., and James M. McCormick. "Economic and Political Explanations of Human Rights Violations." *World Politics* 40, no. 4 (July 1988): 476–98.

Montgomery, John D. *Technology and Civic Life: Making and Implementing Development Decisions.* Cambridge, Mass.: MIT Press, 1974.

Moore, Barrington, Jr. *The Causes of Human Misery.* Boston: Beacon Press, 1970.

Moore, Barrington, Jr. *Privacy: Studies in Social and Cultural History.* Armonk, N.Y.: M. E. Sharpe, 1984.

Moscovici, Serge. *Social Influence and Social Change.* Trans. Carol Sherrard and Greta Heinz. London: Academic Press, 1976.

Moscovici, Serge. *The Age of the Crowd: A Historical Treatise on Mass Psychology.* Cambridge: Cambridge University Press, 1985.

Myers, Ramon H. "Property Rights, Economic Organizations and Economic Modernization During the Economic Reforms." Paper presented at the conference on "China in a New

Era: Continuity and Change," Third International Congress of Professors World Peace Academy, Manila, August 24–29, 1987.

Nathan, Andrew J. "Policy Oscillations in the People's Republic of China: A Critique." *China Quarterly*, no. 68 (December 1976): 720–33.

Nathan, Andrew J. *Chinese Democracy*. New York: Knopf, 1985.

North, Douglass C. *Structure and Change in Economic History*. New York: Norton, 1981.

North, Douglass C. "A Theory of Economic Change." *Science* 219, no. 4581 (January 14, 1983): 163–4.

Nozick, Robert. "Moral Complications and Moral Structures." *Natural Law Forum* 13 (1968): 1–50.

Nozick, Robert. *Anarchy, State, and Utopia*. New York: Basic Books, 1974.

Okun, Arthur M. *Equality and Efficiency: The Big Tradeoff*. Washington, D.C.: The Brookings Institution, 1975.

Olson, Mancur. *The Rise and Decline of Nations: Economic Growth, Stagflation, and Social Rigidities*. New Haven, Conn.: Yale University Press, 1982.

O'Neill, John, ed. *Modes of Individualism and Collectivism*. London: Heinemann, 1973.

Ostrogorsky, George. *History of the Byzantine State*. New Brunswick, N.J.: Rutgers University Press, 1957.

Overton, Willis F., ed. *The Relationship Between Social and Cognitive Development*. Hillsdale, N.J.: Erlbaum, 1983.

Oye, Kenneth A. "Explaining Cooperation Under Anarchy: Hypotheses and Strategies." *World Politics* 38, no. 1 (October 1985): 1–24.

Page, Edward C. *Political Authority and Bureaucratic Power: A Comparative Analysis*. Knoxville: University of Tennessee Press, 1985.

Parenti, Michael. *Democracy for the Few*. New York: St. Martin's, 1977.

Parenti, Michael. *Power and the Powerless*. New York: St. Martin's, 1978.

Parkin, Frank. *Class Inequality and Political Order*. New York: Praeger, 1971.

Pechman, Joseph A., and Benjamin A. Okner. *Who Bears the Tax Burden?* Washington, D.C.: The Brookings Institution, 1974.

Perry, Elizabeth J., and Christine Wong, eds. *The Political Economy of Reform in Post-Mao China*. Cambridge, Mass.: Council on East Asian Studies, Harvard University, 1985.

Peters, R. S. *The Concept of Motivation*. London: Routledge & Kegan Paul, 1958.

Piaget, Jean. *The Construction of Reality in the Child*. New York: Basic Books, 1954.

Piaget, Jean. *The Moral Judgment of the Child*. Trans. Marjorie Gabain. New York: Collier Books, 1962.

Piaget, Jean. *The Psychology of Intelligence*. New York: International Universities Press, 1963.

Piaget, Jean. *The Development of Thought, Equilibration of Cognitive Structures*. New York: Viking Press, 1977.

Piven, Frances Fox, and Richard A. Cloward. *Poor People's Movements: Why They Succeed, How They Fail*. New York: Pantheon, 1977.

Pole, J. R. *The Pursuit of Equality in American History*. Berkeley and Los Angeles: University of California Press, 1978.

Poulantzas, Nicos. *Political Power and Social Classes*. London: New Left Books, 1975.

Pye, Lucian W., and Sidney Verba, eds. *Political Culture and Political Development*. Princeton, N.J.: Princeton University Press, 1965.

Pye, Lucian W. "Political Culture." In *International Encyclopedia of the Social Sciences*, ed. David L. Sills, vol. 12, pp. 218–25. New York: Macmillan and Free Press, 1968.

Pye, Lucian W. *The Dynamics of Chinese Politics*. Cambridge, Mass.: Oelgeschlager, Gunn & Hain, 1981.

Radding, Charles M. *A World Made by Men: Cognition and Society, 400–1200.* Chapel Hill: University of North Carolina Press, 1985.

Rae, Douglas, et al. *Equalities.* Cambridge, Mass.: Harvard University Press, 1981.

Rawls, John. "Distributive Justice: Some Addenda." *Natural Law Forum* 13 (1968): 51–71.

Rawski, Thomas G. *China's Transition to Industrialism: Producer Goods and Economic Development in the Twentieth Century.* Ann Arbor: University of Michigan Press, 1980.

Raz, Joseph. *The Morality of Freedom.* Oxford: Clarendon Press, 1986.

Rejai, Mostafa, and Kay Phillips. *World Revolutionary Leaders.* New Brunswick, N.J.: Rutgers University Press, 1983.

Rest, James R. *Development in Judging Moral Issues.* Minneapolis: University of Minnesota Press, 1979.

Richman, Barry M. *Industrial Society in Communist China.* New York: Vintage Books, 1969.

Riskin, Carl. "Maoist Economics in Retrospect." Paper presented at the Columbia University Seminar on Modern China, April 10, 1986.

Rosenberg, Shawn W. *Reason, Ideology and Politics.* Princeton, N.J.: Princeton University Press, 1988.

Rosenberg, Shawn W., Dana Ward, and Stephen Chilton. *Political Reasoning and Cognition: A Piagetian View.* Durham, N.C.: Duke University Press, 1988.

Rychlak, J. F., volume ed. *Dialectic: Humanistic Rationale for Behavior and Development.* Volume 2 of *Contributions to Human Development*, ed. K. F. Riegel and H. Thomae. Basel: S. Karger, 1976.

Sabine, George H. *A History of Political Theory*, 3rd ed. New York: Rinehart & Winston, 1961.

Sagan, Eli. *At the Dawn of Tyranny: The Origins of Individualism, Political Oppression, and the State.* New York: Knopf, 1985.

Salaman, Graeme. *Work Organization and Class Structure.* Armonk, N.Y.: M. E. Sharpe, 1981.

Schelling, Thomas C. *Micromotives and Macrobehavior.* New York: Norton, 1978.

Schlaefli, Andre, James R. Rest, and Stephen J. Thoma. "Does Moral Education Improve Moral Judgment? A Meta-Analysis of Intervention Studies Using the Defining Issues Test." *Review of Educational Research* 55, no. 3 (Fall 1985): 319–52.

Schopenhauer, Arthur. *On the Basis of Morality.* Trans. E.F.J. Payne. Indianapolis: Bobbs-Merrill, 1965 (first published in 1841).

Schurmann, Franz. *Ideology and Organization in Communist China.* Berkeley and Los Angeles: University of California Press, 1966.

Schwartz, Barry. *Psychology of Learning and Behavior.* New York: Norton, 1978.

Schwartz, David C. *Political Alienation and Political Behavior.* Chicago: Aldine, 1973.

Sen, Amartya. *Resources, Values and Development.* Cambridge, Mass.: Harvard University Press, 1984.

Sen, Amartya. *On Ethics and Economics.* Oxford: Basil Blackwell, 1987.

Shackleton, J. R., and Gareth Locksley, eds. *Twelve Contemporary Economists.* New York: Wiley, 1981.

Sharp, Andrew. *Political Ideas of the English Civil Wars 1641–1649.* New York: Longman, 1983.

Shils, Edward. "Primordial, Personal, Sacred and Civil Ties." *British Journal of Sociology* 8, no. 2 (June 1957): 130–45.

Shils, Edward, ed. *The Intellectuals and the Powers and Other Essays.* Chicago: University of Chicago Press, 1972.

Sidel, Ruth. *Women and Child Care in China.* Baltimore: Penguin Books, 1972.

Smith, Richard A. "Class Structure and Economic Rationality: Problems of Industrial Reform in China." Paper presented at the Columbia University Seminar on Modern China, February 12, 1987.

Solinger, Dorothy J. *Chinese Business Under Socialism: The Politics of Domestic Commerce, 1949–1980*. Berkeley and Los Angeles: University of California Press, 1984.

Solinger, Dorothy, et al., eds. *Three Visions of Chinese Socialism*. Boulder, Colo.: Westview Press, 1984.

Sombart, Werner. *Why Is There No Socialism in the United States*. Trans. Patricia M. Hocking and C. T. Husbands. White Plains, N.Y.: International Arts and Sciences Press, 1976 (first published in 1906).

Starr, John Bryan. *Ideology and Culture: An Introduction to the Dialectic of Contemporary Chinese Politics*. New York: Harper & Row, 1973.

Starr, John Bryan. *Continuing the Revolution: The Political Thought of Mao*. Princeton, N.J.: Princeton University Press, 1979.

Talmon, J. L. *The Origins of Totalitarian Democracy*. New York: Praeger, 1960.

Tawney, R. H. *Equality*. London: Allen & Unwin, 1931.

Thurow, Lester C. *The Zero-Sum Society: Distribution and the Possibilities for Economic Change*. New York: Basic Books, 1980.

Tiger, Lionel. *The Manufacture of Evil: Ethics, Evolution, and the Industrial System*. New York: Harper & Row, 1987.

Tokuda, Noriyuki. "Prospects for Chinese Politics in Terms of System Reform Under Deng Xiaoping." Paper presented at the conference on "China in a New Era: Continuity and Change." Third International Congress of Professors World Peace Academy, Manila, August 24–9, 1987.

Tomkins, Alan J. "Psychology and the Constitution." *Psychology Today* 21, no. 9 (September 1987): 48–50.

Tönnies, Ferdinand. *Community and Society*. Trans. and ed. Charles P. Loomis. New York: Harper & Row, 1963.

Tu, Ching-I, ed. *Tradition and Creativity: Essays on East Asian Civilization*. New Brunswick, N.J.: Transaction Books, 1987.

Tung Chi-ping and Humphrey Evans. *The Thought Revolution*. New York: Coward-McCann, 1966.

Unger, Robert Mangabeira. *Law in Modern Society: Toward a Criticism of Social Theory*. New York: Free Press, 1976.

Veatch, Robert M. *The Foundation of Justice: Why the Retarded and the Rest of Us Have Claims to Equality*. New York: Oxford University Press, 1986.

Verba, Sidney, and Gary R. Orren. *Equality in America: The View from the Top*. Cambridge, Mass.: Harvard University Press, 1985.

Verba, Sidney, et al. *Elites and the Idea of Equality: A Comparison of Japan, Sweden, and the United States*. Cambridge, Mass.: Harvard University Press, 1987.

Walder, Andrew G. *Communist Neo-Traditionalism: Work and Authority in Chinese Industry*. Berkeley: University of California Press, 1986.

Walker, Lawrence J. "Cognitive and Perspective-taking Prerequisites for Moral Development." *Child Development* 51, no. 1 (March 1980): 131–9.

Walzer, Michael. *Spheres of Justice: A Defense of Pluralism and Equality*. New York: Basic Books, 1983.

Weber, Max. *Economy and Society*, vol. 2. Ed. Guenther Roth and Claus Wittich. New York: Bedminster Press, 1968.

Weiner, Myron. "The Political Economy of Industrial Growth in India." *World Politics* 38, no. 4 (July 1986): 596–610.

White, Lynn T., III. "The End of China's Revolution: A Leadership Diversifies." Paper presented at the conference on "China in a New Era: Continuity and Change." Third International Congress of Professors World Peace Academy, Manila, August 24–9, 1987.

Whyte, Martin King. "Bureaucracy and Modernization in China: The Maoist Critique." *American Sociological Review* 38, no. 2 (April 1973): 149–63.

Wiedemann, Kent M. "China in the Vanguard of a New Socialism." *Asian Survey* 26, no. 7 (July 1986): 774–92.

Wilbur, Charles K., ed. *The Political Economy of Development and Underdevelopment*. New York: Random House, 1988.

Wildavsky, Aaron. *The Politics of the Budgetary Process*. Boston: Little, Brown, 1964.

Wilensky, Harold L. *The Welfare State and Equality: Structural and Ideological Roots of Public Expenditures*. Berkeley and Los Angeles: University of California Press, 1975.

Williamson, Jeffrey G., and Peter H. Lindert. *American Inequality: A Macroeconomic History*. New York: Academic Press, 1980.

Williamson, Oliver E. *Markets and Hierarchies: Analysis and Antitrust Implications*. New York: Free Press, 1975.

Wilson, Richard W. *Labyrinth: An Essay on the Political Psychology of Change*. Armonk, N.Y.: M. E. Sharpe, 1988.

Wilson, Richard W., Amy Auerbacher Wilson, and Sidney L. Greenblatt, eds. *Value Change in Chinese Society*. New York: Praeger, 1979.

Winch, Peter. *Ethics and Action*. London: Routledge & Kegan Paul, 1972.

Wood, Michael. *In Search of the Trojan War*. New York: New American Library, 1985.

Wright, Moorhead, ed. *Rights and Obligations in North–South Relations*. New York: St. Martin's, 1986.

Wrightson, Keith. *English Society 1580–1680*. New Brunswick, N.J.: Rutgers University Press, 1982.

Young, Michael. *The Rise of the Meritocracy, 1870–2033*. New York: Penguin Books, 1961.

Index